Paula
Deen
Cuts
the Fat

By Paula Deen

Paula Deen Cuts the Fat

250 Favorite Recipes All Lightened Up

Paula Deen *and* Melissa Clark

PDV

Paula Deen Ventures
2391 Downing Ave.
Thunderbolt, GA 31404

First Paula Deen Ventures hardcover edition, September 2015.

LCCN: 2015909501

ISBN: 978-1-943016-02-2

Paula Deen Ventures and colophon are registered trademarks of Paula Deen Ventures, Inc.

PRODUCED BY WILSTED & TAYLOR PUBLISHING SERVICES
Production manager Christine Taylor
Copy editor Lynn Meinhardt
Designer and compositor Nancy Koerner
Proofreaders Nancy Evans and Melody Lacina
Indexer Thérèse Shere

Manufactured in the United States of America

20 19 18 17 16 15   10 9 8 7 6 5 4 3 2 1

This book is dedicated to

Michael,

Michelle,

and Anthony,

who've helped me be the best new me possible.

Contents

** Starred recipes are
Paula's 50 Classic Recipes
Made Healthier*

◀ *The original Bag Lady team.*

3 Hearty, Warming and Fresh, Cooling Soups   65

7 Fish and Shellfish   189

8 Vegetables and Side Dishes   223

9 Breakfast and Brunch 259

10 Breads, Quick Breads, and Biscuits 289

11 Pies and Cakes 313

12 Other Tempting Desserts and Beverages 339

Paula Deen Cuts the Fat

Cookin' and Eatin' and Healthy

*W*ow, how's that for an opener? I look at this photo of me and I think, how did I not realize that I was so fat? Truth is, like many folks, I was busy and content, and of course I never stepped on a scale.

Looking Back

Growing up in Albany, Georgia, I was fearless. I liked roller skatin', swimmin', and eatin', and I had lots of friends. In high school, I was the pretty cheerleader with the handsome boyfriend. I entered beauty pageants and weighed 118 pounds with a 36-23-36 figure. I had a steady boyfriend when I was a high-school senior, but it took only one look at my future husband, Jimmy Deen, who had graduated the year before, and I was a goner. With his dark eyes and hair, he was a heartthrob. The minute I graduated from high school we got engaged, and my parents were devastated. They had misgivings about Jimmy; they picked up on the fact that he was controlling and not very directed in terms of what he was going to do for a job. But I had my heart set on being his wife. We got married in the fall of 1965, and my daddy gave me the choice of having either a big wedding or a stove and refrigerator, because he couldn't afford both. Needless to say, I took the stove and refrigerator, and that's probably when my destiny was set.

The following year, my son Jamie was born, and two years later Bobby came along. At age twenty-three, I had just begun to cope with my daddy's death when my mother passed away. I had a sixteen-year-old brother to finish raising, two babies under the age of three, and a husband who really liked his cold beer.

For years I remained in an unhappy marriage. The only place I felt happy was in my kitchen. I spent a lot of time bellied up to my stove, and I came to realize that I was good at cookin'; I had a knack for knowing what ingredients would go together and how to make things taste good. Cookin' became a source of comfort to me.

At age forty-two, I started my own catering company, The Bag Lady. That name was not the most complimentary thing to call myself, was it, y'all? But I think it indicates how I felt about myself at the time. I was working sixteen- and sometimes even twenty-hour days, because my life was all about building a business and being able to buy groceries. I knew I wasn't capable of fixing Jimmy and me, so I finally told him it was over, and he moved out.

Over the years, I slowly put on weight. By the time Jamie, Bobby, and I opened our first restaurant, The Lady & Sons, I was comfortable with who I was. What I weighed was the *last* thing on my mind; my thoughts were only on scratchin' out a livin'. We were so busy that we never had time to sit down and eat; whatever was convenient, we'd grab. One of our staples in the restaurant was a "handle sandwich": a chicken leg on a slice of white bread, drizzled with hot sauce. You could keep stirring a pot with one hand and eat the sandwich with the other until all you had left was the "handle"—the chicken bone. My days as a shapely girl were long gone at that point. I knew I was getting way too heavy, but I was focused on building up the business.

I worked hard to compile many of my favorite recipes, and with the support of friends and family, I published *Favorite Recipes of The Lady & Her Friends* and sold copies in the restaurant. I was so proud of this little cookbook, which I printed at the local copy shop. One rainy afternoon, an editor from a large New York City publishing house came into the restaurant and offered to publish the book. I had been discovered, and every day I thank God for this blessing. The book led to cooking shows, and soon I was juggling two full-time jobs in addition to running what was now a very successful restaurant. My weight continued to creep up.

In 2009, during a routine physical, my doctor told me I had type 2 diabetes. It took me such a long time to come to grips with that fact. My gosh, I loved my life, and I loved that it was centered around down-home Southern cookin'. I didn't want to change; I really fought that idea tooth and nail. But change is one thing we're guaranteed in life, although most of us don't like it—especially if we're in a place that we're happy with. My recipes and cooking shows were all about decadent, delicious foods, even though I didn't eat the way I cooked on the shows all the time. Some folks think that what they see in a twenty-two-minute show is what it must really be like in my everyday life. But I don't go around lickin' sticks of butter and munchin' cake all day long. Even so, I had definitely built my whole life and my career around indulgent food. I knew I needed to lose weight and get healthy. I just couldn't wrap my mind around it.

I thought I *had* been eating in moderation. Looking back, to me "moderation" meant eating two biscuits instead of three. So even though I believed I was eating moderately, I came to realize that I wasn't. I was eating as much as I wanted and whatever I wanted, without giving it any thought. And I love to eat when I'm celebrating something. Great food had always been such a big part of my life, as comfort, as a way to share my love with my family and all the other people I cared about, and as my livelihood. But now I had to wonder if I'd be able to keep on cooking and enjoying scrumptious food.

I started to learn about how to improve my diet and how I should watch my starches and cut way back on sugar and fats. Everyone knows I'm a biscuit lover, and my brand-new recipe, *Everyday Whole-Wheat Biscuits* (page 296), is absolutely delicious. And speaking of delicious, you just have to try my *Flourless Chocolate Fudge Cake* (page 331), which is out of this world. You won't believe it uses only half a cup of sugar!

I learned that activity would also help my blood sugar levels, so I was determined to start getting some exercise. Exercise is a really hard thing for me: I just don't enjoy it. Bobby is the only one in my family who is really into it. If he doesn't get his workout, he feels like his day is not complete. I guess I was used to getting my exercise through runnin' around and stayin' active. Now, after a long day, when I get home late at night, dead tired after shooting a show, it's so hard to get on the treadmill and do a mile and a quarter. But I just force myself to do it, and I do feel a lot better afterward.

I had been doing some things that might have invited diabetes, but diabetes is not only caused by what you eat. Genetics, age, stress levels, and, of course, lifestyle can contribute to its onset. It's like a puzzle, and if the puzzle pieces fit, there is a good chance you'll develop the condition.

My husband, Michael, adores sweets: That's his downfall. He will go for days and not eat much of anything, but then he'll have a huge helping of dessert. If I bake cookies, he won't eat one or two; he'll eat twelve. That's why it's great that I've come up with dessert recipes we can both eat. My *Peanut Butter and Jelly Cookies*

(page 349) have a fantastic peanuty flavor but don't have any butter 'tall. I use rasp-berry preserves in the middle to keep the sugars down. They're so yummy, my grandbabies ask for them whenever they come over. Yet in spite of Michael's tre-mendous sweet tooth, he will probably never be diabetic. Although he's in the right age range, his other factors don't line up; his puzzle pieces just don't fit.

It was great to finally discuss my diabetes and then my weight loss in public, but getting to that point wasn't at all easy. Some people responded negatively to my news, because I was seen as the face of Southern home-style cooking. They said, "What does she expect? She goes around lickin' on a stick of butter." But really, I don't. Those weeks when I shoot my shows, yes, pretty much everything that goes into my mouth is rich. People do love seeing decadent food being made on TV. But I never suggested that anyone should eat that way every single day, or even most days. I provide viewers with recipes, and of course it is up to them to decide how often they make them and how much they eat. But when you do decide to make one of these special dishes—oh my gosh, it's going to be good, and it's going to be the real thing. I was brought up on this kind of cookin', and it's what I know.

I don't see why our Southern cuisine gets such a bad rap, other than that we enjoy some fried foods and desserts. I have had the opportunity to travel around the United States a lot in the past ten years, and in no other section of the country have I found a place where people eat more vegetables than in the South. Y'all know how good our produce is—we eat our okra, cucumbers, butter beans, toma-toes, field beans and peas, and corn. And we love our collards and turnip and mustard greens, which have great health benefits; in fact, collards may discourage colon cancer. The South is farmland, and vegetables are what we grow. My grand-mother cooked for herself every day, even after my granddaddy died, and she lived to be ninety-one. We should all be so lucky! So I spend a lot of time defending Southern home-style cooking. And now with dishes like **Roasted Root Vegetable Salad with Honey, Goat Cheese, and Walnuts** (page 59), which incorporates pep-pery baby arugula, and **Eggplant Lasagna** (page 118), which replaces noodles with thin slices of grilled eggplant, my veggies are even healthier than before!

I did decide to give up sweet tea, on the off chance that it would lower my blood sugar a little. Now, sweet tea to a Southern girl is like a diamond to anyone else; we just love our sweet tea. I would start drinking it at eleven o'clock in the morning, and I'd have it all day long because it tasted so good. At night, there was

◄ *It's amazing how small changes can give you big results.*

even a glass by my bed. Later I calculated that I was consuming at least a gallon of tea with at least two cups of sugar a day, just from the tea! I tell y'all, it was hard for me to give it up, but somehow I managed to do it. I probably couldn't even drink a glassful now; it would seem like I was drinking syrup.

In the past, I wanted to eat everything I loved, but I came to see that there could be a happy medium. At a certain point, you have to ask yourself if you want quality versus quantity. I realized that I could have a small portion of something rich once in a while, as long as I paid attention to what I ate the rest of the time. I even figured out how to make some of my all-time favorites, such as **Family Reunion Deviled Eggs** (page 8), a little bit lighter. And I've managed to cut the fat in **The Lady & Sons Chicken Potpie** (page 159) and my classic **Paula's Chicken and Dumplin's** (page 156) without losing any of their great flavors. I don't even notice the difference! And Michael was really pleased that I could fit **Savannah Baked Red Rice** (page 101), one of his favorites, into our healthier lifestyle. All I had to do was substitute olive oil for the butter and use turkey sausage and low-sodium chicken broth. That made a big difference in the fat and salt content without losing the flavor we both love.

And I'm really working on the moderation thing. When I first started watching what I ate, I gave up rice, potatoes, bread, and desserts to jump-start my metabolism. At first it was very hard: It can make you feel singled out, like, "Why am I the only one in my family who has to do this?" And you can dive into self-pity. It definitely took some adjustment. I'd be craving my usual big portions and lots of carbs and sweets, but I'd keep telling myself I had to cut back because now that my condition was out in the open, people were looking to me for some answers.

Once I started to lose weight, I began to feel better about eating less, and I started to feel better physically. People would see me out and about and tell me how good I was lookin', and I won't deny that that was a boost to my spirits and helped me keep on truckin'. Their reaction also made me realize that I could make a difference by encouraging folks who were in the same situation.

It wasn't easy to lose weight. I think that anybody can lose it, but it takes one hell of a person to keep it off! My favorite food in the whole world is potatoes, but for a while at first I gave up everything white—potatoes, rice, biscuits, bread, and pasta. I would eat only veggies and protein six days a week. Oh my gosh, was that *hard*! Then I gave myself one day a week to eat whatever I wanted—Saturday. I just *lived* for Saturdays. I'd go to a local restaurant and have me a wonderful cheeseburger with a side of broccoli instead of French fries. I would just sit and suck on that hamburger roll; it was so incredibly good. Nowadays, I'll just have my **Better Burgers** (page 141) made with extra-lean ground beef to satisfy my craving.

The rest of the week, I watched everything I ate. Michael and I would have a nice big salad every night with regular dressing because that doesn't have any carbs in it. We'd add about four ounces of shrimp, chicken, or steak and pile on a bunch of great veggies, such as cucumbers, tomatoes, and onions, and also raisins or dried cranberries, or even some nuts. It really is delicious! Two other salads we enjoy often are my **Double Green Salad with Green Goddess Dressing** (page 38) and my brand-new **Kale Caesar Salad** (page 50).

These days, I'll have some starch here and there and watch my portions and change my plate around. For instance, I'll have one piece of toast and scrambled eggs, or sometimes I'll fix myself an **Ultimate Egg Sandwich** (page 271). Another favorite is the **Fruity Yogurt Smoothie** (page 284) that Bobby concocted, with bananas, berries, and yogurt, all pureed in a satisfying shake.

I watch my carbs and pile my plate with scrumptious veggies, and I make sure to get some exercise. At this point, I'm not really dieting; I just don't eat nearly as much as I used to, and I watch my starches. I hardly ever have French fries anymore; I'll order a side of coleslaw instead, and I'm okay with it. In fact, raw cabbage is one of the best vegetables for your health, and my **Easy Coleslaw** (page 32) tastes just as good as the heavier versions.

My body and my appetite have learned to adjust, y'all. And I'm as surprised as you are. It's amazing how, over time, little changes can give you big results. Just this past weekend I had some girlfriends to visit, and one of them made a sugar-free dessert. It was so good, you'd never know it was sugar free. And I've managed to slim down even my richest desserts, like **Gooey Butter Cake** (page 328), by using less butter so that I can still enjoy them. My new recipes for fruit pies—like my **Apple Cherry Pie** (page 316) with dried cherries—are a great way to satisfy a sweet tooth with a lot less sugar and fat. So far, by making these adjustments, I've lost forty pounds over the last year, and I feel great. It definitely gets easier the more you do it, and the more you get used to not piling your plate high with everything in sight. I really do feel that if *I* can do it—given that I'm surrounded by food 24/7, and my job is cookin', eatin', and talkin' about food from sunrise to sunset—then *anybody* can do it.

I realize that I will never again be that 118-pound, 36-23-36 girl I once was. I think we all have a weight that we have to own, and that's where we're supposed to be. I also acknowledge that I am not going to live forever, nor do I want to die with a piece of lettuce in my mouth! I want to live life to the fullest, and one of life's biggest pleasures is eating. That's why it's great that you can make small changes in what and how much you eat, as opposed to giving up everything. Then that one day a week—usually when my family's over—I'll eat what I want.

But it's interesting; over time, what I want to eat has changed. Hard as it is to believe, your body does get used to smaller portions and feeling satisfied without being uncomfortably full. I'll now have two of my *Southwest Chicken Enchiladas* (page 172) and feel totally satisfied because they're so rich tasting. I poach the chicken meat and dip the tortillas in hot chicken broth instead of frying them, so they're actually healthy. And I'll limit myself to one of my *Cheddar Chive Muffins* (page 305). I adore these savory treats; sharp Cheddar and chives are so fantastic in a buttermilk muffin, and my family loves them too.

Now believe me, I still struggle with making the right food choices. It sure ain't always easy. I have found that it helps to lose weight together, and Michael has been enjoying my lightened-up dinners. Jamie and Bobby have dropped so much weight eating leaner—so it really has been a family thing. They absolutely love my *Slow Cooker Ribs* (page 132), an easy way to get tender, lip-smacking ribs just like Daddy used to make. They're sweet, salty, and tangy all at once!

Since I made a commitment to take care of myself, wonderful things have happened. It's like God has put me just where I needed to be. I feel so grateful for all the good things that the Lord has sent my way. And I want to thank everyone for being steadfast and loyal, and for sending me nothing but good wishes, love, and support.

Looking Ahead

We Southerners like to show our love by feeding people, particularly when someone is under a lot of stress. That's how you give a piece of yourself; it's immediate gratification for someone who's a people-pleaser. And offering a big ol' spread of down-home cookin' is a great way to share, even if you don't have a lot of money sitting in your bank account.

Food is also a powerful vehicle to get your family together. If I haven't seen my children in a while, I call them and say, "Hey, y'all, I'm going to be making something delicious tonight. And Bobby, you'll be proud of me; it's even low carb! Would ya'll come eat supper?" And almost always they'll say, "Yes, ma'am, we'll be there!" So many memories come out of that group of people gathered around my table. Michael really enjoys the fruits of my labor too. I love to feed him and to hear him say that he's crazy about a certain dish. One of our biggest pleasures is sitting down and having great food together. And it's even better now that we are eating healthier, because we don't leave the table feeling like we've overindulged.

I try to make every meal that I serve a celebration, because I believe a good Southerner always greets her guests at the door with a big smile and a big plate. Nowadays, I offer starters that are lighter in fats, such as my **Southern Tomato Sandwiches** (page 13). A little less butter makes a big difference in health, without sacrificing a bit of taste! The same is true for my **Mini Hot Browns** (page 9) that feature lean turkey, bacon, tomato, and cheese. Another new party favorite is **Boiled Shrimp with Curried Yogurt Dip** (page 25). The dip, made with Greek yogurt, is out of this world—nothing could go better with tender boiled shrimp!

I adore Thanksgiving, Christmas, and New Year's Day because everybody on both sides of the family comes, so we have around forty people. I invite my daughters-in-law's folks too; that way, Jamie and Bobby don't have to choose whose house to go to. I just thrive on feeding our extended family. Before we start, we all stand up and hold hands, and the circle is so big that it stretches across our den, through the kitchen, and around the living room. One of the children says grace, and then we all dig in. I tell y'all, being with my family at times like these is the most important thing in the world to me.

At Thanksgiving everyone brings a dish, which allows us all to show off our cooking skills. I make the meats and two sides, with a special emphasis on vegetables, given my new style of eatin'. Everybody devours my **Mashed Sweet Potatoes with Bourbon** (page 230) and no one even guesses that they are a lighter version, using maple syrup and orange juice for sweeteners. Then the day after Thanksgiving I make my **Southern Turkey Chili in a Biscuit Bowl** (page 180) with lean ground turkey instead of beef. The smiles on everyone's faces tell me I have a hit on my hands, so I want to pass this dish along to you!

I like to serve my crowd-pleasing **Roast Leg of Lamb with Mint** (page 148) on Christmas Eve, and for Christmas dinner, I always have a standing rib or tenderloin. With it I serve salad, lots of veggies, and some desserts that the kids love. Since I've been eating lighter, at these celebrations I'll have moderate portions of my favorite dishes, while watching my carbs, starches, and fats, and I'll feel perfectly satisfied. I've found that I hardly miss cutting out dessert. But on special occasions I'll have a piece of my lighter but scrumptious **Vanilla Buttermilk Pie** (page 321) or **Coconut Cake** (page 334). One big bonus of having lost weight is that I have so much more energy now. My days tend to run from early morning till late at night, with lots of travel thrown in, and sometimes, before I got healthier, I would just feel beat. But now I can go for hours on end without getting nearly as tired.

This past New Year's Day, I cooked up the best pot of collard greens I've ever put in my mouth. I made them with fresh pigs' tails. I served the collards with candied yams, black-eyed peas, rice with country-style ribs, baked ham, and coleslaw. I always cook the same thing on New Year's: black-eyed peas for luck, collard greens for financial success, and a hog jowl for health—go figure! That New Year's Day meal was better than Thanksgiving and Christmas put together. Again, I ate moderately and watched my carbs, and I felt better than ever starting off a brand-new year with a healthy focus and being so much slimmer and trimmer.

I anticipate being able to share my love of good food with y'all for many, many years to come. I am also thrilled about sharing the lighter recipes on the pages that follow. You'll notice that I'm using low-fat cream cheese or Greek yogurt in some dishes and about a third less butter and other fats. I'm replacing some sugar with honey and using less sugar and salt overall, cut by about a third to a half. You'll see some whole-wheat flours and pastas; panfrying or sautéing instead of deep-frying; an emphasis on delicious veggies; and a reduction in carbs throughout. My strategy is balance. It's not a "diet," but instead it's moderate eating without losing any of the delicious tastes and flavors that we all love. And while it's no secret that I love mayonnaise (over the years it has featured in I don't know how many dozens of my recipes), when I first set about lightening up my diet, I figured I'd better give light mayonnaise a try. And you know what I found out? It was just not for me. I would rather eat a dish made with a little less of the real stuff than use the same amount of the light stuff. And that has been the case with most other light products (with the notable exception of low-fat cream cheese and turkey bacon, both of which I use throughout this book). As far as low- and no-sugar items go, it's been hit-or-miss. Some work for me (sugar-free fruit preserves can be wonderful), and some don't. Now I realize that making these kinds of substitutions is a personal, case-by-case decision that depends on your specific dietary needs and your individual tastes. So to that end, I've made sure that the recipes in this book can work well with both the full-fat and full-sugar/carb products and their lighter cousins. If you use the low-fat/sodium/sugar products, these already lightened recipes (most of which have been reduced in fat or calories by at least 30 percent) will be even lighter. These choices keep food interesting and help keep you on the path to healthier eating. Experiment with the different options and find out what works for you. That's exactly what I did, and the changes have been nothing short of a miracle.

The recipes in this book will let everyone re-create the Southern meals I'm known for, with a little less butter, salt, and sugar. From my rich-tasting *Deviled Crab Salad* (page 48) to my unbelievably good whole-wheat *The Lady's New Cheesy Mac* (page 98), from *Pan-Seared Pork Loin with Tomato Gravy* (page 129) to my sweet-salty *Holiday Baked Ham* (page 124), from luscious *Creamy Peanut Butter Pie* (page 320) to *Peaches and Cream Cheesecake* (page 337), I just know you're gonna love my new take on these mouthwatering dishes. And I call out fifty of my favorite classic recipes that I've lightened up (such as my biscuits, pimiento cheese, and shrimp and grits) so y'all can find them easily.

Always keep in mind that you can enjoy good cookin' and eatin' and still be healthy—and I'm living proof of that!

With all my gratitude and love,

Paula Deen

Gettin' It Started
Apps and Snacks

Everyone who knows me knows I love a good party. And in my mind, no celebration is complete without a tempting array of appetizers. Spread out those little bites and the good times are sure to get started. That is what Southern hospitality is all about, y'all.

My new way of eating sure hasn't stopped me from entertaining. Just as I've rearranged my plate for better eating, I have redesigned my party menu too. In this chapter you'll still find classic party recipes such as *Family Reunion Deviled Eggs* (page 8) and *Southern Tomato Sandwiches* (page 13). You'll just find them made a little bit lighter. It's about moderation, y'all, not deprivation. A tablespoon less of butter here and there makes a real difference in health without changing the great taste of these dishes.

I'm also excited to unveil some fresh new recipes for you. My latest party hit is *Boiled Shrimp with Curried Yogurt Dip* (page 25). The Greek yogurt–based dip is creamy and tart and bursting with curry flavor. I tell you, tender boiled shrimp have found their perfect match in this dip.

If you haven't discovered the beauty of figs, I guarantee my *Bacon-Wrapped Figs* (page 5) will do the trick. Sweet, juicy figs wrapped in salty, crispy bacon are just about too delicious for words. Of course, anything wrapped in bacon is a winner in my book, but figs are a winner on their own. Fresh figs are a great source of vitamins and minerals and all sorts of other nutrients, but most important, figs are jam-packed with good-for-you fiber. They are so tasty I like to snack on them even without dressing them up.

I think my cleverest new appetizer offering is **Mini Hot Browns** (page 9). They are a smaller, finger-food version of the classic Kentucky hot brown that I love so much. Lean turkey, bacon, tomato, and cheese are sandwiched in between two whole-wheat bagel halves. The hot browns look so cute coming out on a great big platter. People just snap them up!

When you're figuring on what appetizers to set out, make sure you take into account what your main meal might be. If you're fixing to make something on the heavier side, like slow-cooked ribs or a great big tray of enchiladas, make sure you serve some lighter options up front. But if you have a leaner meal planned, like salad and fish, go ahead and pull out all the stops with your appetizers. It's all about balance.

When you find that balance in your daily diet, I reckon you'll find that you're not really doing without. Go on ahead and have your appetizers *and* your dessert! Just make sure the whole picture keeps your fat, sugar, carb, and calorie count in a healthful range. I tell you, I was so happy to learn this lesson I figured I had something to celebrate. So naturally, I got right on to planning my next party.

Crabby Shrimp Dip

This seafood dip is just as pretty as a picture. Its creamy, pale pink color looks fantastic in a dainty white bowl. But don't be fooled by its delicate appearance; this dip is zesty and decadently rich. My son Jamie introduced me to an Asian chili sauce called Sriracha that I think adds just the right zing to the dip without overpowering the seafood. But if you can't get your hands on Sriracha (which is sold in the international foods aisle of many supermarkets), go on ahead and use any old tomato-based chili sauce.

In a medium bowl, beat together the cream cheese, sour cream, lemon juice, chili sauce, Worcestershire sauce, and garlic until smooth. Fold in the crabmeat, shrimp, and scallions. Season to taste with salt and serve with crisp crackers and celery sticks.

Serves 8

1 package (8 ounces) low-fat cream cheese (Neufchâtel), at room temperature

¼ cup regular or light sour cream

2 tablespoons fresh lemon juice

1 to 2 teaspoons Sriracha or other chili sauce

½ teaspoon Worcestershire sauce

1 small garlic clove, finely chopped

6 ounces crabmeat, picked over to remove bits of shell

6 ounces cooked shrimp, peeled, deveined, and chopped

¼ cup chopped scallions (white and light green parts)

Salt to taste

Crackers and celery sticks for serving

HEALTHY DIPPERS

I can't stress enough the importance of choosing the right cracker or chip to dip into a delicious dip like this one. You can blow your healthy diet by choosing a fried, salty chip, and there are some excellent baked chips out there. Or better yet, load up the tray with crisp veggies for dipping.

Ham Biscuits

2½ cups self-rising flour,
 plus more for dusting

¼ cup cornstarch

½ teaspoon salt

1 tablespoon sugar

4 tablespoons (½ stick)
 cold unsalted butter,
 cut into small bits

1 cup buttermilk

½ cup milk

¾ cup finely chopped ham

1 tablespoon finely chopped
 fresh chives

These lighter-than-air biscuits are helped along by a little dose of cornstarch, which makes them just as tender as can be. While I used to mix my ham biscuits using heavy cream, these biscuits use buttermilk, which is naturally lower in fat. Filled with salty ham and fresh chives, they are a welcome sight for guests at any special gathering. But you don't need a special occasion to bake these biscuits. They are so easy to whip up that the only occasion I need is waking up with a hankering for them.

1. Preheat the oven to 450°F. Lightly grease a rimmed baking sheet with cooking spray.

2. In a large bowl, whisk together the flour, cornstarch, salt, and sugar. Cut in the butter with a fork or your hands until the mixture resembles coarse meal. Stir in the buttermilk and milk until just combined. Fold in the ham and chives.

3. Turn the dough out onto a lightly floured surface and, with the palms of your hands, knead the dough gently six or seven times, adding just enough flour as needed to keep the dough from sticking to your hands.

4. Pat the dough into a rectangle shape until it's about ½ inch thick. Using a 3-inch round biscuit cutter, cut the dough into biscuits, placing them at least 1 inch apart on the prepared baking sheet and spraying the tops with cooking spray. Gather the scraps and pat out again (do this only once). You should be able to get 16 biscuits from the dough. Bake until golden brown, about 12 minutes. Split the biscuits and serve them up while they're still warm.

Makes 16 biscuits

Bacon-Wrapped Figs

These sweet and salty morsels can be made in no time flat, which pretty much describes how quickly they will disappear when you set them out for your guests. When fig season is at its peak in late summer, you can bet on my serving bacon-wrapped figs. Sometimes, when I'm feeling a bit fancy, I serve them with the dipping sauce drizzled on the platter to create a pretty design right under the figs.

4 turkey or regular bacon slices, cut in half lengthwise, then each half cut into thirds to make 3-inch strips

6 fresh Black Mission or Brown Turkey figs, stems removed and figs quartered

¼ cup spicy brown mustard

¼ cup honey

1. Position an oven rack 5 to 6 inches from the heat. Preheat the broiler on high. Lightly grease a rimmed baking sheet with cooking spray.

2. Wrap the bacon around the figs so the seam is on the skin side of the figs. Place the figs, seam side down, on the prepared baking sheet and place the baking sheet on the prepared oven rack. Broil until the bacon is crisp and browned, about 6 minutes.

3. Meanwhile, to make the dipping sauce, in a small bowl, combine the mustard and honey and stir well.

4. Serve the figs immediately with toothpicks and the dipping sauce.

Makes 24 wrapped figs

2 tablespoons olive oil

¼ cup finely chopped fennel

2 cups loosely packed
chopped spinach

1 scallion (white and light green
parts only), chopped

½ teaspoon Paula Deen's
House Seasoning (see below)

2 tablespoons dry white wine

¼ cup grated Parmesan cheese

2 tablespoons whole-wheat
or regular panko bread crumbs

12 oysters on the half shell

1 lemon, cut into wedges,
for serving

Paula Deen's House Seasoning

*This seasoning of mine is good
to have on hand to punch up
meat, fish, poultry, veggies,
well, just about anything,
I'd say. Here's a recipe for a
healthy amount that should
last you a while in your pantry.*

1 cup salt

¼ cup freshly ground
black pepper

¼ cup garlic powder

In a small bowl, combine
the salt, pepper, and garlic
powder. Store in an airtight
container for up to 6 months.

Makes 1½ cups

Oysters Rockefeller

*Classic oysters Rockefeller is made with Pernod, an anise-flavored
liqueur from France. You can get a similar flavor using fresh fennel
instead and cooking it down with a little dry white wine. To make
this just the easiest party dish ever, have your fish market shuck
the oysters for you. Your guests will be so impressed when you
bring these out all dressed up with bright yellow lemon wedges.*

1. Position an oven rack in the upper third of the oven.
   Preheat the oven to 450°F. Line a rimmed baking sheet
   with a layer of lightly crumpled aluminum foil.

2. In a medium skillet, heat the oil over medium heat. Add
   the fennel and cook, stirring frequently, until the edges start
   to turn golden, about 2 minutes. Add the spinach, scallion,
   and House Seasoning and cook, stirring, for 30 seconds,
   until the spinach is wilted. Increase the heat to medium-high,
   add the white wine, and cook for 1 minute, until the wine
   has bubbled away. Place the spinach mixture in a medium
   bowl and let it cool to room temperature.

3. Meanwhile, in a small bowl, combine the Parmesan and
   bread crumbs.

4. Arrange the oysters on the prepared baking sheet, bringing
   the foil up and around the bottoms of the shells to keep them
   upright. Top the oysters with the spinach mixture, followed
   by the Parmesan mixture. Bake until the oysters are browned
   on the tops, 10 to 12 minutes.

5. Serve on pretty plates with the lemon wedges on the side.

Serves 4

Family Reunion Deviled Eggs

12 large eggs,
   hard boiled and peeled

2 tablespoons regular
   or light mayonnaise

¼ cup low-fat Greek yogurt

2 teaspoons Dijon mustard

¼ teaspoon hot sauce

Salt and freshly ground
   black pepper to taste

2 tablespoons chopped scallions
   (light and dark green parts)

Sweet paprika, for garnish

These tasty snacks always make me think fondly of my family and all the good times and good food we've shared. I've managed to make this treat just a little bit better for us by stirring in some low-fat Greek yogurt with the mayo. I like the nice kick of acidity it brings to the table. Don't think you have to save these for a special occasion. I like these deviled eggs at lunchtime, served on a bed of chopped fresh lettuce.

1. Halve the eggs lengthwise and pop the yolks out into a medium bowl. Arrange the whites on a pretty serving platter.

2. Mash the yolks with the mayonnaise, yogurt, mustard, hot sauce, and salt and pepper to taste until everything is thoroughly combined and smooth. Stir in the scallions.

3. Spoon the filling back into the egg whites and serve them with a pretty little dusting of paprika.

Makes 24 deviled eggs

Mini Hot Browns

This homey appetizer is just the thing for a casual get-together. It's a mini and lighter version of the classic Kentucky hot browns I love so much. If you're not familiar with a traditional hot brown, well, it is just about the most scrumptious sandwich: turkey, bacon, and tomato smothered in a thick, cheesy sauce. It's decadent, y'all. But you can feel pretty good about taking a couple of these mini versions down. And that sure is a good thing. Because I find them just about irresistible! I bet you will too.

2 tablespoons canola
    or safflower oil

2 tablespoons all-purpose flour

1 cup milk

¾ cup shredded Cheddar cheese

Salt and freshly ground
    black pepper to taste

5 mini whole-wheat bagels,
    separated into halves
    and toasted

½ pound sliced smoked turkey

10 slices (about ½ inch thick)
    plum tomato (from about
    3 tomatoes)

Hot paprika, for garnish

1. In a medium saucepan, heat the oil over medium-high heat. Whisk in the flour and cook, stirring with the whisk, for 1 minute. Add the milk, bring to a boil, and cook, stirring with the whisk, until thickened, about 3 minutes. Stir in the cheese until melted. Season to taste with salt and pepper.

2. Preheat the broiler. Place the bagel bottoms, cut side up, in a large baking dish. Divide the turkey and tomatoes among the bagels and top with the cheese sauce. Put the bagel tops on top. Broil until browned and bubbling, about 5 minutes. Sprinkle with a little paprika and serve hot and melty.

Makes 10 sandwiches

SMALLER CAN BE BETTER
I know my mantra used to be "the bigger, the better," but I've learned a thing or two. These mini hot browns are the perfect example of built-in portion control. I used to make my hot browns large and overstuffed. Finishing one sandwich would leave me so full. Now, I eat one or two of these mini versions, taking my time between bites, and I realize I'm satisfied before I've eaten too much.

Everyone's Favorite Pimiento Cheese

This pimiento cheese started out in life as my Bobby's favorite. Along the way, I decided to change the name because the fan club just kept on growing. Well, in homage to Bobby, I have made this staple of mine better for you by subbing out Greek yogurt for mayonnaise. You'll find this cheese is as creamy as it ever was without the added fat and calories the mayo brought along with it. And with that small change, it's once again Bobby's favorite pimiento cheese!

In a medium bowl, whisk together the yogurt, pimientos, onion (if using), House Seasoning, Worcestershire sauce, vinegar, and dry mustard. Add the Cheddar, Monterey Jack, and cream cheese and stir well until the mixture is smooth and evenly combined. Serve with whole-grain crackers and lots of crisp veggies.

Makes about 2 cups cheese

½ cup Greek yogurt

3 tablespoons chopped pimientos

1 teaspoon grated onion (optional)

½ teaspoon Paula Deen's House Seasoning (see page 6)

½ teaspoon Worcestershire sauce

½ teaspoon cider vinegar

¼ teaspoon dry mustard

1 cup shredded Cheddar cheese

1 cup shredded Monterey Jack cheese

3 ounces low-fat cream cheese (Neufchâtel), at room temperature

Whole-grain crackers and crisp veggies for serving

Georgia Caviar

1 cup cooked black-eyed peas
(from dried or canned
black-eyed peas)

1 cup fresh or frozen corn,
thawed

1 cup canned no-salt-added
diced tomatoes, drained

1 cup chopped red bell pepper

¼ cup chopped Vidalia
or other sweet onion

1 jalapeño pepper, seeded
and finely chopped

½ cup bottled Italian dressing

¼ teaspoon salt

⅛ teaspoon freshly ground
black pepper

Baked tortilla chips,
for serving

If you want good luck and prosperity throughout the year, any Southerner will tell you: Eat your black-eyed peas on New Year's Day. Legend has it that during the Civil War, Union soldiers burned all the crops near Vicksburg, Virginia, except the black-eyed peas. They mistook the peas for animal feed, thereby leaving the local people with some food to get them through those trying times. From this story, these little coin-shaped beans have come to represent good fortune throughout the year. And this here recipe is one of my favorite ways to enjoy my beloved black-eyed peas. It's a crunchy, tangy, healthy dip that I've made just a little bit healthier by cutting down on the bottled dressing, using no-salt-added canned tomatoes, and pairing it up with baked tortilla chips instead of fried. This recipe is the perfect example of how small changes really do add up to big results.

In a medium serving bowl, stir together the black-eyed peas, corn, tomatoes, red bell pepper, onion, jalapeño, dressing, salt, and pepper. Serve with tortilla chips.

Serves 8

Southern Tomato Sandwiches

It's not a party in the South until the tomato sandwiches are served!
These days, I swap out the mayo with heart-healthy avocado, which
gives the sandwiches a nice creaminess but is so much better for you.
Remember, it's still just as important to drain your tomatoes well
so that they don't make your bread all soggy. Also, be sure to cover
your sandwiches with a damp towel if you've made them ahead of
time so that the bread doesn't dry out. And, whatever you do, make
sure you grab yourself a sandwich as the platter walks out the
kitchen door because these treats will go fast.

2 small tomatoes,
   such as Roma (plum)
   tomatoes

8 slices soft whole-wheat bread

1 large ripe avocado, halved
   and pitted

¼ teaspoon Paula Deen's House
   Seasoning (see page 6),
   plus ⅛ teaspoon more
   to sprinkle on the tomatoes

½ teaspoon finely chopped
   fresh flat-leaf parsley

1. Thinly slice the tomatoes crosswise and drain them
   thoroughly between layers of paper towels.

2. Use a biscuit cutter or cookie cutter (a little larger than the
   diameter of the tomato slices) to cut rounds from the bread.

3. Scoop the avocado flesh into a medium bowl. Add the
   ¼ teaspoon of the House Seasoning and the parsley and
   mix until smooth.

4. Spread the avocado onto one side of each bread round.
   Sprinkle the tomato slices with the remaining ⅛ teaspoon
   House Seasoning. Place a tomato slice on a bread round,
   avocado side up, and top with another bread round, avocado
   side down. You can prepare these sandwiches several hours
   before you serve them. If you do, cover the sandwiches
   with a damp paper towel and refrigerate them until you're
   ready to serve.

Makes 4 sandwiches

Pimiento Cheese–Stuffed Mushrooms

1 pound medium button
mushrooms (about 24),
stems removed

½ cup Everyone's Favorite
Pimiento Cheese
(see page 11)
or jarred pimiento cheese

1 tablespoon dried
bread crumbs

*I haven't got enough fingers on my hands to count the many ways
I put pimiento cheese to use. I bake it into casseroles, stir it through
mac and cheese, slather it on toast, and stuff it into beautiful baked
button mushrooms for a scrumptious party appetizer.*

1. Position an oven rack in the upper third of the oven.
   Preheat the oven to 350°F.

2. Spoon the cheese evenly among the mushroom caps and top
   with the bread crumbs. Each mushroom should hold about
   1 teaspoon of stuffing. Place on a rimmed baking sheet and
   bake for 15 minutes, until the bread crumbs are golden.

Makes about 24 stuffed mushrooms

Cheese-Stuffed Baby Bell Peppers

6 baby bell peppers, preferably a
mix of red, orange, and yellow,
sliced in half lengthwise and
seeded

2 teaspoons olive oil

¼ cup soft goat cheese

¼ cup part-skim ricotta cheese

2 tablespoons grated
Parmesan cheese

1½ teaspoons chopped fresh
thyme

½ teaspoon freshly ground
black pepper

Large pinch of salt

2 tablespoons chopped fresh
basil (optional)

*Whenever I make these mellow and sweet bell peppers, I like to serve
them in a rainbow of colors—red, yellow, and orange. It makes the
platter so pretty when you bring it out. I also take care not to char
them too much so that their lovely colors shine through.*

1. Preheat the broiler. Place the bell pepper halves on a baking
   sheet and brush both sides of the peppers with the oil. Broil
   until slightly charred but not completely tender, 1 to 2
   minutes per side. Reduce the oven temperature to 375°F.

2. In a medium bowl, stir together the goat cheese, ricotta,
   Parmesan, thyme, black pepper, and salt. Spoon the mixture
   into the bell pepper halves. Return them to the oven and bake
   until the cheese is melted and the bell peppers are tender, 10
   to 15 minutes. Garnish with the chopped basil, if you'd like.

Serves 6

*With my precious twenty-four-year-old
blue-and-gold macaw, Lady Bird.* ▶

Benne Seed Wafers

¾ cup benne seeds

½ cup all-purpose flour

¼ teaspoon baking powder

¼ teaspoon salt

4 tablespoons (½ stick)
   unsalted butter,
   at room temperature

⅔ cup packed light brown sugar

1 large egg, lightly beaten

2 teaspoons pure vanilla extract

We Southerners call them benne seeds and the folks up North call them sesame seeds. Whatever the name, I absolutely love their subtle, nutty flavor. I especially love them baked into a buttery treat like this. And speaking of buttery, I have to admit that I was amazed when I first tasted these wafers. I never would have thought they would turn out so rich and delicious with only four tablespoons of butter. But, my goodness, was I wrong. And I've never been so happy to be mistaken. I enjoy these wafers on their own, or set them out at parties with my favorite pimiento cheese dip (see page 11).

1. Preheat the oven to 350°F. Line several rimmed baking sheets with parchment paper.

2. Spread the benne seeds on one of the prepared baking sheets and toast until lightly browned and fragrant, about 5 minutes. Transfer to a bowl to cool. Reduce the oven temperature to 325°F.

3. In a small bowl, whisk together the flour, baking powder, and salt. In an electric mixer fitted with the paddle attachment, beat the butter and brown sugar together until fluffy. Add the egg and beat until combined. Beat in the flour mixture just until combined. Stir in the vanilla and cooled benne seeds.

4. Drop rounded ½ teaspoons of dough onto the prepared baking sheets, about 1 inch apart. Bake for about 10 minutes, until the wafer edges are golden. Transfer to a wire rack to cool completely. The wafers will keep crisp in an airtight container for about 2 weeks.

Makes about 60 wafers

TOP TOAST

Make sure you do take the time to toast the benne seeds because that really brings out their flavor. You can do it in the oven as I do here, or you can toss them into a dry skillet and cook them for about 2 minutes over a medium heat, while shaking the pan.

Cheddar and Currant Cheese Ball

A cheese ball is a guaranteed party hit. Put one out on the serving table and you'll find half the party hovering over it. This Cheddar cheese ball gets its creamy texture from low fat cream cheese and a nice kick of sweetness from dried currants.

1. In an electric mixer fitted with the paddle attachment, or using a hand-held mixer, beat together the cream cheese, Cheddar, Parmesan, scallions, Worcestershire sauce, pepper, and salt until combined. Beat in ⅓ cup of the pecans and the currants.

2. Scrape the mixture onto a large sheet of plastic wrap. Form into a ball and chill until semifirm, about 30 minutes. Just before serving, coat the outside of the cheese ball with the remaining ¼ cup pecans and the parsley. Serve with the crackers.

Serves 12

1 package (8 ounces) low-fat cream cheese (Neufchâtel), at room temperature

1 cup shredded extra-sharp Cheddar cheese

½ cup grated Parmesan cheese

¼ cup finely chopped scallions

1 teaspoon Worcestershire sauce

¼ teaspoon freshly ground black pepper

⅛ teaspoon salt

⅓ cup plus ¼ cup finely chopped toasted pecans

½ cup dried currants

¼ cup chopped fresh parsley

Crackers, for serving

KEEPIN' IT REAL
Even though I'm watching my fat intake, I still use real whole milk cheese in recipes, just a little bit less of it. The low-cal, low-fat stuff is just not the same to me. The one exception I make, however, is the low-fat cream cheese called Neufchâtel. I find it tastes so good and still lends a creamy, rich texture to any dish I use it in.

CHEESE RING

3 ounces low-fat cream
    cheese (Neufchâtel),
    at room temperature

½ cup regular or light mayonnaise

1 cup cottage cheese

5 cups shredded sharp
    Cheddar cheese

½ cup chopped scallions
    (white and light green parts),
    plus more for garnish

½ teaspoon garlic powder

Freshly ground black pepper
    to taste

⅛ teaspoon cayenne pepper

1 cup finely chopped pecans

PEPPER JELLY

1½ teaspoons pectin powder
    (from two-part pectin
    system such as Pomona's
    Universal Pectin)

1½ cups sugar

¾ cup finely chopped red, yellow,
    or orange bell peppers

¼ cup finely chopped
    jalapeño peppers

1 cup cider vinegar

¼ cup fresh lemon juice

2 teaspoons calcium water
    (from two-part pectin system
    such as Pomona's Universal
    Pectin), prepared according
    to package directions

Three-Cheese Ring with Pepper Jelly

My favorite condiment to serve with a cheese ring is a sweet and spicy pepper jelly. By using a two-part pectin system for making jelly the sugar-free way, I didn't have to give up on the pepper jelly. Instead of using sugar to gel, it uses calcium. I tried it here to great success. This pepper jelly is seriously good. If you're watching your sugar intake, this is a great new way for you to make your homemade jellies.

1. To prepare the cheese ring: In a food processor, pulse together the cream cheese, mayonnaise, cottage cheese, and 3 cups of the Cheddar. Add the scallions, garlic powder, black pepper, and cayenne. Process until smooth and creamy. Scrape the mixture into a large bowl and stir in the remaining 2 cups Cheddar and ½ cup of the pecans.

2. Grease a 4-cup ring mold lightly with cooking spray and spoon the mixture into the mold. Cover with plastic wrap and refrigerate for 2 to 3 hours.

3. Meanwhile, to make the pepper jelly: In a small bowl, combine the pectin powder with ½ cup of the sugar and mix well.

4. In a medium saucepan over medium-high heat, bring the bell peppers, jalapeño, vinegar, and lemon juice to a boil. Reduce the heat and simmer, covered, for 5 minutes. Add the prepared calcium water and stir well. Bring the mixture back to a boil, add the pectin-sugar mixture, and stir vigorously until the sugar has fully dissolved. Add the remaining 1 cup sugar, stirring to combine for 1 to 2 minutes. Keep the mixture at a hard boil, without stirring, for 1 minute more.

5. Remove the pan from the heat and let it cool to room temperature. Pour the jelly into a jar or bowl, cover, and refrigerate for 1 to 2 hours, until the jelly has set.

6. Unmold the cheese ring and garnish with the remaining ½ cup pecans and some scallions. Serve with the pepper jelly.

Makes one 4-cup ring mold / Makes 1½ cups pepper jelly

Honey-Glazed Spicy Pecans

½ teaspoon salt

¼ teaspoon ground cinnamon

⅛ teaspoon ground nutmeg

⅛ teaspoon ground allspice

⅛ teaspoon freshly ground black pepper

2 cups whole pecans

2 tablespoons honey

1 tablespoon egg white, lightly beaten

I reckon pecans are just about my favorite nut. So most of the time, I enjoy them just as they are. But every once in a while I like to gussy them up a bit. And when I do, I turn to my spice drawer. These sweet and spicy nibbles, made with just a touch of honey and no sugar at all, are like a little flavor explosion. Pair them up with a nice tall glass of bubbles and you have yourself a party just waiting to happen. If you happen to have any left over, toss them into a salad the next day.

1. Preheat the oven to 325°F. Line a rimmed baking sheet with aluminum foil.

2. In a small bowl, stir together the salt, cinnamon, nutmeg, allspice, and pepper.

3. In a medium bowl, whisk together the honey and egg white. Add the pecans and toss until evenly coated. Sprinkle the spice mixture over the nuts and toss well.

4. Spread the nuts in a single layer on the prepared baking sheet. Bake, stirring once or twice, until the nuts are golden, 12 to 15 minutes. While still warm, transfer the nuts to a medium bowl, breaking up any clumps with your fingers. Cool completely and store in an airtight container for up to 1 week.

Makes 2 cups pecans

White Bean and Sun-Dried Tomato Dip

The tangy, sun-dried tomatoes in this white bean dip make it something really special. Set this out on the table, then go on ahead and watch your guests fall all over it.

1. In a food processor, pulse the garlic until it is roughly chopped. Add the beans and pulse until combined. Add the oil, lemon juice, and sour cream and pulse until combined, stopping to scrape down the sides of the bowl with a rubber spatula. Season to taste with salt and pepper.

2. Add the sun-dried tomatoes to the processor and pulse until just combined. Be careful not to overmix. Taste for seasoning and adjust. Scoop the dip into a bowl and serve at room temperature garnished with chopped parsley. I like to serve this dip with baked whole-wheat pita chips.

Serves 4

1 garlic clove

1 can (15½ ounces) cannellini or other white beans, rinsed and drained

2 tablespoons olive oil

1 tablespoon fresh lemon juice

2 tablespoons regular or light sour cream

Salt and freshly ground black pepper to taste

6 sun-dried tomato halves in olive oil, finely chopped

Chopped fresh flat-leaf parsley, for garnish

Pickled Shrimp

When I'm invited round to friends' houses, I like to show up with a homemade treat in a pretty little mason jar. And pickled shrimp is a fine example of a homemade goody that is always welcome. In this version I use already-cooked shrimp, which makes it ever so easy. All you need to do is make up the brine, put everything together in a jar, and let the flavorings work their magic.

¾ cup white wine vinegar

¾ cup water, plus more as needed

1 tablespoon black peppercorns

1 tablespoon coriander seeds

1 teaspoon cumin seeds

¼ teaspoon salt

6 garlic cloves, peeled

½ cup fresh lime juice

1½ pounds medium or large shrimp, cooked, peeled, and deveined

1 red onion, thinly sliced

2 jalapeño peppers, sliced (remove the seeds for a milder pickle)

1. In a small saucepan, combine the vinegar, the ¾ cup water, the peppercorns, coriander seeds, cumin seeds, salt, and garlic and bring to a boil over medium-high heat. Reduce the heat to medium and simmer for 5 minutes. Let the liquid cool to room temperature and add the lime juice.

2. Meanwhile, in a 1½-quart jar (or nonreactive bowl), layer the shrimp, red onion, and jalapeños. Pour the liquid into the jar, adding up to ¼ cup water, if necessary, to cover the whole lot. Refrigerate for 8 hours or overnight before serving. Keeps for up to 3 days in the refrigerator.

Serves 6 to 8

Mexican 5-Layer Dip

1 large ripe avocado,
  halved and pitted

1 teaspoon fresh lime juice

¼ teaspoon Paula Deen's
  House Seasoning
  (see page 6)

1 can (16 ounces) refried beans

1 cup regular or light sour cream

1 cup drained fresh tomato salsa
  (from the refrigerator case)

1 cup shredded Mexican-style
  cheese

Baked tortilla chips and crunchy
  veggies (carrots, celery, jicama),
  for serving

You are not going to believe this one, y'all! I managed to cut out an entire cup of mayonnaise from this classic dip of mine, and it is still so creamy and tasty. Just watch out though: You will have to stop yourself from devouring the whole thing before your guests show up. Sometimes I serve this dip with baked tortilla chips, but crunchy veggie sticks make it colorful and even better for you.

1. Scoop the avocado flesh into a small bowl and, using a fork, mash it with the lime juice and House Seasoning.

2. In a medium shallow serving bowl, layer the beans followed by the avocado mixture, then the sour cream and salsa. Scatter the cheese on top and serve with the chips and vegetables for dipping.

Serves 8

Boiled Shrimp
with Curried Yogurt Dip

I have doubled up on the flavor for this app. First, I boil the shrimp with all sorts of fragrant seasonings, like coriander seeds, allspice berries, and garlic. And I boil the shrimp in their shells so they stay nice and plump. Next, I mix up a curry-spiced yogurt dip that beats plain old cocktail dip, hands down. We do love our shrimp down here in Savannah, so when I brought this to a party for the first time, you can bet the guests beelined straight to it.

1. In a medium pot, combine the salt, coriander seeds, peppercorns, allspice, garlic, bay leaves, and 8 cups water and bring to a boil. Boil gently for 5 minutes to bring out the flavors of the seasonings. Add the shrimp and boil until they are pink, about 2 minutes. Drain the shrimp and run briefly under cold water. If you like, you can peel them now, but be sure to leave the tails intact.

2. In a small serving bowl, stir together the yogurt, curry powder, honey, and lemon juice and season to taste with salt. Place the bowl of dip on a serving platter and surround with the plump, pink shrimp.

Serves 4 to 6

1 tablespoon salt,
   plus more to taste for the dip

1 tablespoon coriander seeds

1 teaspoon black peppercorns

1 teaspoon whole allspice berries

2 garlic cloves, peeled and
   lightly crushed

2 bay leaves

1 pound medium shrimp,
   unpeeled

1 container (7 ounces)
   Greek yogurt

1½ teaspoons curry powder

1 teaspoon honey

1 teaspoon fresh lemon juice

2

Salads and Slaws

I have always loved a good, hearty salad. In the past, I have to admit, my salads have skewed toward the heavy side. But now, my new attitude toward food has made me rethink this. Whereas yesterday I might have loaded up my salads with all sorts of sweet tidbits and rich dressings (I do love my mayonnaise), today I'll pile on the dark greens or lean meats and use a lighter dressing to bring it all together. And doggone it if I haven't found I still love my salads.

The key, folks, is to keep it interesting. There's more to salads than just iceberg lettuce. I've opened up my palate to a world of leafy greens. ***Double Green Salad with Green Goddess Dressing*** (page 38) features two that I'm absolutely loving right now: baby spinach and romaine. But I haven't stopped there. My ***Roasted Root Vegetable Salad with Honey, Goat Cheese, and Walnuts*** (page 59) is highlighted by the peppery bite of baby arugula, a leaf that will add interest to just about any dish. A real showstopper on this tour of green leaves is the all-new ***Kale Caesar Salad*** (page 50). The crisp, earthy kale creates a modern twist on the classic dish that is sure to make this salad everybody's favorite.

These days you'll find lots of fresh raw veggies in my salads because they're just the best stuff for you and I adore their snappy texture. Turns out, my love of coleslaw all these years has been darn good for me. Crunchy, raw cabbage tops the list of good-for-you vegetables, and my **Easy Coleslaw** (page 32) is a tasty way to get your fill.

The last hurdle I had to clear with my salads was the dressing. You'll find a lighter style of dressing in these recipes, dressings that feature less oil and a little less mayo. They run the gamut from the fragrant flavor of my herb vinaigrette on **Fresh Corn and Tomato Salad with Herb Vinaigrette** (page 58) to the zinging, mustardy dressing I toss through **Hot French Green Bean and Potato Salad** (page 40). A big thanks goes out to my son Bobby for introducing me to the many healthful benefits of Greek yogurt. I've been adding it to my creamy dressings like the one in **Creamy Tuna and Potato Salad** (page 49). This dressing is so velvety smooth you'd swear I'd added a cup of mayonnaise.

Now, my husband, Michael, he took a little more convincing on the salad front. I had to put my thinking cap on to come up with a new batch of salads that would satisfy this tough critic. So I devised a wickedly delicious **Deviled Crab Salad** (page 48) that's rich, creamy, and tastes of the sea. Even without a drop of cream, he still thinks it tastes so sinful he's just about convinced himself he's not eating salad when he has this delicious concoction.

The highlight of this salad chapter for me has got to be **Picnic Wild Rice Salad with Cranberries and Pecans** (page 45). I will be toting this one around to all my outdoor dining invitations from now on. I've always loved a good rice salad, but I found out that white rice is more of a "sometimes food" for those with type 2 diabetes. That revelation reminded me of the untamed beauty of wild rice. It's packed with protein, it's naturally fat free, and it brings such full flavor to the dish all on its own that I find you don't even need to dress it up too much. All these wonderful health benefits make wild rice a better choice for diabetics and healthy eating in general.

With a wide array of scrumptious salad recipes at our fingertips, even Michael has become a salad guy. It's one of the first things he eats on his plate these days. And that is no small victory.

Black-Eyed Pea Salad

I can toss this scrumptious bean salad together in the blink of an eye. Like any true Southerner, I love buttery black-eyed peas paired up with a tangy dressing. And the romaine lettuce, cucumber, and radishes add a nice crunch to the salad, while the avocado brings a satisfying creaminess. This is the perfect side dish to any barbecue.

1. To make the vinaigrette, in a small bowl, whisk together the vinegar, mustard, and salt. Slowly whisk in the oil until combined and season to taste with pepper.

2. In a large bowl, combine the romaine, black-eyed peas, cucumber, tomato, avocado, scallions, and radishes. Add the vinaigrette and toss through. Give it a taste and adjust the seasonings to your liking.

Serves 6

1 tablespoon balsamic vinegar

1 teaspoon Dijon mustard

½ teaspoon salt

¼ cup olive oil

Freshly ground black pepper to taste

2 cups romaine lettuce, thinly sliced

1 can (15 ounces) black-eyed peas, rinsed and drained

¾ cup chopped cucumber

½ cup chopped tomato

½ cup chopped ripe avocado

¼ cup thinly sliced scallions (white and light green parts)

¼ cup sliced radish

7-Layer Molded Salad

2 packages (0.3 ounce each)
   regular or sugar-free
   lemon gelatin

2 cups boiling water,
   plus 1½ cups cold

1 tablespoon fresh lemon juice

½ cup drained mandarin
   orange segments

¼ cup coarsely chopped walnuts

2 tablespoons raisins

1 banana, peeled and sliced

2 tablespoons chopped
   dried apricots

1 can (8 ounces) crushed
   pineapple, drained well

1 cup cottage cheese

This version of seven-layer salad is cool and creamy and crunchy and chewy. Sometimes I make my molded salads with vegetables, but I decided to make this one chock-full of sweet, yummy fruit. And what a wise decision it was.

1. In a medium heatproof bowl, mix the gelatin with the boiling water until completely dissolved. Stir in the cold water and lemon juice. Refrigerate, covered, until the gelatin is just wiggly but not firmed up (like loose jelly), about 1 hour.

2. Spoon ½ cup of the gelatin into a 6-cup mold. Arrange the orange segments over the top and cover with another ½ cup gelatin. Scatter the walnuts and raisins on top and cover with another ½ cup gelatin. Next, layer the banana and apricots on top of the gelatin.

3. In a small bowl, fold 1 cup of the gelatin into the crushed pineapple and spoon evenly over the banana layer. Fold the cottage cheese into the remaining 1 cup gelatin and spoon over the pineapple layer. Refrigerate until firm, about 4 hours or overnight. Unmold and serve.

Serves 8

Easy Coleslaw

1 container (7 ounces)
   plain low-fat yogurt

¼ cup buttermilk

3 tablespoons balsamic vinegar

1 head green or red cabbage
   (2 pounds), shredded, or 2 bags
   (16 ounces each) shredded
   green or red cabbage

½ cup chopped fresh dill

Salt and freshly ground
   black pepper to taste

This is just as easy and tasty as my classic coleslaw, but it's plenty lighter. I use low-fat yogurt and buttermilk in place of full-fat mayo. And instead of sugar to sweeten up the slaw, I throw in a bit of balsamic vinegar. You're bound to find this in my fridge most days because I tend to make more than I need. That way I can pile some on just about anything throughout the week.

In a large serving bowl, whisk together the yogurt, buttermilk, and balsamic vinegar. Add the cabbage and dill and toss thoroughly to coat. Season to taste with salt and pepper. This salad is best made at least an hour or two before you serve it so the flavors have time to come together.

Serves 12 to 15

BUTTERMILK BOASTS
Buttermilk may sound like it is super fatty, but the truth is it's actually lower in fat and calories than regular milk. It's also a great source of calcium, protein, and many other vitamins and minerals. It is simply the liquid left over after butter has been churned. I like the tangy taste and added creaminess it brings to sauces and marinades. And, of course, we Southerners have long been using it in our baked goods to achieve a light, fluffy texture.

Colorful Broccoli, Bell Pepper, and Carrot Slaw

Pretty as a picture, y'all! And this salad tastes as good as it looks. Next time you're invited over to a friend's house and they ask you to bring a salad, skip the plain green salad and show up with this one. It's called going the extra mile.

1. In a small bowl, whisk together the yogurt, lemon juice, garlic, and salt. Whisk in the oil, parsley, and pepper to taste.

2. Slice each broccoli floret into ¼-inch-thick slabs. In a large serving bowl, combine the broccoli, red bell pepper, yellow bell pepper, carrot, and sunflower seeds. Add the dressing and toss to coat. Let the salad stand for 10 minutes, then give it another toss and serve.

Serves 4 to 6

¼ cup plain yogurt

1 tablespoon fresh lemon juice

1 garlic clove, finely chopped

½ teaspoon salt

1½ tablespoons canola or safflower oil

2 tablespoons chopped fresh flat-leaf parsley

Freshly ground black pepper to taste

1 head broccoli, cut into large florets (2 cups)

½ cup thinly sliced red bell pepper

½ cup thinly sliced yellow bell pepper

1 carrot, grated (about ½ cup)

3 tablespoons sunflower seeds

FLOWER POWER
I sprinkle sunflower seeds into my salads a lot these days. I find them deliciously nutty and I love that they are packed with a whole host of vitamins and minerals. I also like them on their own. I carry them around in my purse to stave off hunger between meals. They're a great portable snack.

All-New Macaroni Salad

This lighter version of my classic macaroni salad features carrots, radishes, and scallions, making it a gorgeous medley of colors. The lemon juice and parsley keep it nice and bright, perfect for spring picnics and summer barbecues. It's a recipe just made to feed a crowd, so whip up a big batch when you're expecting guests.

1. In a large pot of boiling salted water, cook the pasta according to the package directions. Drain well and rinse with cold water until the pasta is no longer warm.

2. In a large bowl, combine the carrots, radishes, olives, parsley, and scallions.

3. In a small bowl, whisk together the mayonnaise, lemon juice, and salt and pepper to taste. Add the cooled pasta to the vegetables and toss. Pour in the dressing and toss until combined. Serve at room temperature or cold.

Serves 10 to 12

1 pound elbow macaroni

2 carrots, grated

¾ cup thinly sliced radishes

½ cup sliced pimiento-stuffed olives

½ cup chopped fresh flat-leaf parsley

2 scallions (white and light green parts), thinly sliced

¾ cup regular or light mayonnaise

3 tablespoons fresh lemon juice

Salt and freshly ground black pepper to taste

Pasta, Chicken, and Veggies Salad

2 boneless, skinless chicken breasts (½ pound each)

2 to 2½ cups low-sodium chicken broth

1 fresh thyme sprig

½ teaspoon black peppercorns

1 bunch thin asparagus (about 1 pound), woody ends trimmed, cut into 1-inch pieces

½ cup sun-dried tomatoes in olive oil, thinly sliced

1 medium yellow squash, cut in half lengthwise and cut across in ¼-inch slices

8 ounces whole-wheat or regular penne

2 tablespoons fresh lemon juice

2 teaspoons white wine vinegar

½ teaspoon finely chopped garlic

¼ cup finely chopped fresh basil

½ teaspoon salt

¼ teaspoon freshly ground black pepper

½ cup olive or vegetable oil

½ cup finely grated Parmesan cheese

Michael just adores a pasta salad with chicken. So in order to sneak some more vegetables into his diet, I decided to create a chicken and pasta salad with some veggies tucked in. When he eats this salad, along with the yummy pasta and chicken, he's munching away at asparagus, sun-dried tomatoes, and squash. And I get a healthy and happy hubby in the bargain!

1. Place the chicken in a deep skillet or saucepan just large enough to hold it and add enough broth just to cover the chicken. Add the thyme and peppercorns to the broth. Bring to a boil over medium-high heat, partially covered, and boil for 1 minute. Turn the chicken breasts over, remove the pan from the heat, and let the chicken sit in the hot liquid, covered tightly, for 15 minutes. Remove the chicken to a plate, tent with aluminum foil, and reserve.

2. Prepare a medium bowl with ice water. In a large pot of boiling salted water, cook the asparagus and sun-dried tomatoes until the asparagus are bright green and crisp-tender, 1 minute. Using a slotted spoon, transfer the asparagus and tomatoes to the bowl of ice water. Add the squash to the boiling water and cook for 1 minute. Using a slotted spoon, remove the squash from the boiling water and, along with the drained asparagus and tomatoes, transfer to a serving bowl that will be large enough to hold the pasta and chicken as well.

3. Return the water to a boil, add the pasta, and cook according to the package directions. Drain the pasta well and set aside to cool.

4. To make the dressing, in a small bowl, combine the lemon juice, vinegar, garlic, basil, salt, and pepper. Slowly whisk in the oil until the mixture is well combined. Stir in ¼ cup of the Parmesan.

5. Slice the chicken breasts in half lengthwise, then crosswise into ¼-inch slices and add to the bowl with the vegetables. Toss with ¼ cup of the dressing. When the pasta is cool, add it to the chicken and veggie mixture. Drizzle with the remaining dressing and toss well to coat. Top with the remaining ¼ cup Parmesan. Serve at room temperature or refrigerate until you are ready to serve.

Serves 4

Pasta and Bean Salad

If you're a bean lover like I am, this salad is for you. It's loaded up with black-eyed peas, kidney beans, chickpeas, and even some fresh green beans to brighten things up. This salad is so satisfying and hearty I usually serve it with a simple piece of grilled fish or chicken and call it a day.

1. Prepare a large bowl with ice water. Bring a large pot of salted water to a boil over medium-high heat. Add the green beans and cook for 2 to 3 minutes, until crisp-tender. Remove the beans from the pot with a slotted spoon and transfer to the ice water. Let the beans cool down for 5 minutes in the ice water, then drain and set aside.

2. Return the large pot of water to a boil and add the pasta. Cook according to the package directions and drain well.

3. Meanwhile, make the dressing. In a small bowl, combine the vinegar, mustard, lime juice, and shallots. Slowly add the oil, whisking until the mixture is well combined. Season to taste with salt and pepper.

4. In a large bowl pretty enough to serve in, combine the green beans or wax beans, pasta, bell pepper, red onion, black-eyed peas, kidney beans, chickpeas, and basil and mix well. Pour half the dressing over the salad and gently stir to coat. Give the salad a taste and adjust the seasonings. Chill the salad until you are ready to serve. Just before serving, add the remainder of the dressing and toss to combine.

Serves 8 to 10

6 ounces green beans or wax beans or a combination of the two, trimmed and cut into thirds (about 1¼ cups)

8 ounces whole-wheat mini pasta shells

3 tablespoons cider vinegar

1 teaspoon Dijon mustard

1 tablespoon fresh lime juice

3 tablespoons finely chopped shallot

3 tablespoons olive oil

Salt and freshly ground black pepper to taste

¼ cup finely chopped red bell pepper

½ cup thinly sliced red onion

¾ cup canned black-eyed peas, rinsed and drained

¾ cup canned kidney beans, rinsed and drained

¾ cup canned chickpeas, rinsed and drained

¼ cup thinly sliced fresh basil, plus more to taste

Double Green Salad with Green Goddess Dressing

DRESSING

2 anchovy fillets

1 garlic clove, finely chopped

⅓ cup buttermilk

¼ cup regular or light mayonnaise

¼ cup fresh flat-leaf parsley leaves

¼ cup fresh basil leaves

2 tablespoons thinly sliced scallion

1 tablespoon chopped fresh tarragon

2 teaspoons fresh lemon juice

¼ teaspoon salt

Freshly ground black pepper to taste

SALAD

6 cups chopped romaine lettuce

6 cups baby spinach

1 cup cherry tomatoes, halved

1 cup chopped cucumber

I've dressed this salad with a lighter version of my scrumptious Buttermilk Green Goddess Dip. It's one of the salads that went a long way toward turning Jamie into a salad guy. He couldn't get over how decadent and delicious it was, even though it is chock-full of good-for-you raw spinach and crunchy romaine. And I couldn't agree more. It feels like a downright treat digging into this plate of greens.

1. To make the dressing: In a food processor or blender, puree the anchovies, garlic, buttermilk, mayonnaise, parsley, basil, scallion, tarragon, lemon juice, salt, and pepper to taste until smooth and bright green.

2. To make the salad: In a large salad bowl, combine the romaine, spinach, tomatoes, and cucumber. Pour in the dressing and toss to coat. Serve immediately.

Serves 6

Hot French Green Bean and Potato Salad

½ pound small red potatoes, unpeeled

2 tablespoons low-sodium chicken broth

1 teaspoon, plus 1 tablespoon olive oil

2 teaspoons white wine vinegar

2 teaspoons whole-grain mustard

1 pound green beans, trimmed

Salt and freshly ground black pepper to taste

Sorry, potatoes, but the green beans get top billing in this salad. This recipe is a perfect example of how I've changed the balance on my plate. Although I load up on the greens, I haven't done away with the carbs altogether. You'll notice that I cut up the potato into pretty small pieces. I find that makes it seem like there's more in the bowl— and helps to ensure that I get a little potato in each and every bite.

1. In a medium pot, cover the potatoes with cold salted water. Bring to a boil over medium-high heat and cook until the potatoes are tender, about 15 minutes.

2. Meanwhile, in a medium bowl, whisk together the chicken broth, 1 teaspoon of the oil, the vinegar, and 1 teaspoon of the mustard. In a separate medium bowl, whisk together the remaining 1 tablespoon oil and the remaining 1 teaspoon mustard.

3. When the potatoes are done, remove with a slotted spoon. Add the green beans to the same pot and cook until crisp-tender, 2 to 3 minutes. Drain.

4. Meanwhile, when the potatoes are cool enough to handle, cut into quarters lengthwise and then slice crosswise into ¼-inch pieces. Add to the bowl with the broth mixture and toss until the dressing has been absorbed. Add the green beans to the bowl with the oil and mustard and toss to coat. Add the potatoes to the green beans and toss gently to combine. Season to taste with salt and pepper.

Serves 4 to 6

Nutty Couscous Salad
with Oranges

I've found that a light, fluffy couscous salad makes for a nice change of pace in my weekday meals, and it's so easy to make. The trick with couscous is that you need to layer it up with lots of strong flavors from nuts, fruits, and fresh herbs; otherwise it can be pretty bland. I use oranges and pistachios here, but feel free to experiment with different nut and fruit combos to suit your mood.

1. In a small pot, bring the water to a boil over medium-high heat. Stir in the couscous, remove from the heat, and cover with a tight-fitting lid. Let the couscous stand until it has absorbed the water, about 5 minutes. Fluff with a fork and cool to room temperature. Place the couscous in a medium serving bowl.

2. Add the orange zest to the couscous. Peel the oranges and slice crosswise into ½-inch-thick rounds, removing any seeds. Pull apart the segments of the rounds, discarding the fibrous pieces. Add to the couscous.

3. Toss in the pistachios, scallion, parsley, oil, lemon juice, salt, and cayenne. Taste and adjust the seasonings if you like.

Serves 4

1 cup water

⅔ cup dry whole-grain or regular couscous

2 medium oranges, plus ½ teaspoon finely grated orange zest

⅓ cup unsalted pistachios, roasted and coarsely chopped

3 tablespoons thinly sliced scallion

2 tablespoons chopped fresh flat-leaf parsley

2 tablespoons olive oil

1 teaspoon fresh lemon juice

½ teaspoon salt

⅛ teaspoon cayenne pepper

NUTS ABOUT NUTS
You'll notice that a great number of my salads feature nuts. That is no accident! They are an important and satisfying protein source that I feel good about adding to my dishes. And they do the trick in helping me feel more full from a lighter-style meal.

Barley Salad with Feta, Tomatoes, and Scallions

I've always loved barley in my soups. But I've discovered how delicious it is in a fresh salad too. Barley's nuttiness pairs up perfectly with a tangy lemon dressing, and its slightly chewy texture sits so nicely next to crisp fresh veggies. Not to mention, it's good for you! Barley is packed full of fiber and other nutrients and is especially good for those of us with type 2 diabetes because it helps to regulate glucose and insulin. Now, I call that a win-win.

1. In a large bowl, combine the barley, tomatoes, cucumber, parsley, scallions, and feta.

2. In a small bowl, whisk together the oil, lemon juice, and salt and pepper to taste.

3. Pour the dressing over the salad and toss until well coated. Serve at room temperature.

Serves 4 to 6

3½ cups cooked barley, at room temperature

2 plum tomatoes, chopped

1 cucumber, peeled and chopped

¼ cup chopped fresh flat-leaf parsley

2 thinly sliced scallions (white and light green parts)

1 cup crumbled feta cheese

6 tablespoons olive oil

1 tablespoon fresh lemon juice

Salt and freshly ground black pepper to taste

1 cup quinoa, rinsed and drained

2 tablespoons dry white wine

2 cups water

¼ cup sliced blanched almonds

2 tablespoons white wine vinegar

1 teaspoon Dijon mustard

1 teaspoon honey

1 teaspoon finely grated
  orange zest

2 tablespoons olive oil

Salt and freshly ground
  black pepper to taste

1 cup seedless red grapes,
  cut in half widthwise

2 tablespoons chopped fresh
  flat-leaf parsley

SUPER GRAIN
If you're not familiar with
quinoa, I highly recommend
you give it a whirl. This
seed from South America is
prepared like other grains
such as barley and rice.
What makes it a super
grain, though, is its
staggering protein count.
I'm nuts about this nutty
staple, whether it's dressed
up with lots of fixings or
served just as is. And while
you used to find it only in
health food stores, these
days you can buy it in most
groceries and supermarkets.

Quinoa Salad
with Grapes and Almonds

When I was told that I needed to curb my carbs, I was at a loss at first. Carbs were a central part of my diet, and I didn't know where to turn. But then I collected myself and decided the best two people to talk to about this dilemma were my boys, Jamie and Bobby. Well, I am so glad I did. They opened me up to a whole world of grains that are better for me. And quinoa is one of them. It's a funny-looking thing, but it's got a lovely nutty flavor and a wonderful chewy yet crunchy texture. This salad of quinoa, sweet red grapes, and toasted almonds is out of this world. You can substitute couscous for the quinoa—just follow the directions on the package to cook it.

1. In a medium saucepan, toast the quinoa for a couple minutes over medium heat, stirring often, until it is fragrant and the individual grains have separated. Carefully add the wine and water to the pan. Bring to a boil over high heat, then reduce the heat to low, cover the pan, and simmer for 15 to 20 minutes, until the liquid is absorbed and each grain has a visible little thread. Fluff the quinoa with a fork, then cover and allow it to sit off the heat for 10 minutes. Scrape the quinoa into a medium serving bowl and cool to room temperature.

2. In a small skillet, toast the almonds over medium-low heat until golden brown, shaking the pan occasionally to avoid burning. Set aside to cool.

3. In a small bowl, whisk together the vinegar, mustard, honey, and orange zest. Slowly add the oil, whisking until it is completely incorporated. Season to taste with salt and pepper.

4. When the quinoa has cooled, stir in the grapes, vinegar dressing, and the parsley. Toss well to combine.

5. Add the almonds just before serving. Serve at room temperature or chilled.

Serves 4

Picnic Wild Rice Salad
with Cranberries and Pecans

I think it's no secret that nuts are high up on my list of favorite foods, and pecans are high up on my favorite list of favorite nuts. I highly recommend you toss this salad together while the rice is still warm. That way the rice will soak up more of the dressing and you get lots of flavor in every bite. And here's a secret: If you don't have any wild rice, try this with brown or white rice on their own. The flavors are so good no one will be the wiser.

¾ cup pecans

½ cup fresh orange juice

3 tablespoons white wine vinegar

3 tablespoons olive oil

2 cups wild and brown rice mix, cooked according to the package directions

1 cup chopped scallions (white and light green parts)

¾ cup dried cranberries

Salt and freshly ground black pepper to taste

1. Preheat the oven to 350°F.

2. Spread the nuts in a single layer on a rimmed baking sheet and bake until toasted and aromatic, 5 to 7 minutes. When they are cool enough to handle, coarsely chop the nuts.

3. Meanwhile, in a small bowl, whisk together the orange juice, vinegar, and oil.

4. In a large bowl, combine the rice with the chopped nuts, scallions, cranberries, and orange dressing. Toss to coat well and season to taste with salt and pepper.

Serves 10 to 12

PILE ON THE PROTEIN
You can make a satisfying one-dish lunch out of most salads by adding meat or seafood to them. My top choice for this salad is grilled chicken.

Watermelon Cucumber Salad with Fresh Basil

4 teaspoons fresh lime juice

1 tablespoon olive oil

4 cups 1-inch watermelon cubes

2 cucumbers, peeled, seeded, and cut into 1-inch chunks

1 tablespoon chopped fresh basil

Salt to taste

Super refreshing, y'all, this salad is a must-serve at summer barbecues or picnics; it just cools you right down. If you're starting out with your watermelon and cukes straight out of the fridge, you can serve the salad right away. Otherwise, make sure you chill it for a bit so it's nice and cool and crunchy. And if you're taking it with you to the beach or park, make sure to surround it with plenty of ice packs in the cooler.

1. In a small bowl, whisk together the lime juice and olive oil.

2. In a medium bowl, toss the watermelon and cucumbers with the lime dressing and the basil. Season to taste with salt and serve chilled.

Serves 4

Deviled Crab Salad

5 tablespoons olive oil

2 tablespoons fresh lemon juice

2 teaspoons Dijon mustard

Paula Deen's House Seasoning
(see page 6) to taste

1 pound lump crabmeat,
picked over for bits of shell

½ cup chopped yellow
bell pepper

2 tablespoons chopped fresh
chives

1 head butter lettuce

Hot paprika, for garnish

Although I had my doubts that a deviled crab salad could possibly be as good without a cup of mayo in the dressing, this recipe proves me wrong. A simple lemon juice, mustard, and olive oil dressing makes for a salad that's just as delicious as my old recipe, but much better for you. I mound the crab salad on top of soft butter lettuce leaves. Served on my good china, this makes for one elegant luncheon salad.

1. In a small bowl, whisk together the oil, lemon juice, mustard, and House Seasoning. Place the crabmeat in a medium bowl and, using a rubber spatula, gently fold in 5 tablespoons of the dressing, the bell pepper, and chives. Season with more House Seasoning, if you think it needs it.

2. Divide the lettuce leaves among six plates, with the stems facing inward and the leaves fanning out. Mound the crabmeat in the center of the plates (on top of the stems) and sprinkle with paprika.

Serves 6

Creamy Tuna and Potato Salad

What's better than a classic potato salad? Why, a classic potato salad with tuna thrown in. This salad is more like a meal. It's got your protein, it's got your veggies, and it's got your carbs. I like to serve this for lunch when I've got the ladies over for a game of cards and some good old-fashioned gossip.

1. In a large pot, cover the potatoes with cold salted water. Bring to a boil over medium-high heat, then reduce the heat to medium and gently simmer for 15 to 20 minutes, until the potatoes are tender and can be pierced easily with the tip of a sharp knife. Drain well and set the potatoes aside to cool to room temperature.

2. In large bowl, combine the yogurt, mayonnaise, feta, lemon juice, mustard, salt, and dill and mix well. Add the tuna, scallion, red onion, olives, radishes, and carrots and lightly mix. Add the potatoes and toss gently to combine. Season to taste with salt and pepper.

Serves 4 to 6

1¾ pounds small red potatoes or small Yukon gold potatoes, cut into 1-inch cubes

¾ cup nonfat Greek yogurt

2 tablespoons regular or light mayonnaise

½ cup creamy feta cheese

1 tablespoon fresh lemon juice

4 teaspoons Dijon mustard

½ teaspoon salt, plus more to taste

1½ tablespoons chopped fresh dill

2 cans (5 ounces each) tuna packed in water, drained

1 scallion (white and light green parts), thinly sliced

2 tablespoons finely chopped red onion

½ cup pitted black olives, sliced

½ cup sliced radishes

¼ cup coarsely grated carrots

Freshly ground black pepper to taste

Kale Caesar Salad

3 tablespoons olive oil

1 garlic clove

2 anchovy fillets

½ teaspoon Worcestershire sauce

2 tablespoons fresh lemon juice

¼ teaspoon dry mustard

Salt and freshly ground black pepper to taste

1¼ pounds Tuscan kale, center stalks removed, leaves thinly sliced (5 to 6 cups)

¼ to ⅓ cup finely grated Parmesan cheese

2 hard-boiled eggs, crumbled

We Southerners love our dark leafy greens—kale is no exception. Nowadays, instead of always cooking my greens down as we do in traditional Southern cooking, I sometimes like to enjoy them fresh and crisp. This salad is a delicious new take on the Caesar salad, but with a heartier flavor from the kale. It's so delicious and so darn good for you too.

1. In a blender or food processor, puree the oil, garlic, anchovies, Worcestershire sauce, lemon juice, dry mustard, and salt and pepper to taste until smooth. This dressing can be made ahead and refrigerated until you're ready to use it.

2. When you are ready to serve, place the kale in a large serving bowl. Set aside 1 tablespoon of the Parmesan for sprinkling. Toss the kale with the dressing and as much of the remaining Parmesan as you need to suit your taste. Sprinkle the top of the salad with the egg and the set-aside Parmesan.

Serves 4 to 6

SUPER TUSCAN

My Italian friends have known for some time now just how delicious this kale is. You'll sometimes see it called Lacinato, black, or dinosaur kale, but I prefer to call it Tuscan because it's the Italians who brought it to us. You'll find it's a bit sweeter than regular curly kale so it works great sliced into a salad.

Greek Spinach Salad

Throughout the world people enjoy different variations of this famous salad. Most recipes include tomato, cucumber, red onion, feta, and olives. But, did you know that in Greece this salad doesn't usually include lettuce greens of any kind? Well, I've kept the main players, but here they are joined with one of my own favorite green leaves: baby spinach. I think that the silky texture of the baby spinach leaf is a nice complement to all the crunchy bits in the salad. This is one of my go-to lunches throughout the summer. I just get myself a great big mixing bowl, throw everything in together, and give it a good toss for one of the quickest and tastiest lunches I know.

1. In a small bowl, whisk together the vinegar, oregano, salt, and red pepper flakes. Whisk in the oil until well combined.

2. In a large bowl, combine the spinach, tomato, cucumber, feta, red onion, and olives. Add the dressing and toss to combine.

Serves 4

1½ tablespoons red wine vinegar

½ teaspoon dried oregano

¼ teaspoon salt

⅛ teaspoon crushed red pepper flakes

3 tablespoons olive oil

8 cups baby spinach

1 tomato, cut into large chunks

1 small cucumber, peeled and cut into large chunks

1 cup feta cheese, cut into cubes

¼ cup thinly sliced red onion

3 tablespoons sliced pitted kalamata olives

Beet and Vidalia Onion Salad
with Creamy Horseradish Dressing

You can always boil beets, but I prefer to roast them. They have a richer, sweeter flavor when roasted. It's also easier. Just wrap them in aluminum foil with their skins on and toss them in the oven. The skins will literally slip off when they are done. As an added bonus, they also retain more of their nutrients when cooked in the oven than they would if you boiled them.

1. Preheat the oven to 400°F. Place the beets on a large sheet of aluminum foil and sprinkle with salt to season. Wrap the beets tightly in the foil and place the packet on a rimmed baking sheet.

2. Roast until tender, about 45 minutes. Once the beets are cool enough to handle, slip off the skins. Thinly slice the beets and cool completely.

3. In a small bowl, whisk together the sour cream, horseradish, vinegar, the ½ teaspoon salt, and the sugar. Whisk in the oil. Whisk in 1 to 2 teaspoons water, as needed, until the dressing has a drizzling consistency.

4. Spread the lettuce on a large serving plate. Layer the beet and onion slices over the lettuce and drizzle the dressing over the vegetables. Sprinkle with dill and serve.

Serves 4

½ pound small beets

½ teaspoon salt, plus more for seasoning the beets

2 tablespoons regular or light sour cream

2 teaspoons prepared horseradish

1½ teaspoons white wine vinegar

½ teaspoon sugar

3 tablespoons canola oil

4 cups torn butter lettuce

½ small Vidalia onion, thinly sliced

1 tablespoon chopped fresh dill

Baby Greens with Slow-Roasted Tomatoes and Mozzarella

2 pints cherry tomatoes, sliced in half lengthwise

2 teaspoons plus 2 tablespoons olive oil

Salt and freshly ground black pepper to taste

2 teaspoons red wine vinegar

½ teaspoon Dijon mustard

1 garlic clove, cut in half

8 cups baby lettuce

6 ounces mozzarella cheese, shredded

If this is what eating healthy tastes like, well then, sign me up! This delicious salad is brimming with flavor. By slow cooking the tomatoes, their natural sugars caramelize to create a sweet tasty bite that sits so well with the creamy mozzarella and the zinging mustard dressing. If you can find fresh mozzarella (look for it in the deli or cheese section of your supermarket), this is a great place to use it.

1. Preheat the oven to 250°F.

2. In a medium bowl, toss the tomatoes with 2 teaspoons of the oil and season very lightly with salt and pepper. Arrange the tomatoes, cut side up, on a rimmed baking sheet and roast for 2½ hours, until thoroughly wrinkled with just a bit of juice remaining.

3. When the tomatoes are done, in a small bowl, whisk together the remaining 2 tablespoons oil, the vinegar, and mustard. Season to taste with salt and pepper.

4. Rub the bottom and sides of a salad bowl with the cut side of the garlic. Add the lettuce, tomatoes, mozzarella, and dressing and toss gently to combine and coat.

Serves 6

Sugar Snap Peas, Almonds, and Mint Salad

When sugar snap peas are at their very sweetest in my spring garden, I love to pluck them off the vine for this bright green salad. You don't need to do much to these lovely veggies. Just throw in some fresh herbs, squeeze on some lemon juice and a little drizzle of olive oil, and you've got yourself a beautiful fresh salad with loads of satisfying crunch.

1. Prepare a medium bowl with ice water. In a large pot of boiling salted water, cook the sugar snap peas until they are bright green and crisp-tender, 1½ to 2 minutes. Drain immediately and transfer to the ice water. Let the sugar snap peas cool down for 5 minutes, then drain and set aside.

2. In a small food processor, puree the almonds, mint, basil, shallot, lemon juice, and oil until the mixture forms a paste. Season to taste with salt and pepper. Scrape into a large bowl and add the drained sugar snap peas. Toss well to coat.

3. To serve the salad, place a butter lettuce leaf or ½ cup mesclun greens on each of four dishes. Top the lettuce with the sugar snap peas. Then pretty up the plate with a lemon slice and a mint sprig.

Serves 4

1 pound sugar snap peas (about 4 cups), ends trimmed and strings removed

1½ tablespoons slivered almonds

½ cup fresh mint leaves

½ cup fresh basil leaves

1½ teaspoons finely chopped shallot

¾ teaspoon fresh lemon juice

1½ tablespoons canola oil

Salt and freshly ground black pepper to taste

4 leaves butter lettuce or 2 cups mesclun greens

Thinly sliced lemon, for garnish

Mint sprigs, for garnish

ICE BATH

Having a bowl of ice water on hand after blanching vegetables provides an easy way to cool down vegetables quickly. And that's important when you're shooting for snappy, bright green veggies. It can be a matter of seconds in overcooking delicate vegetables like snap peas, asparagus, and green beans.

Butternut Squash Salad with Apple, Pecans, and Parmesan Dressing

1 small butternut squash
(about 2 pounds), peeled,
seeded, and cut into 1-inch
cubes

4½ tablespoons olive oil

1 teaspoon salt

¼ teaspoon ground allspice

Large pinch of cayenne pepper

2 tablespoons fresh lemon juice

1 small shallot, finely chopped

5 ounces baby arugula

1 small Granny Smith apple,
cored and thinly sliced
(about 1 cup)

⅓ cup toasted chopped pecans

½ cup finely grated Parmesan
cheese

Throughout the fall months, this is the salad you will find me eating most often. It hits the spot when I'm craving starch and satisfies that urge without skyrocketing my sugar and carb intake. It also fills me up, like I've eaten a plate of potatoes, without the negative health effects. But besides all that, it just plain tastes good. There's nothing quite like roasted squash on a cool evening. It's warming, comforting, and downright tasty.

1. Preheat the oven to 400°F.

2. In a large bowl, toss together the squash, 1½ tablespoons of the oil, ½ teaspoon of the salt, the allspice, and cayenne. Spread the squash on a large rimmed baking sheet. Roast, tossing occasionally, until tender and golden, about 35 minutes. Cool.

3. In a small bowl, whisk together the lemon juice, shallot, the remaining ½ teaspoon salt, and the remaining 3 tablespoons oil.

4. In a large bowl, toss together the arugula, cooled squash, apple, pecans, and dressing. Add the Parmesan and toss once more before serving.

Serves 4 to 6

Fresh Corn and Tomato Salad with Herb Vinaigrette

3 ears of corn, husks and silk removed

2 ripe tomatoes, chopped

1½ teaspoons Dijon mustard

2 teaspoons red wine vinegar

¼ teaspoon salt, plus more to taste

3 tablespoons olive oil

3 tablespoons chopped mixed fresh herbs, such as basil, chives, parsley, and mint

Freshly ground black pepper to taste

Corn and tomato is a classic pairing that speaks for itself. There's no need to get fussy here because the natural sweetness of the combo will make any dish sing. This is one of those simple salads I make throughout the summer. It takes almost no effort, but the payoff is big. When I've got the grill going, I grill my corn instead of boiling it. The smoky char-grill flavor is a nice way to change up this summer stunner.

1. In a large pot of boiling salted water, cook the corn until tender, about 5 minutes. Cool completely, then cut the kernels from the ears with a sharp knife. Place the kernels in a large bowl along with the tomatoes.

2. In a small bowl, whisk together the mustard, vinegar, and salt. Whisk in the oil until well combined. Stir in the herbs and pepper to taste. Taste and adjust the seasonings, if you like.

3. Pour the dressing over the corn salad and toss to combine.

Serves 4

Roasted Root Vegetable Salad with Honey, Goat Cheese, and Walnuts

Next time you're looking to clean out the hardy veggies at the bottom of your pantry, this is the salad to help you along. Whatever you've got lots of—parsnips, turnips, you name it—will be welcome in this dish. I roast the veggies until they get deeply browned on the outside so they come out nice and caramelized. Then I toss them with some baby arugula, cider vinegar, a touch of honey, crunchy walnuts, and creamy goat cheese. There certainly is a whole lot to love about this salad.

1. Preheat the oven to 400°F.

2. Toss the root vegetables and red onion with 1½ tablespoons of the oil, the rosemary, salt, and pepper. Spread on a rimmed baking sheet. Roast, tossing occasionally, until golden brown and tender, 30 to 40 minutes. Cool to room temperature.

3. In a small bowl, whisk together the vinegar, honey, and the remaining ⅓ cup oil. Season to taste with salt and pepper.

4. In a large bowl, combine the baby arugula, the roasted and cooled vegetables, the celery, walnuts, and goat cheese. Add the dressing and toss to coat.

Serves 6

1½ pounds root vegetables, such as parsnips, turnips, and carrots, peeled and cut into 1-inch chunks (about 3 cups)

1 small red onion, halved lengthwise and thinly sliced

⅓ cup plus 1½ tablespoons olive oil

2 fresh rosemary sprigs

¾ teaspoon salt, plus more to taste

¾ teaspoon freshly ground black pepper, plus more to taste

1½ tablespoons cider vinegar

1 teaspoon honey

10 cups baby arugula

½ cup thinly sliced celery

⅓ cup toasted chopped walnuts

¾ cup crumbled goat cheese (3 ounces)

Arugula and Peach Salad
with Poached Chicken

This salad certainly is a taste sensation. Peppery arugula, sweet peaches, and tender poached chicken all together in one bowl. I like to call this my "ladies who lunch" salad because my girlfriends always request it when we get together at my house. And I am only too happy to oblige.

1. To make the chicken: In a large deep skillet, combine the white onion, carrot, celery, garlic, thyme, salt, and 4 cups water over medium-high heat. Bring to a boil, then add the chicken and just enough extra water to cover the chicken completely. Reduce the heat to medium-low and simmer for 10 minutes. Remove from the heat, cover, and let the chicken stand until it's cooked through, 15 to 20 minutes. Cool in the water completely and, using your hands or two forks, shred into bite-size pieces.

2. To prepare the salad: In a small bowl, whisk together the vinegar, salt, pepper to taste, and oil until combined.

3. In a large bowl, toss together the arugula, peaches, red onion, almonds, cooled chicken, and dressing. Serve immediately.

Serves 6

POACHED CHICKEN

1 small white onion, quartered

1 carrot, cut into 2-inch chunks

1 celery stalk,
cut into 2-inch chunks

3 garlic cloves,
smashed and peeled

4 fresh thyme sprigs

1 tablespoon salt

1¼ pounds boneless, skinless
chicken breasts (about 3)

SALAD

3 tablespoons white wine vinegar

¾ teaspoon salt

Freshly ground black pepper to
taste

⅓ cup olive oil

10 cups loosely packed
baby arugula

2 ripe peaches, pitted and cut
into 1-inch chunks

½ small red onion, thinly sliced

¼ cup toasted sliced almonds

PICK POACH
Poaching is a super-healthy way to cook your chicken. There's not a drop of oil involved! And the chicken always comes out moist and flavorful.

Asparagus and Goat Cheese Salad

1 bunch asparagus
(about 1 pound),
woody ends trimmed

2 tablespoons pine nuts
or slivered almonds

1 small garlic clove,
finely chopped

2 teaspoons fresh lemon juice,
plus the finely grated zest
of 1 lemon, for garnish

½ teaspoon white wine vinegar

2 tablespoons olive oil

⅓ cup crumbled goat cheese

½ cup seeded and finely
chopped tomatoes (2 small
or Roma tomatoes)

Salt and freshly ground
black pepper to taste

This salad looks so gorgeous on the plate it's almost too pretty to eat. I like to use thin asparagus spears, but any size will work. Just make sure you cook the asparagus only until tender, so it is still snappy when you bite into it. That snap is a nice contrast next to the creamy goat cheese and the sweet soft tomato.

1. Prepare a large bowl with ice water. In a large pot of boiling salted water, cook the asparagus for 1 to 2 minutes, until crisp-tender. Drain immediately and transfer to the ice water. Let the asparagus cool down for 5 minutes in the ice water, then drain and set aside.

2. In a small skillet, toast the pine nuts over low heat, shaking the pan frequently to avoid burning, Toast until the pine nuts are fragrant and golden, about 5 minutes.

3. In a small bowl, combine the garlic, lemon juice, and vinegar. Whisk in the oil until well combined.

4. Lay the asparagus on a pretty white serving dish. Drizzle with the lemon dressing and layer with the pine nuts, goat cheese, and tomatoes. Season to taste with salt and pepper and garnish with the lemon zest.

Serves 4

Tomato Aspic
with Yogurt Chive Dressing

This fancy molded salad is perfect for a summer dinner party. The aspic tastes so fresh and bright, it's like biting into a just-picked tomato from the garden—but without the seeds. I like to use low-sodium tomato juice and then add more salt if needed. That way I'm in control of the sodium in the dish. If you haven't got chives on hand, feel free to substitute almost any other fresh green herb, such as parsley, basil, or mint.

2 packages (¼ ounce each) powdered plain gelatin

4 cups low-sodium tomato juice

¼ cup fresh lemon juice, plus ¼ teaspoon finely grated lemon zest

1 teaspoon hot sauce

1 container (7 ounces) low-fat Greek yogurt

¼ cup chopped fresh chives

2 tablespoons olive oil

Pinch of salt

1. In a small saucepan, combine the gelatin and ½ cup of the tomato juice and let it sit for 2 minutes. Place the pan over medium heat and warm, stirring occasionally, until the gelatin is completely dissolved, about 5 minutes.

2. In a medium bowl, combine the remaining 3½ cups tomato juice, the lemon juice, and hot sauce. Whisk in the hot gelatin mixture until combined. Pour into a 6-cup gelatin mold and refrigerate until set, 3 to 4 hours.

3. In a blender or food processor, combine the yogurt, 2 tablespoons of the chives, the oil, lemon zest, and salt and puree until smooth. Serve the aspic in slices with a dollop of the dressing and a sprinkling of the remaining 2 tablespoons chives.

Serves 12

3

Hearty, Warming and Fresh, Cooling Soups

*I*n today's fast-paced, fast-food world, more and more people are missing out on what I think is one of the kitchen's simplest comfort foods: soup. And that is a crying shame, I tell you. While homemade soups may take a little more prepping time up front, when you've got your fridge or freezer stocked with soup, you've got yourself one of the quickest, easiest, and healthiest meals you can think of.

Soups are so simple to whip up and it always makes sense to make them in large quantities so you wind up with lots of leftover soup for freezing. When I've got a rainy weekend day on my hands, I spend a few hours throwing together a couple of big ol' pots of soup. Then I freeze them up in small labeled containers. That way I've got a healthy meal on hand for the next month or so. If your fridge and freezer are stocked with soup, you'll find yourself more likely to skip the fast food. Instead, you'll be reaching for an instant meal that just needs reheating on the stove or in the microwave.

Come January or February, I like to use the root vegetables lurking in my pantry for *Winter Vegetable Soup* (page 78). The soup is just perfect on a cold day. It's a chunky, hearty blend of carrots, parsnips, butternut squash, and more. Why, if you name a winter vegetable, chances are you'll find it in this soup. When cold season is in full swing, I'm never without *Down-Home Chicken Noodle Soup* (page 72). What kind of a grandma would I be to my grandbabies if I didn't have the ultimate cure for the sniffles?

But soup is not just for the winter months. In the warm weather, I love to make use of the beautiful tomatoes, bell peppers, and cucumbers in my garden by pulling together a bright and zippy **Cajun Gazpacho** (page 70). It's my Southern take on the traditional Spanish chilled soup. I swear **Cool Cucumber Soup** (page 80) is like an air conditioner in a soup bowl. It's a fresh, minty mouthful that never fails to cool me down, even on the hottest Savannah afternoon.

These days, I like to use lots of healthy beans and grains in my soups. They are super hearty and so good for you. Take, for instance, my **Beef and Vegetable Barley Soup** (page 88). The beef is fall-apart delicious on its own, but paired up with the nutty taste and firm texture of the barley, it's made that much better. For something a bit more exotic, I turn to **Mexican Chicken and Tortilla Soup** (page 75). When I smell this chili powder–infused soup bubbling away, my mouth positively waters thinking about the meals ahead.

Soup is not just a convenience food. It is the ultimate Southern comfort food. And that's why I like to have a pot on the stove when guests stop by. An offer of homemade soup says, "So glad you're here, now stay awhile." From **Old-Fashioned Black Bean and Ham Bone Soup** (page 69) to a modern-day **Chickpea and Vegetable Soup with Orzo** (page 92), soups of all stripes and varieties are a friendly welcome any old day of the year.

Confederate Bean Soup

This is the soup for all the baked bean lovers out there, myself included. It offers a good taste of warming Southern hospitality. One spoonful in and you'll feel your cares melt away. As with all my favorites, I've amended this dish to fit my new and improved diet. I said see you later to the cream and pork sausage and I now use a mix of turkey kielbasa and milk. And I've added coarsely chopped mustard greens, which I think make this rendition even better than the old one. Soup's up, folks.

1. In a medium saucepan, cook the bacon until crisp, about 5 minutes. Add the onion, bell pepper, and celery and cook, stirring, until soft, about 7 minutes. Stir in the garlic and tomato paste and cook, stirring, for 1 minute. Add the baked beans, pinto beans, kielbasa, and water. Simmer over medium heat for 15 minutes.

2. Stir in the milk and simmer for 10 minutes more. Add the mustard greens for the last 5 minutes of cooking time. Season to taste with pepper and ladle into bowls.

Serves 6

2 turkey or regular bacon slices, cut into ½-inch pieces

1 small onion, chopped

1 green bell pepper, chopped

1 celery stalk, chopped

3 garlic cloves, finely chopped

1 tablespoon tomato paste

1 can (16 ounces) vegetarian baked beans

1 can (15½ ounces) pinto beans, rinsed and drained

½ pound turkey kielbasa or other turkey sausage, cubed

1 cup water

1 cup milk

6 cups coarsely chopped mustard greens or spinach

Freshly grated black pepper to taste

New Savannah Gumbo

1½ tablespoons unsalted butter

1½ tablespoons all-purpose flour

1 large onion, chopped

2 green bell peppers, chopped

2 celery stalks, chopped

1 teaspoon salt,
plus more to taste

4 garlic cloves, finely chopped

2 teaspoons dried thyme

8 ounces chicken sausage

1¼ pounds boneless, skinless
chicken breasts (about 3),
cut into ½-inch pieces

¼ teaspoon cayenne pepper,
plus more to taste

4 cups low-sodium chicken broth

1 can (28 ounces) no-salt-added
stewed tomatoes

2 cups fresh or frozen sliced okra

½ pound medium shrimp,
peeled and deveined

1 teaspoon filé powder (optional)

2½ cups cooked brown or white
rice, for serving

It was a snap to make this gumbo better for me. It really involved only two big changes. First off, I had to cut down the butter and flour in the roux. Check. And I needed to change the meats I used in order to cut the fat but keep the protein and flavor. Double check. With these tweaks, I ended up with a delicious new alternative to my classic Savannah gumbo.

1. In a large pot, melt the butter over medium heat. Whisk in the flour and cook, stirring occasionally, until the mixture turns a deep hazelnut brown, about 15 minutes. Reduce the heat to medium-low and add the onion, bell peppers, celery, and salt to taste. Cook until the vegetables are very soft, about 15 minutes. Stir in the garlic and thyme and cook for 1 minute.

2. Add the sausage, chicken, salt, and cayenne. Pour in the chicken broth and tomatoes. Bring the mixture to a simmer and cook until the chicken is almost cooked through, about 15 minutes. Add the okra and cook until tender, 10 minutes. Add the shrimp and simmer until just cooked through, about 5 minutes. Remove from the heat and stir in the filé powder (if using). Taste and adjust the seasonings.

3. To serve, spoon some rice into soup bowls. Spoon the gumbo over the top.

Serves 10

FILÉ POWDER

If you can get your hands on some filé powder, which is a traditional ingredient in the South, it will help to thicken up your gumbo and give it an authentic, earthy flavor. Don't sweat it if you can't find it, though. The roux and the okra will do a fine job of thickening the stew.

Old-Fashioned Black Bean and Ham Bone Soup

This smoky, hammy bean soup is one of Jamie's and Bobby's favorite dishes. I don't know how they know I'm making it, but they never fail to show up on my doorstep when I've got a pot of this going on the stove. No matter. I always make a double batch; enough to feed the troops on the day it's made and plenty to stow away in the freezer for reheating. I like topping my black bean soup with a creamy guacamole, but if you're in a hurry, some cut-up avocado with a spritz of fresh lemon or lime will do just fine.

1. To make the soup: Rinse the beans in cold water. Place in a medium saucepan and add enough water to cover the beans by about 3 inches. Bring just to a boil over medium-high heat, then remove the pan from the heat and cover. Let the beans stand for 1 hour. Drain and set aside.

2. In a large pot, heat the oil over medium heat. Add the onion, celery, carrots, and parsnip and cook, stirring, for 5 to 7 minutes, until the vegetables have softened. Add the garlic, thyme, and cumin and cook until fragrant, about 1 minute. Add the red wine and scrape the bottom of the pan to get up all the brown bits. Cook for 2 minutes. Add the beans, beef broth, water, bay leaf, and ham hock. Bring to a boil over medium-high heat, then reduce to a simmer. Cover the pot and cook for 1½ hours.

3. Take the ham hock out of the soup. Cut the meat off the hock into bite-size pieces and return the meat to the soup. Continue cooking, covered, 30 minutes more, or until the beans are very tender. Remove the bay leaf and season to taste with salt and pepper.

Serves 4 to 6

THICK AND THIN
If you would like the soup a bit thicker, simmer it, partially covered, for an extra 15 to 20 minutes.

2 cups dried black beans

2 tablespoons olive oil

1 large onion, finely chopped

2 celery stalks, finely chopped

2 carrots, finely chopped

1 parsnip, finely chopped

1 large garlic clove, finely chopped

¼ teaspoon dried thyme

½ teaspoon ground cumin

¼ cup dry red wine

4 cups low-sodium beef broth

3 cups water

1 bay leaf

1 smoked ham hock

Salt and freshly ground black pepper to taste

Guacamole

1 ripe avocado, halved and pitted

1 teaspoon fresh lemon juice

¼ teaspoon Paula Deen's House Seasoning (see page 6) or other seasoned salt

½ teaspoon chopped fresh cilantro (optional)

Scoop the avocado flesh into a blender or food processor and puree with the lemon juice, seasoned salt, and cilantro (if using) until smooth. Serve dolloped on top of the soup.

Makes ⅔ cup guacamole

Cajun Gazpacho

8 fresh okra, sliced crosswise
    into ¼-inch-thick slices,
    or ½ cup sliced frozen okra

1 teaspoon fresh lemon juice

2 cups 1-inch watermelon cubes

1 cup chopped red bell peppers

2 tablespoons chopped red onion

2 tablespoons red wine vinegar

2 tablespoons olive oil

1 small garlic clove, chopped

1 cup low-sodium tomato juice

Hot sauce to taste

Salt and freshly ground
    black pepper to taste

This watermelon gazpacho has got all the signature elements of good Cajun cooking. It's slightly sweet, tangy, and it packs a spicy punch in the end. But most of all, it's a light, bright, cooling way to cap off a hot day in the South. Or wherever you may be sweating it out in the sunny summertime.

1. Bring a small saucepan of lightly salted water to a boil. Add the okra and cook for 1 minute (if you are using frozen, cook according to the package directions). Drain and run under cold water to cool down. In a small bowl, toss the okra with the lemon juice. Refrigerate until you are ready to use it.

2. In a blender, working in batches, puree the watermelon, bell peppers, red onion, vinegar, oil, and garlic until smooth. Pour into a large bowl, whisk in the tomato juice and hot sauce, and season with salt and pepper. Chill for at least 1 hour. Serve cold, garnished with the okra.

Serves 4

With my boys, Jamie and Bobby, and beautiful daughters-in-law, Claudia, Bobby's wife, and Brooke, Jamie's wife (left and right).

Broccoli Chowder

Like many mamas out there, I used to get my boys to eat their veggies by serving their broccoli covered in creamy melted Cheddar. And did it ever work! These days, I serve this satisfying chowder to my grandbabies and the veggie-cheese combo still works its magic. Of course, this soup is not just for kids, so grab yourself a spoon and join in. You'll be glad you did.

1. In a large skillet over medium heat, melt the butter. Add the onion, carrot, and celery and cook, stirring, until soft, 7 to 10 minutes. Stir in the flour and cook for 2 minutes. Add the dry mustard and garlic powder (if using). Slowly stir in the chicken broth. Bring to a boil. Add the potatoes and salt. Cook until the potatoes are fork-tender, 15 to 20 minutes. Stir in the broccoli and cook until tender, about 10 minutes. Remove the soup from the heat and let it cool a bit.

2. Ladle 3 cups of the soup into a blender or food processor and puree until smooth. Return to the pot and warm over medium heat. Stir in the yogurt and Gouda and cook until the cheese is melted and the soup is smooth. Season with pepper, if you like, and serve.

Serves 6

2 tablespoons (¼ stick) unsalted butter

1 large onion, chopped

1 carrot, chopped

1 celery stalk, chopped

2 tablespoons all-purpose flour

¾ teaspoon dry mustard

½ teaspoon garlic powder (optional)

6 cups low-sodium chicken broth

1 large russet potato, peeled and chopped

1 teaspoon salt

2 heads broccoli, stems and florets chopped into bite-size pieces (4 cups)

¾ cup low-fat Greek yogurt

1½ cups shredded Gouda or Swiss cheese

Freshly ground black pepper to taste

Down-Home Chicken Noodle Soup

1 tablespoon olive oil

1 large onion, coarsely chopped

4 carrots, thinly sliced

4 celery stalks, thinly sliced

2 garlic cloves, smashed and peeled

1 whole chicken (3½ to 4 pounds), rinsed and patted dry, cut into 8 pieces, and skin removed

1 tablespoon salt, plus more to taste

4 fresh thyme sprigs

1 bay leaf

Freshly ground black pepper to taste

8 ounces whole-wheat egg noodles

Chopped fresh dill, for serving

Now I ask you, who does not love a homemade chicken soup? It's just so much better than the canned variety that I make sure to have some in my freezer at all times. And this here is the simple, down-home recipe I turn to most of the time. It's basically the same chicken soup I've been making for years on end. One of the few changes I've made is to take the skin off the bird before adding it to the pot. Every little bit helps when you are trying to cut the fat out of your diet.

1. In a large pot, heat the oil over medium heat. Add the onion, half the carrots, half the celery, and the garlic. Cook until lightly browned and tender, about 10 minutes. Add the chicken, 8 cups water, salt, thyme, bay leaf, and pepper to taste. Simmer gently, skimming off any foam that rises to the top of the pot, until the chicken is cooked through, about 1 hour.

2. Strain the soup into a large bowl. Discard the vegetables and set the chicken aside to cool. When the chicken is cool enough to handle, pick the meat off the bones, discarding the bones.

3. Return the strained liquid to the pot and bring to a boil over high heat. Add the remaining carrots and celery. Simmer over medium heat until the vegetables are almost tender, about 5 minutes. Stir in the noodles and cook the noodles according to the package directions. Stir in the shredded chicken in the last 2 minutes of cooking time. Season to taste with salt and pepper, ladle into bowls, and garnish with dill.

Serves 6

Creamy Cauliflower and Vidalia Soup

2 tablespoons olive oil

1 large Vidalia onion, thinly sliced

1 carrot, chopped

1 head cauliflower (2½ pounds), coarsely chopped

3 tablespoons fresh flat-leaf parsley leaves, finely chopped

2 teaspoons salt

3 cups low-sodium chicken or vegetable broth

1½ cups milk

¾ cup shredded Swiss cheese

Freshly ground black pepper to taste

Large pinch of nutmeg

Soups are a great way to eat your vegetables. There's something about a thick, creamy soup that seems to satisfy me more than just plain veggies. A soup like this one is warming and filling, without being too heavy. With a nice crusty hunk of whole-wheat bread, this is a meal that won't leave you wanting for more.

1. In a large pot, heat the oil over medium heat. Add the onion and cook until golden, 5 to 7 minutes. Add the carrot and cook for 5 minutes more.

2. Stir in the cauliflower, parsley, salt, and chicken broth. Bring to a boil. Reduce the heat to medium-low, cover the pot, and simmer until the cauliflower is very tender, about 20 minutes. Pour in the milk.

3. Transfer the soup to a blender or food processor and puree until smooth (or use an immersion blender to puree right in the pot). Return the soup to the pot over medium heat. Whisk in the Swiss cheese and cook until the soup is hot and the cheese is completely melted. Taste and adjust the seasonings. Ladle the soup into bowls and sprinkle with pepper and nutmeg.

Serves 4

Mexican Chicken and Tortilla Soup

I reckon this soup is something like the Mexican version of our Down-Home Chicken Noodle Soup (page 72). It's soothing and warm but has a spicy edge to it. I make sure to add the tortilla chips to the individual serving bowls so that they don't go all soggy on me. That little bit of crunch adds such a nice texture to the soup.

1. In a large pot, heat the oil over medium heat. Add the onions and cook until very tender, about 10 minutes. Stir in the garlic and chili powder and cook for 1 minute. Pour in the chicken broth, tomatoes, and salt. Bring to a simmer. Reduce the heat to low and cook for 15 minutes. Stir in the chicken, beans, and corn. Bring to a simmer and cook for 10 minutes more.

2. Place the tortilla chips in the bottom of individual serving bowls. Ladle the soup over the chips. Sprinkle with the avocado and scallions. Finish with a dollop of the yogurt. Serve with lime wedges.

Serves 6

1 tablespoon olive oil

2 cups finely chopped onions

2 garlic cloves, finely chopped

1 tablespoon chili powder

6 cups low-sodium chicken broth

1 can (14½ ounces) no-salt-added diced tomatoes

1 teaspoon salt, plus more to taste

3 cups shredded cooked chicken breast

1 can (15 ounces) black beans, rinsed and drained

1 cup frozen corn kernels

3 cups baked tortilla chips

¾ cup chopped ripe avocado

6 tablespoons sliced scallions (white and light green parts)

6 tablespoons Greek yogurt

Lime wedges, for serving

Italian Wedding Soup
with Turkey Meatballs

While you certainly can make the meatballs in this soup with regular white meat turkey, for a supremely moist meatball, I highly recommend dark meat turkey if you can get your hands on it. Or try a mix of white meat turkey and lean ground beef. I like to finish off this soup with grated Parmesan cheese, but you'll be pleased as punch with the flavor even without it.

1. In a medium bowl, combine the ground turkey, bread crumbs, egg, sage, and House Seasoning. Mix gently with your hands and form into 1-inch balls. Refrigerate until ready to use.

2. In a large pot, heat the oil over medium-high heat. Add the onions, carrots, and celery and cook, stirring occasionally, until the vegetables start to soften, 5 to 7 minutes. Add the chicken broth and Worcestershire sauce and bring to a boil.

3. Add the meatballs to the boiling broth and cook for 5 minutes, until just cooked through. Using a slotted spoon, transfer the meatballs to a bowl and reserve. Add the orzo to the broth and boil until just tender, about 7 minutes. Add the spinach, return the meatballs to the soup, and cook for 1 minute, until the spinach is wilted.

Serves 8

1 pound ground dark meat turkey

⅓ cup plain bread crumbs

1 large egg, lightly beaten

1 tablespoon chopped fresh sage
 or 1 teaspoon dried

1 teaspoon Paula Deen's House
 Seasoning (see page 6)

3 tablespoons olive oil

1 cup chopped onions

1 cup chopped carrots

1 cup chopped celery

6 cups low-sodium chicken broth

1 teaspoon Worcestershire sauce

¾ cup whole-wheat
 or regular orzo

1 bag (5 ounces) baby spinach,
 chopped

Winter Vegetable Soup

2 tablespoons canola oil

4 cups coarsely chopped Swiss chard (ribs removed before chopping)

1 cup sliced carrots

½ cup chopped onion

1 can (28 ounces) no-salt-added whole peeled tomatoes, coarsely chopped with their juice

¾ cup chopped parsnip

¾ cup chopped celery root

4 cups low-sodium chicken broth

1 large bay leaf

½ teaspoon salt

¼ teaspoon freshly ground black pepper

1 small butternut squash (1 pound), peeled, seeded, and cut into ½-inch cubes

1 can (19 ounces) cannellini beans, rinsed and drained

Tabasco sauce to taste

This healthy, hearty soup can take whatever veggies you've got in the fridge. I usually throw in some parsnip, celery root, carrot, and winter squash. But if I've got other root vegetables rolling around in there, they might make it into the pot too. By pureeing half the beans with half the soup mixture, the soup takes on a thick texture that makes it a meal on its own. Where I come from, we call this stick-to-your-ribs eating.

1. In a large pot or Dutch oven, heat the oil over medium heat. Add the Swiss chard, carrots, and onion and cook for 5 to 6 minutes, stirring occasionally, until the vegetables have softened. Add the tomatoes and their juice, the parsnip, celery root, chicken broth, bay leaf, salt, and pepper. Bring the soup to a boil, then reduce the heat to a simmer and add the squash. Simmer for 20 minutes.

2. Place half of the cannellini beans and ½ cup of the soup broth in a blender or food processor and puree until smooth. Add the bean puree and the remaining whole beans to the soup. Stir well to combine. Remove the bay leaf, ladle the soup into bowls, and serve with Tabasco to taste.

Serves 6 to 8

Creamy Potato Leek Soup

I always think this soup gives the impression that you worked so hard over it when in truth it takes just about no time to fix. The buttery leeks are the perfect partner to the creamy potatoes and cauliflower. Topped off with a sprinkling of paprika and ladled into a special china bowl, why it looks positively beautiful coming to the table. No need to let your guests know how quickly you whipped it up. Just sit back and enjoy the praise, and the soup, of course.

1. In a large pot or Dutch oven, melt the butter over medium heat. Add the leeks and cook, stirring occasionally, until they are well softened, 7 to 8 minutes. Add the cauliflower, potatoes, chicken broth, and a pinch of salt and bring the mixture to a boil. Then reduce to a simmer and cook for 20 to 30 minutes, until the potatoes are completely softened.

2. Working in batches, transfer the soup to a blender or food processor and puree until smooth (or use an immersion blender to puree right in the pot). Return the soup to the pot and stir in the milk. Warm the soup over low heat just until heated through. Season to taste with salt and pepper, then ladle the soup into pretty soup bowls and sprinkle with paprika.

Serves 4 to 6

2 tablespoons (¼ stick) unsalted butter

4 medium leeks (white and light green parts), thoroughly cleaned and thinly sliced

2 cups cauliflower florets

2 medium Yukon gold potatoes, peeled and cut into ½-inch cubes

4 cups low-sodium chicken broth (or substitute water if you like)

Salt and freshly ground black pepper to taste

1 cup milk

Paprika, for garnish

8 ounces chicken andouille
  sausage, cubed

1 tablespoon olive oil

2 cups chopped onions

1 cup chopped carrots

4 cups low-sodium chicken broth

4 cups water

2 teaspoons salt

2 cans (15 ounces each)
  black-eyed peas,
  rinsed and drained

1 bunch collard greens (1 pound),
  stems removed and leaves
  coarsely chopped

Tabasco sauce to taste

Collard Greens Soup with Black-Eyed Peas and Sausage

You know how the pot liquor you cook your greens in is usually the best part of the meal? Well, this soup is basically your pot liquor turned into a soup. And it's downright delicious. Collards, andouille sausage, and black-eyed peas. Honey, it doesn't get much more Southern than this.

1. In a large pot over medium-high heat, brown the sausage until golden, about 10 minutes. Transfer to a bowl.

2. Add the oil to the pot. Stir in the onions and carrots and cook until very soft, about 10 minutes. Add the chicken broth, water, salt, black-eyed peas, and sausage. Bring to a boil over high heat. Reduce the heat to medium-low and simmer for 20 minutes. Stir in the collards and cook for 10 minutes more. Season to taste with hot sauce.

Serves 6

3 cucumbers (about 2 pounds),
  peeled, seeded, and chopped

One container (7 ounces)
  low-fat Greek yogurt

½ cup low-sodium chicken broth

4 teaspoons champagne or
  white wine vinegar

1 tablespoon chopped fresh mint,
  plus 4 small sprigs for serving

1 small garlic clove, finely
  chopped

Salt and white pepper to taste

Cool Cucumber Soup

I could eat this pretty, pale green soup all day long on a hot summer day. It is zesty, creamy, and, well, cool as a cucumber.

1. In a blender or food processor, working in batches, puree the cucumbers, yogurt, chicken broth, vinegar, chopped mint, and garlic until smooth. Season to taste with salt and pepper and pour the soup into a large bowl. Cover with plastic wrap and refrigerate for at least 1 hour or up to overnight.

2. Serve chilled, decorated with the sprigs of mint.

Serves 4

Cozy Tomato Soup with Parmesan Crisps

Tomato soup and grilled cheese sandwiches always bring my mind back to lazy lunches with my two baby boys. Seems like yesterday, y'all. So when I make this tomato soup with Parmesan crisps, I give a call over to my boys just to say howdy. They love that I've redesigned this recipe. Like me, they are eating healthier these days too. Good to know that mother and sons can still share this bowl of memories.

2 tablespoons (¼ stick) unsalted butter

1 onion, thinly sliced

¾ teaspoon salt

1 can (28 ounces) no-salt-added crushed tomatoes

3 cups water

1 cup grated Parmesan cheese

1 cup milk

⅓ cup chopped fresh basil

1. In a large pot, melt the butter over medium heat. Add the onion and ¼ teaspoon of the salt. Cover and cook over medium-low heat, tossing occasionally, until the onion is very tender, about 15 minutes.

2. Stir in the tomatoes and water. Increase the heat to medium and simmer, uncovered, for 20 minutes.

3. Meanwhile, heat a large nonstick skillet over medium-high heat. Sprinkle ¼ cup of the Parmesan into the skillet in an even, pancake-shape mound. Flatten the mound with the back of a spatula. Repeat with a second ¼ cup of the cheese. Cook until the cheese is lacy and the edges and bottom are golden, 1 to 2 minutes. Carefully flip with a thin, flexible spatula. Cook until crisp and golden, about 1 minute. Transfer the crisps to a paper towel–lined plate. Repeat with the remaining cheese. Let the crisps cool and then break them into bite-size pieces.

4. Transfer the soup to a blender or food processor and puree until smooth (or use an immersion blender to puree right in the pot). Return the soup to the pot over medium heat. Stir in the milk and cook until hot. Ladle into bowls and top with the cheese crisps and basil.

Serves 4

Mushroom Soup with Wild Rice

3 tablespoons olive oil,
plus more as needed

1 large leek (white and light
green parts), thoroughly
cleaned and thinly sliced

1 cup finely chopped carrots

1 cup thinly sliced celery

1 pound mixed mushrooms,
such as cremini and shiitake,
chopped

3 garlic cloves, finely chopped

1 tablespoon finely chopped
fresh rosemary

¼ cup dry sherry

6 cups low-sodium vegetable
broth

1 cup uncooked wild rice

1½ teaspoons salt,
plus more to taste

½ teaspoon freshly ground
black pepper, plus more to taste

Fresh lemon juice to taste

It seems like there is just no end to the types of mushrooms out there in the world. And this soup is a fine place to taste them all. Have fun with it. Try exotic mushrooms like cremini or shiitake or stick with the classics like brown or button. Whichever way you go, this warming soup will have you feeling snug as a bug in no time flat.

1. In a large pot, heat the oil over medium heat. Cook the leek, carrots, and celery until soft, about 5 minutes. Add the mushrooms and cook until the mushrooms and vegetables have released their liquid and are brown and caramelized, about 15 minutes. You may need to add a little more oil because the mushrooms really soak it up.

2. Add the garlic and rosemary and cook for 1 minute. Add the sherry and cook until almost evaporated. Stir in the vegetable broth, rice, salt, and pepper. Simmer over medium-low heat until the rice is tender, about 45 minutes. Season the soup with a squeeze of lemon and more salt and pepper, if you like.

Serves 4

Corn and Sweet Potato Chowder

Sometimes I make this hearty corn and potato chowder into a meal by adding cooked cubed chicken. The chicken transforms this tasty starter into a satisfying meal that both the young ones and the grownups can enjoy together.

1. In a large pot, heat the butter over medium heat. Add the onion, celery, chile, and salt to taste. Cook until the vegetables are tender, 5 to 7 minutes. Add the thyme and cook for 1 minute. Stir in the tomato paste and cook for 1 minute.

2. Add the sweet potatoes, red potatoes, chicken broth, and salt. Simmer until the potatoes are tender, about 25 minutes. Add the corn and simmer 5 minutes more. Pour in the milk and cook until hot. Season to taste with salt and pepper.

Serves 6

1 tablespoon unsalted butter

1 onion, finely chopped

1 celery stalk, finely chopped

1 poblano chile, seeded and chopped

1 teaspoon salt, plus more to taste

1 teaspoon dried thyme

1 tablespoon tomato paste

2 sweet potatoes, peeled and cubed

2 red potatoes, peeled and cubed

4 cups low-sodium chicken broth

1½ cups fresh or frozen corn kernels

2 cups milk

Freshly ground black pepper to taste

Light and Creamy Shrimp Bisque

3 tablespoons unsalted butter

1 pound large shrimp,
   peeled and deveined,
   shells reserved

¼ cup brandy

6 cups water

1 teaspoon salt,
   plus more to taste

3 fresh thyme sprigs

1 bay leaf

2 celery stalks, thinly sliced

2 large leeks (white and light
   green parts), thoroughly
   cleaned and thinly sliced

2 garlic cloves, finely chopped

2 tablespoons all-purpose flour

2 tablespoons tomato paste

1 cup milk

½ cup half-and-half

Large pinch of cayenne pepper

1 tablespoon fresh lemon juice

Chopped fresh flat-leaf parsley,
   for serving

Adding the shrimp shells to flavor the bisque broth adds great flavor to this soup. It tastes like it just jumped out of the sea. But don't limit yourself to shrimp for this bisque. Any shellfish would be delicious: crab, lobster, crawfish, you name it. I used to make my bisques with cups and cups of half-and-half. Yet I've found that a half cup is really all you need to create a smooth and decadently creamy soup.

1. In a large pot, melt 1 tablespoon of the butter over high heat. Add the shrimp shells and cook, stirring, until lightly browned, about 5 minutes. Remove the pot from the heat and add the brandy. Return the pot to the heat and simmer until the liquid evaporates. Stir in the water, ½ teaspoon of the salt, the thyme sprigs, and bay leaf. Simmer, uncovered, for 15 minutes. Strain the liquid into a bowl and discard the solids.

2. Return the empty pot to the stove. Add 1 tablespoon of the remaining butter. Add the shrimp and cook until they are pink but not quite cooked through, about 2 minutes. Remove with a slotted spoon to a bowl. Add the remaining 1 tablespoon butter, the celery, leeks, garlic, and a large pinch of salt to the pot. Cook over medium heat until soft, 5 to 7 minutes. Stir in the flour and tomato paste and cook, stirring, for 2 minutes.

3. Slowly pour in the reserved shrimp broth. Bring to a simmer and cook for 5 minutes. Stir the shrimp back into the pot and simmer until the shrimp are just cooked through, about 2 minutes.

4. Working in batches, transfer the soup to a blender or food processor and puree until smooth (or use an immersion blender to puree right in the pot). Return the soup to the pot and stir in the milk, half-and-half, cayenne, and the remaining ½ teaspoon salt. Simmer until hot, then add the lemon juice. Ladle into bowls and sprinkle with parsley.

Serves 6

Beef and Vegetable Barley Soup

1½ pounds boneless beef chuck,
cut into 1-inch chunks

Salt and freshly ground
black pepper to taste

3 tablespoons all-purpose flour

2 tablespoons olive oil

¾ cup finely chopped onion

¾ cup finely chopped celery

¾ cup finely chopped carrot

3 garlic cloves, finely chopped

8 cups low-sodium beef broth

2 cups water

1 bay leaf

1 cup pearl barley

1 small russet potato,
peeled and chopped

1 cup fresh green beans, chopped

1 cup frozen peas

Soups like this one are what I look forward to in the chilly winter months. A bowl of this robust soup is just what you need after a day out in the elements. And it sure does stick to your ribs. The barley and beef combine to keep you satisfied for a good long while. So I make sure to take my time in eating this dish. That way, I won't gobble up too much and find that I've eaten past the point of fullness.

1. Season the meat with salt and pepper and toss lightly with the flour. Heat a large pot over medium-high heat and add 1 tablespoon of the oil. Add the beef and cook, in batches, until well browned all over, about 10 minutes. Remove with a slotted spoon to a large bowl.

2. Reduce the heat to medium and add the remaining oil. Add the onion, celery, carrot, garlic, and a pinch of salt. Cook until soft, 5 to 7 minutes. Stir in the beef broth, water, and bay leaf. Bring to a boil. Return the beef to the pot, reduce the heat to medium-low, and simmer, covered, for 20 minutes. Stir in the barley and potato and simmer until the meat and barley are tender, about 40 minutes. Add the green beans and peas and cook for 10 minutes more. Taste and adjust the seasoning.

Serves 8

MORE VEGGIES, PLEASE
One of the biggest changes you'll see in my soups
is that I now take every opportunity to throw extra
vegetables into the pot. I don't leave it at onion, carrot,
and potato. Now you'll see lots of green beans, dark leafy
greens, and peas added just before serving, making my
soups so much better for you.

Split Pea and Bacon Soup

I love that I can make this soup at the drop of a hat. Because I don't have to soak the split peas, I can get right on this soup whenever I get a hankering for it. Besides being downright delicious, split peas happen to be very, very good for you. They have a low glycemic level so they fill you up for a longer time, which keeps your appetite under control. And they are a great source of protein and fiber, not to mention vitamins and minerals.

1 tablespoon olive oil

6 turkey or regular bacon slices, coarsely chopped

1 large onion, finely chopped

2 celery stalks, finely chopped

2 large carrots, finely chopped

2 garlic cloves, finely chopped

1 teaspoon fresh thyme

½ teaspoon dried marjoram

½ teaspoon finely chopped fresh rosemary

¼ teaspoon cayenne pepper, or more to taste

8 cups low-sodium chicken broth

1 pound dried green split peas, rinsed and drained

1 bay leaf

Salt and freshly ground black pepper to taste

1. In a large pot or Dutch oven, heat the oil over medium-high heat. Add the bacon and cook until crisp, about 5 minutes. Drain the bacon on a paper towel–lined plate. Crumble and set aside.

2. Reduce the heat to medium-low and add the onion, celery, carrots, garlic, thyme, marjoram, rosemary, and cayenne. If you used turkey bacon and the pot seems dry, grease it with cooking spray. Cook, stirring, until the vegetables are tender, about 6 minutes. Add the chicken broth, split peas, and bay leaf and bring the soup to a boil. Reduce the heat to medium-low, cover, and simmer until the peas are tender, about 1 hour. Lift the cover occasionally to give the soup a stir.

3. Remove the bay leaf. Working in batches, transfer the soup to a blender or food processor and puree until smooth (or use an immersion blender to puree right in the pot). Return the soup to the pot and warm over medium-low heat until heated through. Season to taste with salt and black pepper and garnish with the crumbled bacon.

Serves 4 to 6

DON'T BLOW YOUR TOP
Be extra careful if you puree soups in a blender or food processor. Best idea is to let the soup cool down first. But if you do puree it while it's hot, start slowly with little pulses so that the soup doesn't explode out the top of the blender. Or, better yet, use an immersion blender and puree the soup right in the pot.

Hearty Lentil and Spinach Soup

Don't let anybody tell you that a vegetarian soup can't be a satisfying meal. There's a reason this recipe has the word "hearty" in the title. Lentils get about 30 percent of their calories from protein. And spinach is no slouch in that department either. This soup is comforting and earthy with a bright side, thanks to the red wine vinegar stirred in just before serving. Paired up with a crusty piece of bread, this soup is a mighty fine one-pot meal.

1. In a large pot, heat the oil over medium heat until shimmering, about 3 minutes. Add the celery, carrot, and onion and cook, stirring occasionally, until the vegetables have softened, about 10 minutes. Stir in the garlic and tomato paste and cook until fragrant, about 1 minute. Season with the 1½ teaspoons salt and pepper to taste.

2. Add the water, chicken broth, tomatoes with their juice, the lentils, bay leaf, and thyme and stir to combine. Cover and bring to a simmer, about 5 minutes. Once the mixture is simmering, reduce the heat to low and continue simmering, covered, until the lentils are soft, 30 to 40 minutes more.

3. Taste and season with more salt and pepper, if you like, then stir in the vinegar, adding more if you think it needs it. Add the spinach and stir until it's wilted.

Serves 4 to 6

1 tablespoon olive oil

1 celery stalk, finely chopped

1 carrot, finely chopped

1 onion, finely chopped

2 garlic cloves, finely chopped

1 tablespoon tomato paste

1½ teaspoons salt, or to taste

Freshly ground black pepper to taste

2 cups water

4 cups low-sodium chicken or vegetable broth

¾ cup canned no-salt-added diced tomatoes with their juice

1½ cups green or brown lentils, rinsed

1 bay leaf

½ teaspoon dried thyme

2 teaspoons red wine vinegar, or to taste

2 bags (5 ounces each) baby spinach

THICK AND THIN
If the soup seems thick when you are reheating it, thin it out with extra chicken broth.

Chickpea and Vegetable Soup with Orzo

2 teaspoons olive oil

2 carrots, finely chopped

2 celery stalks, finely chopped

1 onion, finely chopped

2 garlic cloves, finely chopped

2 tablespoons chopped
fresh parsley

1 teaspoon chopped
fresh rosemary

4 cups low-sodium chicken
or vegetable broth

1 bay leaf

½ cup whole-wheat
or regular orzo

1 can (15 ounces) chickpeas,
rinsed and drained

1½ cups grape tomatoes,
coarsely chopped

1 bag (5 ounces) baby spinach

Salt and black pepper to taste

Chopped scallions (dark green
parts only) for garnish (optional)

Grated Parmesan cheese to taste
(optional)

It may have an unusual-sounding name, but orzo is simply a type of pasta that's shaped like a flat grain of rice. Because of its delicate size, it has become my new favorite soup pasta. If you can't find it on your supermarket shelves, go ahead and use small macaroni instead.

1. In a large pot, heat the oil over medium-high heat. Add the carrots, celery, and onion and cook, stirring, until softened, 5 to 7 minutes. Add the garlic, parsley, and rosemary and cook for 1 minute. Add the chicken broth and bay leaf and bring to a boil over high heat.

2. Add the orzo, chickpeas, and tomatoes to the soup. Reduce the heat to a simmer and cover. Simmer for about 10 minutes, or until the orzo is tender. Remove the lid and stir in the spinach. Season to taste with salt and pepper.

3. Ladle the soup into bowls and top with chopped scallions and grated Parmesan, if you like.

Serves 4 to 6

Creamy Butternut Squash Soup

Now, I think it's pretty hard to go wrong with butternut squash soup, but this little beauty takes it up a notch, I tell you. It's velvety smooth and ever so tasty. I really love the surprising zing of the fresh ginger and the cider vinegar. I like to serve it on Thanksgiving Day to start off the great meal. But you don't need a holiday to bring out this simple yet satisfying soup. A cool day is a fine enough excuse for this little gem.

1. In a medium pot, melt the butter over medium-high heat. Add the onion and carrot and cook, stirring, until softened, 5 to 7 minutes. Add the ginger and garlic and cook for 1 to 2 minutes more, until fragrant.

2. Add the squash to the onion mixture and cook, stirring, for 5 minutes. Season with salt, black pepper, and cayenne, then pour in the water and bring to a boil over medium-high heat. Reduce the heat to medium and simmer for 20 to 30 minutes, until the squash is beginning to fall apart.

3. Transfer the soup to a blender or food processor and puree until smooth (or use an immersion blender to puree right in the pot). Add more water if you think it needs to be thinned out. Return the soup to the pot and bring up to a simmer over medium heat. Stir in the vinegar. Have a taste and add more vinegar, salt, and black pepper to taste, if you think it needs it.

Serves 4

1 tablespoon unsalted butter

1 onion, chopped

1 carrot, chopped

1½ tablespoons finely chopped fresh ginger

2 garlic cloves, finely chopped

1 medium butternut squash, halved, seeded, and cut into 1-inch cubes

Salt and freshly ground black pepper to taste

Pinch of cayenne pepper

5 cups water

1 teaspoon cider vinegar

4

Pasta and Rice

Back when I was growing up, pasta meant macaroni noodles, and rice was always plain white. Thank heavens that these days there are so many more interesting options out there when it comes to carbs. As y'all know, I do love them so and I am not about to cut them out of my diet entirely.

To keep carbs in my diet, I had to look at making two big changes. The first was to rethink my plate so that they were no longer the main attraction, but more of a supporting character. I aim for about a fistful each of protein and starch and then fill at least half my plate with veggies of some sort or other. This helps me fill up on heart-healthy vegetables instead of heavy carbs and protein. But I still leave the table satisfied.

Change number two involved varying the types of carbs I chose to eat. Nowadays I try to cook with whole-wheat pastas more often than not. They have an earthy flavor that I find lends so much to a dish. And the health benefits are real. When I discovered that whole-wheat pasta had been linked to lower blood pressure and a decreased risk of type 2 diabetes, I knew I had to give whole wheat a try.

What I've found is that some dishes lend themselves to white-flour pasta, some lend themselves to whole-wheat pasta, and in some you wouldn't know the difference. The whole-wheat macaroni I use in *The Lady's New Cheesy Mac* (page 98) seems tailor-made for that recipe. I actually prefer mac and cheese this way. And my **Creamy Ham and Vegetable Casserole** (page 111) can be made with a white-flour egg noodle or a whole-wheat egg noodle. I think either is absolutely delicious in this recipe. My advice would be to try these recipes with both whole-wheat and white-flour noodles and see which noodles suit you best.

How great is it that you can find all sorts of shapes and sizes of pastas on the supermarket shelves these days? I love experimenting with these different types of pastas to see which work best in different dishes. Some shapes pick up chunky sauces better than others. I wouldn't dream of using a thin spaghetti to make my **Fusilli with Roasted Vegetables and Ricotta** (page 117). That dish needs a thicker noodle to pick up the hearty bits of veggies and cheese that I toss throughout.

When it comes to rice, my options have also grown. You'll find brown and wild rice in my pantry these days. These types of rice are high in fiber and protein, which helps to slow the rate at which the body digests carbs. And that means no more spikes in sugar. Nutty brown rice adds a whole new level of flavor to **New Southern Brown Rice** (page 105). Sure it could be done with white rice, but I tell you, it's even better with brown.

You will even find one recipe in this chapter that doesn't actually contain pasta or rice. I make an out-of-this-world **Eggplant Lasagna** (page 118) that has not a lick of pasta. I just had to share it with you. The secret? I've replaced the noodles with thin slices of roasted eggplant. Now, how clever is that?

Baked Spaghetti

I've been making baked spaghetti for my boys since they were just up to my knees. Now I make this leaner version for my grandkids, Jack, Matthew, and Henry Reed. It suits the way we're all eating these days. It's as full flavored as it always was, but with the whole-grain pasta, lean ground beef, and lower sodium count, it's definitely a modern version of an oldie but a goodie.

1. Preheat the oven to 350°F.

2. In a medium pot, heat 1 teaspoon of the oil over medium heat. Add the onion and cook until soft, 5 to 7 minutes. Add the garlic and cook for 2 minutes. Add the tomatoes, tomato paste, parsley, basil, bay leaf, and oregano. Season to taste with salt and pepper. Bring to a boil over high heat, and then reduce the heat and simmer for 10 minutes.

3. Meanwhile, in a medium skillet, heat the remaining 1 teaspoon oil over medium heat. Add the bell pepper and cook until soft, 5 to 7 minutes. Crumble the ground beef into the skillet. Cook over medium-high heat until no pink color remains. Season to taste with salt and pepper. Drain the fat from the meat and then add the beef mixture to the tomato sauce. Simmer for 5 to 10 minutes more.

4. In a large pot of boiling salted water, cook the pasta according to the package directions. Drain well and, in a medium bowl, toss with the Parmesan while still warm.

5. Cover the bottom of a 13 by 9-inch baking dish with half of the tomato sauce. Add the pasta in an even layer and top with the remaining sauce. Sprinkle with the Cheddar and mozzarella and bake until the cheese is melted and the sauce is bubbling, 30 minutes.

Serves 10

2 teaspoons olive oil

1 large onion, chopped

2 garlic cloves, chopped

1 can (28 ounces) no-salt-added diced tomatoes

1 tablespoon tomato paste

¼ cup chopped fresh parsley

¼ cup chopped fresh basil

1 bay leaf

½ teaspoon dried oregano

Salt and freshly ground black pepper to taste

1 green bell pepper, chopped

1 pound lean ground beef

6 ounces whole-grain or regular angel hair pasta

2 tablespoons grated Parmesan cheese

½ cup shredded Cheddar cheese

½ cup shredded mozzarella cheese

The Lady's New Cheesy Mac

8 ounces whole-wheat
  or regular elbow macaroni
  (2 cups)

2 tablespoons low-fat
  cream cheese (Neufchâtel),
  softened

2 cups shredded sharp
  Cheddar cheese,
  plus more for topping

2 large eggs, lightly beaten

¼ cup milk

1 tablespoon Dijon mustard

½ teaspoon salt

Pinch of cayenne pepper
  (optional)

This new recipe has all my friends and family wondering how on earth I've managed to cut the fat. It's a creamy, delectable little dish that does not taste like it would be good for you. But let me tell you, I have cut the fat like crazy from this classic dish without sacrificing a lick of flavor. Have y'all noticed there is not even one tablespoon of butter in this recipe? I rest my case.

1. Preheat the oven to 350°F. Grease a 9-inch square baking dish with cooking spray.

2. In a large pot of boiling salted water, cook the macaroni according to the package directions. Drain well and return the pasta to the pot. Add the cream cheese and Cheddar while the pasta is still warm. Stir until the cheeses have melted and the pasta is well coated.

3. Whisk together the eggs, milk, mustard, salt, and cayenne (if using) and stir through the pasta mixture. Pour the mixture into the prepared baking dish, top with extra Cheddar, if you like, and bake for 30 to 40 minutes, until the cheese is melted and starting to turn golden brown at the corners of the pan.

Serves 6 to 8

DON'T DOUBLE UP
Here's a good rule of thumb to follow at meal times: Don't double up on your carbs. If you are indulging in a pasta dish like this one, skip the bread and have yourself a nice side salad.

Roasted Tomato Pasta with Basil and Mozzarella

8 ounces whole-wheat or regular pasta, such as penne, fusilli, or farfalle

1 pint (10 ounces) grape tomatoes

3 garlic cloves, finely chopped

1 tablespoon olive oil

½ teaspoon salt, plus more to taste

¼ teaspoon freshly ground black pepper, plus more to taste

½ cup fresh basil, coarsely chopped

½ pound bocconcini (mozzarella balls; see Note), drained and halved

1 teaspoon balsamic vinegar

Grated Parmesan cheese, for serving (optional)

This here is a pasta dish that you can throw together in no time flat. It really is that easy. Get your hands on some ripe grape tomatoes, a creamy mozzarella, and sweet balsamic and this pasta will blow you away. It's like your classic tomato mozzarella salad with pasta thrown in to make it hearty enough for a meal. And here's a little hint: If you toss in the mozzarella while the pasta is still warm, the cheese will begin to melt. Now that is too delicious for words!

1. Preheat the oven to 350°F.

2. In a large pot of boiling salted water, cook the pasta according to the package directions. Drain well.

3. Meanwhile, as the pasta cooks, toss the tomatoes with the garlic, oil, salt, pepper, and ¼ cup of the basil. In a small baking dish, roast the tomato mixture until the tomatoes have collapsed and are tender, 20 to 25 minutes, tossing halfway through.

4. In a large bowl, toss the pasta with the roasted tomatoes (make sure you scrape all the garlic and oil from the pan into the pasta), bocconcini, vinegar, and the remaining ¼ cup basil. Season to taste. Serve warm or at room temperature, topped with Parmesan, if you like.

Serves 4

CHEESE SWAP
Bocconcini are baby-size balls of mozzarella that can be found in the cheese case or many olive bars near the deli section in most supermarkets. If you can't get your hands on bocconcini, though, feel free to substitute an 8-ounce ball of mozzarella, cut into bite-size pieces.

Savannah Baked Red Rice

Michael sure did feel a whole lot better after I found a way to fit Savannah red rice into our healthier lifestyle. He practically lives on this dish! Truth is, it really wasn't all that hard to lighten up his favorite. I swapped olive oil for butter, switched to turkey sausage from pork, and substituted low-sodium chicken broth. Small changes, big difference.

2 tablespoons olive oil

1 cup chopped onions

1 cup chopped green bell peppers

1 cup chopped turkey andouille
   or other smoked turkey sausage
   (about 5 ounces)

1 cup long-grain white rice

1 can (14½ ounces) no-salt-added
   crushed tomatoes

1 cup low-sodium chicken broth

1 teaspoon hot sauce

Salt and freshly ground
   black pepper to taste

1. Preheat the oven to 350°F. Lightly grease a 9-inch square baking dish with cooking spray.

2. In a medium saucepan, heat the oil over medium heat. Add the onions, bell peppers, and sausage and cook until the vegetables soften, 5 to 7 minutes. Stir in the rice, tomatoes, chicken broth, hot sauce, and salt and pepper to taste and bring to a boil, stirring occasionally.

3. Scrape the mixture into the prepared baking dish and cover with aluminum foil. Bake until the rice is tender and the sauce is bubbling, about 40 minutes.

Serves 4 to 6

Jambalaya

We love this ragin' Cajun dish so much in my family, I reckon we have it several times a month. It's got all you need for a well-rounded dinner cooked all together in the same skillet. I always bring it to the table right there in the skillet I cooked it in so I don't have to dirty up another dish. If we don't have shrimp in the house (which is rare, but it happens!), then I throw in cooked cubed chicken instead.

1. In a large skillet, heat the oil over medium heat. Add the onions, bell pepper, celery, and garlic. Cook, stirring, until soft, 5 to 7 minutes. Add the sausage and cayenne and cook for 2 minutes. Stir in the tomato paste and cook for 1 minute.

2. Add 2 cups of the chicken broth, tomatoes, rice, and salt. Simmer, stirring frequently, until the rice is almost tender, about 15 minutes. Stir in the shrimp and cook until the rice is completely tender and the shrimp are cooked through, 5 to 10 minutes more. If the mixture starts to seem dry, add more broth to moisten it up. Season with the Tabasco and serve.

Serves 6

2 tablespoons olive oil

1 cup chopped onions

½ cup chopped green bell pepper

½ cup chopped celery

2 garlic cloves, finely chopped

8 ounces andouille chicken sausage, cubed

½ teaspoon cayenne pepper

1 tablespoon tomato paste

2 to 3 cups low-sodium chicken broth

1 can (14½ ounces) no-salt-added diced tomatoes

¾ cup long-grain white rice

1 teaspoon salt

1 pound medium shrimp, peeled and deveined

½ teaspoon Tabasco sauce

Hoppin' John

Hoppin' John may be a New Year's tradition, but we like to enjoy it any old day of the year. It's a simple dish for simple folk, and it's quite possibly the best darn rice and beans recipe out there. I was surprised to find that it worked so well with brown rice. But it did, and that's the way you'll find me making it these days.

2 tablespoons (¼ stick) unsalted butter

1 cup chopped onions

½ cup chopped green bell pepper

¼ cup chopped celery

2 garlic cloves, finely chopped

½ teaspoon dried thyme

1 can (15 ounces) black-eyed peas, rinsed and drained

2 cups cooked white or brown rice

½ cup low-sodium chicken broth

½ teaspoon salt, plus more to taste

Tabasco sauce to taste

1. In a large skillet, melt the butter over medium heat. Add the onions, bell pepper, and celery. Cook, stirring, until the vegetables are almost tender, about 5 minutes. Stir in the garlic and thyme and cook for 1 minute.

2. Stir in the black-eyed peas, rice, chicken broth, and salt. Simmer until the broth is absorbed and the peas are hot, about 5 minutes. Season with Tabasco and some more salt, if you think it needs it.

Serves 4 to 6

A PAULA DEEN CLASSIC

New Southern Brown Rice

This is a modern take on the classic Southern brown rice I grew up with in Albany, Georgia. Now, I believe that there is a time and a place for everything and I haven't forsaken the beloved dish my mama used to make for Bubba and me. It will always have a special place in my heart. But this variation, made with brown rice and fresh mushrooms instead of white rice and canned mushrooms, gives me a new, healthier way to enjoy an old favorite.

2 tablespoons (¼ stick) unsalted butter

¾ cup chopped onion

1 cup sliced cremini mushrooms

1 cup long-grain brown rice

2 cups low-sodium beef or chicken broth (or substitute water if you like)

¼ teaspoon salt

1 tablespoon chopped fresh parsley (optional)

1. In a medium saucepan, heat the butter over medium-low heat. Add the onion and mushrooms and cook until soft and golden, 8 to 10 minutes. Increase the heat to medium, add the rice, and cook, stirring to coat with the butter, for about 2 minutes. Carefully pour in the beef broth and add the salt. Bring to a boil over high heat. Reduce to a simmer, cover, and cook gently until most of the liquid has been absorbed and the rice is tender, about 45 minutes.

2. Remove from the heat and let stand, covered, for 5 minutes. Fluff with a fork, stir through the parsley (if using), and serve.

Serves 4 to 6

ADD SOME GREEN
There's nothing stopping you from adding a little green vegetable to this dish. If you'd like a boost of vitamins in your rice, throw in some peas or a handful of baby spinach during the last couple minutes of cooking time.

Brown Rice Pilaf

2 tablespoons olive oil

¾ cup finely chopped red onion

⅓ cup finely sliced celery

1 garlic clove, finely chopped

½ cup coarsely grated carrots

1 heaping teaspoon fresh thyme

1 cup long-grain brown rice

2 cups water

1 bay leaf

½ teaspoon salt,
  plus extra if you like

¼ teaspoon freshly ground black
  pepper, plus more to taste

½ cup cooked peas

⅓ cup dried cherries, chopped

1 to 2 tablespoons torn fresh mint
  leaves

1½ teaspoons finely grated
  lemon zest

1 to 2 tablespoons toasted
  sunflower seeds

This pretty pilaf is an absolute riot of color. Red onion, celery, carrot, peas, dried cherries, and mint leaves are nestled right into the brown rice. And you know what comes along with all that color? Tons of flavor, that's what. This is no shrinking violet of a pilaf. So when you're looking for something bold to set next to your meat, try this dish on for size.

1. In a medium saucepan, heat the oil over medium heat. Add the red onion, celery, garlic, carrots, and thyme. Stir to combine and cook gently for 5 minutes, until the vegetables are softened. Add the rice and cook, stirring to coat, for 1 minute. Slowly add the water, bay leaf, salt, and pepper. Bring to a boil, then cover and reduce to a simmer. Cook for 45 minutes, until almost all the liquid is absorbed and the rice is tender and moist. Remove from the heat and stir the peas and cherries into the rice mixture. Cover and let it sit for 5 minutes.

2. Remove the bay leaf, add the mint and 1 teaspoon of the lemon zest, and fluff the mixture with a fork. Give the rice a taste and add more salt and pepper if you think it needs it. Sprinkle the sunflower seeds and the remaining ½ teaspoon lemon zest over the top before serving.

Serves 4 to 6

Perlow

1 tablespoon vegetable oil

1 turkey or regular bacon slice, chopped

1 large green bell pepper, chopped

1 onion, chopped

2 garlic cloves, chopped

½ cup long-grain white rice

1 can (14½ ounces) no-salt-added diced tomatoes

4 dashes hot sauce, or to taste

Salt and freshly ground black pepper to taste

1 pound boneless, skinless chicken thighs (about 4 to 5), each cut into 4 pieces

½ cup chopped scallions (dark green tops only)

I knew this dish represented a carb overload for my new diet and I just couldn't eat it the way I used to. Well, I just refused to have to give it up. So after some careful consideration, this is what I came up with. It's an absolutely delicious alternative to the old perlow I used to enjoy. All I've really done is switch the rice amount with the meat amount. Where I used to make this with 1½ cups rice to ½ cup meat, I now use ½ cup rice and 1 pound lean meat for four servings. That switcheroo gives me the protein my body needs with a good hit of the carbs I love so much. Give up my perlow? No way. I've just made it work for me today.

1. In a Dutch oven, heat the oil over medium-high heat. Add the bacon and cook until just colored, about 2 minutes. Add the bell pepper and onion and cook until soft, about 5 minutes. Add the garlic and cook until fragrant, 30 seconds. Add the rice, tomatoes, hot sauce, ¾ cup water, and salt and pepper to taste. Stir everything together and nestle the chicken pieces into the pot. Bring to a boil, cover, reduce the heat to medium-low, and cook until the rice is tender and the chicken cooked through, about 30 minutes.

2. Remove from the heat, stir, replace the lid, and let the perlow stand for 5 minutes. Serve garnished with the scallions.

Serves 4

Mexican Rice Bake

This colorful, spicy dish always makes me think fiesta. So I always make tons of it. I don't know who can resist this rice bake when it comes bubbling out of the oven smelling like chiles and cheese. It makes my mouth water just thinking about it! I like to dress it up with a sprinkling of fresh cilantro and scallions and fresh lime wedges on the side. Presentation is everything, y'all.

1. Preheat the oven to 350°F.

2. In a medium Dutch oven or heavy-bottomed pan, heat the oil over medium-high heat. Add the onion, bell pepper, and jalapeño. Cook, stirring, until soft, about 5 minutes. Add the garlic and cook until fragrant, about 1 minute. Stir in the cumin, chili powder, and oregano. Cook until fragrant, 1 to 2 minutes.

3. Add the rice to the pan and toast for 2 minutes, stirring continuously. Pour in the chiles, tomatoes, and chicken broth. Bring to a simmer.

4. Pour the rice mixture into a 13 by 9-inch baking dish. Cover with aluminum foil and bake for 30 to 40 minutes, until the rice is soft. Uncover and add the Cheddar in an even layer on the top. Return the rice to the oven, uncovered, to brown for 10 to 15 minutes. Garnish with chopped cilantro and scallions. Serve with lime wedges.

Serves 10 to 12

1 tablespoon olive oil

1 onion, chopped

1 red bell pepper, chopped

1 jalapeño pepper, finely chopped

2 garlic cloves, finely chopped

1 teaspoon ground cumin

2 teaspoons chili powder

½ teaspoon dried oregano

2 cups long-grain white rice

1 can (4 ounces) chopped green chiles

1 can (14½ ounces) no-salt-added diced tomatoes

1¾ cups low-sodium chicken or vegetable broth

2 cups shredded Cheddar cheese

Chopped fresh cilantro, for garnish

Chopped scallions (green tops only), for garnish

Lime wedges, for serving

SPICY SHORTCUT
If you've got some in your pantry, you can substitute two 10-ounce cans of spicy diced tomatoes, such as Ro*Tel, for the can of regular diced tomatoes and the can of chiles called for in this recipe.

Dirty Rice

1 cup long-grain brown rice

2 cups water

¾ teaspoon salt

1 tablespoon olive oil

½ pound extra-lean ground beef
or ground turkey

½ pound chicken livers, cleaned
and finely chopped

½ teaspoon freshly ground
black pepper

1 tablespoon unsalted butter

½ cup chopped green bell pepper

½ cup chopped yellow bell pepper

½ cup finely chopped celery

4 scallions (white and light green
parts), chopped

1 garlic clove, finely chopped

Hot sauce to taste

Chopped fresh parsley, for serving

I like to call this dish my Southern chicken soup because it is so packed with vitamins and minerals, you can scare a cold away just by looking at it. While I already knew that brown rice and chicken livers tasted great, what I didn't know was that this dish just about has it all: antioxidants, vitamin A, vitamin C, fiber, iron, protein, and on and on. Next time you feel a sniffle coming on, try this little remedy on for size.

1. In a medium saucepan, combine the rice, water, and ¼ teaspoon of the salt. Bring to a boil over medium-high heat. Reduce to a simmer, cover, and cook until most of the liquid has been absorbed and the rice is tender, about 45 minutes. Remove from the heat and let stand, covered, for 5 minutes.

2. Meanwhile, in a large skillet, heat the oil over medium-high heat. Add the meat and cook, breaking it up with a fork, until well browned, 5 to 7 minutes. Add the chicken livers and cook, turning once, until no longer pink, 2 to 3 minutes. Season with another ¼ teaspoon of the salt and ¼ teaspoon of the black pepper. With a slotted spoon, transfer the mixture to a paper towel–lined plate to drain.

3. Return the skillet to the heat. Add the butter and let it melt. Add the green bell pepper, yellow bell pepper, the celery, scallions, and garlic. Cook until the vegetables have softened, 5 to 7 minutes. Stir in the cooked rice and the meat mixture, and cook until warmed through. Season to taste with the hot sauce and the remaining ¼ teaspoon salt and ¼ teaspoon black pepper. Stir in the parsley just before serving.

Serves 6 to 8

Creamy Ham and Vegetable Casserole

This noodle casserole is one of Michael's favorites. He loves the creamy sauce and the salty ham so much he doesn't even notice he's stuffing himself full of good-for-you cabbage too. Healthy and decadent? Yes, sir, that is a perfect dish for the new Paula.

1. Preheat the oven to 350°F. Grease a 13 by 9-inch baking dish with cooking spray.

2. In a large pot of boiling salted water, cook the noodles according to the package directions. Drain well.

3. In a large skillet, heat the oil over medium heat and cook the onion and bell pepper until soft, 5 to 7 minutes.

4. Meanwhile, remove the tough outer leaves of the cabbage. Halve the cabbage and remove the core. Rinse in between the layers until no grit remains. Slice the cabbage into thin ribbons either by hand or using the grater attachment on a food processor.

5. Add the cabbage ribbons to the vegetable mixture in three batches, waiting for each batch to begin wilting before adding the next. Cook, stirring, over medium-high heat until the cabbage is translucent, 10 to 15 minutes. Season to taste with salt and pepper.

6. In a large bowl, whisk together the milk, sour cream, eggs, and 1 cup of the Cheddar. Add the cooled pasta and stir to combine and coat. Stir in the vegetable mixture and the ham.

7. Spoon into the prepared baking dish and cover with the remaining ½ cup Cheddar and the Parmesan. Cover with aluminum foil and bake for 20 minutes. Uncover the dish and place under the broiler until lightly browned, 1 to 2 minutes.

Serves 12

1 package (12 ounces) extra-wide egg noodles, whole wheat or regular

1 teaspoon olive oil

1 onion, chopped

1 red bell pepper, chopped

1 medium head green cabbage

Salt and freshly ground black pepper to taste

½ cup milk

1 cup regular or light sour cream

3 large eggs

1½ cups shredded Cheddar cheese

4 ounces chopped ham (about 1 cup)

⅓ cup finely grated Parmesan cheese

WHOLE-WHEAT NOODLES
I love whole-wheat egg noodles. There, I said it. As unbelievable as this may sound, I think I actually prefer them to the white variety. They've got a hearty flavor but are still soft like regular egg noodles. To my taste, this is the best type of whole-wheat noodle out there and I highly recommend you give it a try.

Baked Ziti

1 pound whole-wheat
   or regular ziti

1 tablespoon olive oil

¾ pound lean bulk Italian-style
   turkey or pork sausage or use
   sausage links and squeeze the
   meat out of the casings

¾ cup chopped onion

1 tablespoon finely chopped garlic

1 teaspoon dried oregano

1 teaspoon crushed
   red pepper flakes

½ teaspoon dried thyme

1 can (28 ounces) no-salt-added
   crushed tomatoes

4 cups loosely packed chopped
   fresh kale (3 to 4 large leaves)

Salt and freshly ground
   black pepper

1 cup part-skim ricotta cheese

¾ cup shredded mozzarella
   cheese

⅓ cup grated Parmesan cheese

Baked ziti is one of those satisfying, decadent dishes that whole families just crave. And mine is no different. Jamie and Brooke love when I feed Jack and Matthew this meal because now I bake it with healthy kale right in the mix. This ziti is meaty, cheesy, and packed with vitamins. I'm not sure who loves it more—the kiddos or Grandma!

1. Preheat the oven to 375°F.

2. In a large pot of boiling salted water, cook the ziti according to the package directions. Drain well.

3. In a large deep skillet, heat the oil over medium heat and add the sausage meat. Cook, breaking the sausage up with a wooden spoon, for about 8 minutes, or until the meat is no longer pink. Remove the sausage from the skillet with a slotted spoon and transfer it to a paper towel–lined plate to drain.

4. Add the onion, garlic, oregano, red pepper flakes, and thyme to the skillet and cook, stirring occasionally, until the onion is tender, 3 to 5 minutes. Add the tomatoes and simmer for 5 minutes. Stir in the cooked sausage and the kale. Season to taste with salt and pepper.

5. Remove the pan from the heat, add the cooked pasta, and stir in the ricotta. Pour the mixture into a 13 by 9-inch baking dish. Sprinkle with the mozzarella and then the Parmesan. Bake until the cheese is melted and golden brown, 25 to 30 minutes.

Serves 8

TAKE A WALK

After a hearty meal of cheesy pasta, I find it's a good idea to take a nice brisk walk. Michael and I so enjoy our evening walks together. They give us a great chance to catch up on the events of the day, all while burning the calories we just took in over dinner.

Lightened-Up Tuna Casserole

2 cans (5 ounces each)
tuna in water

1 can (10¾ ounces) low-fat
condensed cream of
mushroom soup

½ cup shredded Cheddar cheese

¾ cup whole-wheat elbow
macaroni, cooked and drained

½ cup milk

2 tablespoons chopped pimiento

2 scallions (white and light green
parts), chopped

Pinch of crushed red pepper
flakes

Freshly ground black pepper
to taste

½ cup crushed baked potato chips

Remember how I told you that some dishes actually work better with whole-wheat pasta instead of white-flour pasta? Well, this here is one of them. You can barely tell that I use whole-wheat macaroni in this tuna casserole. The only hint is a little bit of extra chew, which works nicely next to the soft tuna. I just love a one-dish meal like this. It's big on flavor and light on the washing up.

1. Preheat the oven to 400°F. Lightly grease an 8-inch square baking dish with cooking spray.

2. In a large bowl, mix together the tuna, soup, Cheddar, macaroni, milk, pimiento, scallions, red pepper flakes, and pepper to taste. Scrape the mixture into the prepared baking dish and top with the potato chips. Bake for 20 minutes, until the chips are golden and the casserole is bubbling.

Serves 4

Turkey Tetrazzini

This stove-top tetrazzini is thoroughly modern and fantastically delicious. Instead of heavy cream or a creamy soup base, I make a roux and pour in milk. And in place of a cracker or bread crumb topping, I sprinkle over a light Parmesan, parsley, and lemon zest topping that really brightens up this easy weeknight dinner. Don't forget about this dish the day after Thanksgiving. It's a great place to use your leftover turkey.

1. In a small bowl, toss together the Parmesan, parsley, and lemon zest. Cover and refrigerate until ready to use.

2. In a Dutch oven or large deep skillet, heat the oil over medium heat. Add the mushrooms and cook, stirring frequently, until all the liquid has evaporated, about 5 minutes. Add the garlic and cook for 30 seconds, until fragrant. Add the flour and cook, stirring, for 1 minute (the pan will get pretty dry but that's okay). Add the milk, chicken broth, sherry (if using), and sage. Raise the heat to medium-high and bring to a boil. Cook, stirring, until the sauce coats the back of a spoon. Reduce the heat to medium, add the turkey, and cook, stirring occasionally, until the turkey is cooked through, about 5 minutes.

3. Meanwhile, in a large pot of boiling salted water, cook the pasta according to the package directions. About 2 minutes before the pasta is done, add the broccoli to the pot and cook until the broccoli is tender and the pasta is done, about 2 minutes. Drain well and add both to the pan with the turkey and sauce. Toss over medium heat until the pasta and broccoli are thoroughly coated with the sauce.

4. Serve in shallow bowls with the reserved Parmesan mixture passed alongside.

Serves 4

¼ cup grated Parmesan cheese

¼ cup chopped fresh parsley

½ teaspoon finely grated lemon zest

3 tablespoons olive oil

8 ounces button mushrooms, sliced

2 garlic cloves, finely chopped

2 tablespoons all-purpose flour

1 cup milk

1 cup low-sodium chicken broth

1 tablespoon sherry (optional)

1 tablespoon chopped fresh sage or 1 teaspoon dried

1 pound turkey cutlets, cut into 1-inch cubes

8 ounces linguine

2 cups broccoli florets

Fusilli with Roasted Vegetables and Ricotta

Besides grilling, roasting is one of my favorite ways to cook vegetables. They always turn out golden and sweet. This simple dish is a great way to serve roasted veggies. Just toss them through store-bought or homemade marinara and the pasta shape of your choice and dollop on ricotta. It's fast and fantastic, y'all.

1. In a large pot of boiling salted water, cook the fusilli according to the package directions. Drain well.

2. Preheat the oven to 450°F. Line a rimmed baking sheet with parchment paper and grease the paper with cooking spray.

3. Combine the zucchini, broccoli, tomatoes, bell pepper, red onion, and garlic on the baking sheet. Spray the vegetables with cooking spray and season to taste with salt and pepper. Toss well to coat the vegetables.

4. Roast until the tomatoes have shriveled and the veggies are golden, about 15 minutes. Discard the garlic cloves.

5. In a medium saucepan, heat the marinara sauce until warm. Toss the pasta with the sauce to coat, then add the vegetables and toss again. You can either fold in the ricotta now or everyone can add a scoop to their bowls. Garnish with fresh basil.

Serves 4 to 6

8 ounces whole-wheat or regular fusilli

1 zucchini, quartered lengthwise and then sliced crosswise into ¼-inch-thick pieces (about 2 cups)

1 small head broccoli, cut into florets (about 4 cups)

1 pint (10 ounces) grape tomatoes, cut in half

1 yellow bell pepper, finely chopped

1 red onion, halved and cut into ½-inch slices

3 garlic cloves, peeled and smashed

Salt and freshly ground black pepper to taste

1½ cups store-bought marinara sauce

1 cup part-skim ricotta cheese

Fresh basil, for garnish

Eggplant Lasagna

2 large eggplants (about 3½ pounds), peeled and sliced lengthwise into ¼-inch-thick slices

Salt and freshly ground black pepper to taste

2 tablespoons olive oil

6 ounces thinly sliced cremini mushrooms

1 large onion, chopped

2 garlic cloves, finely chopped

2 teaspoons fresh thyme

½ teaspoon dried oregano

1 can (28 ounces) low-sodium whole plum tomatoes in puree

6 fresh basil leaves, torn

2 cups part-skim ricotta cheese

½ package (5 ounces) chopped frozen spinach, thawed and squeezed of excess liquid

2 tablespoons chopped fresh flat-leaf parsley

1 large egg yolk

¾ cup grated Parmesan cheese

1½ cups shredded mozzarella cheese

I like to make this dish in the late summer or early fall when my garden provides me with a bounty of beautiful eggplant. I swap out the pasta noodles and use thin eggplant slices to create my layers. Then I pretty much follow a classic lasagna recipe, with the addition of mushrooms. The eggplant, mushrooms, and spinach make it so healthy and pretty, like a little celebration right there in a casserole dish. And because I believe every good celebration should feature cheese, I fill this lasagna with three of my favorites: ricotta, Parmesan, and mozzarella.

1. Position one oven rack in the top third of the oven and another rack in the bottom third of the oven. Preheat the oven to 450°F.

2. Lay the sliced eggplant in a single layer on two rimmed baking sheets. Generously grease both sides of the eggplant with cooking spray and season to taste with salt and pepper. Place one baking sheet on the top rack and the other on the bottom rack and roast the eggplant for 15 minutes. Flip the eggplant slices over and switch the pans from one rack to the other. Roast until the eggplant slices are soft and golden, about 10 minutes. Remove the baking sheets from the oven and reduce the temperature to 375°F.

3. In a large skillet, heat the oil over medium-high heat. Add the mushrooms and cook until soft and beginning to brown, about 5 minutes. Add the onion, garlic, and thyme and cook until the onion is tender, 5 to 6 minutes. Add the oregano, tomatoes, and basil and season to taste with salt and pepper. Reduce the heat to medium-low and simmer for 20 minutes.

4. Meanwhile, in a large mixing bowl, combine the ricotta, spinach, parsley, egg yolk, and Parmesan and season to taste with salt and pepper.

5. Spread one-third of the tomato sauce into the bottom of an 11 by 7-inch baking dish. Lay enough eggplant slices to cover the bottom in a single layer, about 4 slices. Top with half of

the ricotta mixture and cover with another layer of eggplant. Begin the layering again and finish with the remaining sauce. Sprinkle the shredded mozzarella over the top of the dish and cover with aluminum foil. Bake the lasagna for 25 minutes, then remove the foil and continue baking for another 15 to 20 minutes, until golden on top and bubbling. Let the lasagna rest for 5 to 10 minutes before serving.

Serves 4 to 6

COOK OUTSIDE
If it's a warm night and you just can't find the will to turn your oven on, well, just take your eggplant outside and cook it on the grill. The grilled eggplant will give the dish a nice smoky taste.

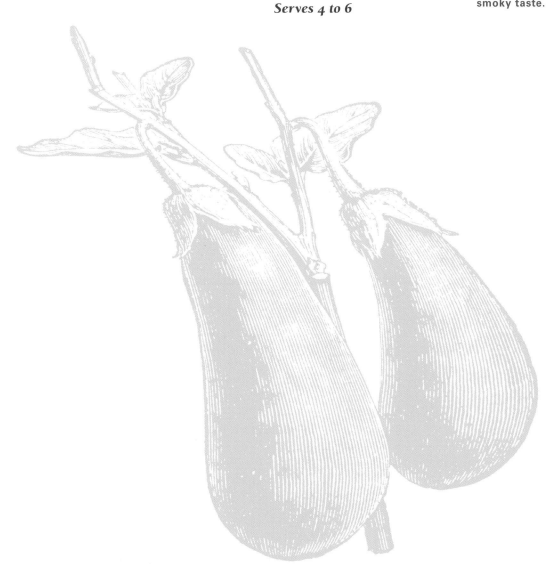

Pork, Beef, and Lamb

*I*f you're married to a meat and potato lover like I am, chances are the pages in this chapter will be dog-eared and splattered from overuse. It doesn't matter if it's beef, pork, or lamb, you can be sure Michael will be the first one to the dinner table if he smells meat cooking in the house. Add to that my two boys, Jamie and Bobby, and you have yourself a household of committed carnivores. So it almost goes without saying that I needed to find a way to build a healthy diet that featured its share of meat. This turned out to be easier than I was figuring on.

While beef is an important source of protein, it can also be a source of saturated fat, which is not the best for anyone, much less a diabetic. So when I'm in the mood for a good plate of beef, I mostly stick with leaner cuts. My **Better Burgers** (page 141) are a great example of this. I make them with extra-lean ground beef, which gives me the protein I need without all the bad fats tagging along for the ride. These tasty burgers have a deep meaty flavor that is pure heaven.

When I do indulge in a fattier cut of beef on special occasions, I make sure that I trim the meat of excess fat before I cook it. This is an important first step in putting together my **Slow Cooker Brisket** (page 140), which bubbles away in my slow cooker all day, making the house smell so inviting. By the time my guests and I sit down to enjoy this meal, the meat is falling-off-the-bone tender and oh so flavorful.

◀ *With my Captain Mike.*

But red meat does not have to mean beef. I have become a true convert to lamb. This lightly gamy, luscious meat tends to be just a little bit healthier than most cuts of beef because it usually contains less marbling. That means you can cut away the fat around the edges and be left with a pretty darn lean piece of meat without having to give up on flavor. There is just nothing quite as special as **Roast Leg of Lamb with Mint** (page 148). I like to serve this classic roast on Christmas Eve or Easter. But, really, anytime I roast this up, I get myself in a holiday frame of mind that just makes me happy.

For me, the real star of any meat chapter is pork. My goodness, but do I love me some pork! From Boston butt to lean tenderloin to baked ham, it is all near and dear to my heart. And miracle of all miracles, it is actually one of the healthiest meat choices. Now how about that? All these years I've been touting the virtues of one of the better meats.

More often than not, it's a good old pork chop I sit down to. The taste of a pan-fried pork chop just can't be beat. To really make the most of this cut, I suggest you brine your pork chops first. And to make fast work of it, try my **Quick Brined Pork Chops** (page 126). With just thirty minutes of brining, the chops turn out moist, bursting with flavor, and so tender you could cut them with a butter knife.

The leanest of the pork cuts is the tenderloin. That's why I like to top off a tenderloin with cream gravy as I do in **Pan-Seared Pork Loin with Tomato Gravy** (page 129). This lean meat absolutely sits up and sings when it's paired up with the spicy, creamy gravy. This cut also lends itself to flavor-packed spice rubs. **Spice-Rubbed Roasted Pork Tenderloin** (page 130) is a testament to that. In that recipe, I hit the tenderloin with a double punch of flavor by brining it first, then marinating it in a spice rub before roasting until the meat is juicy and golden.

But what better way to eat your pork than in the form of a traditional **Holiday Baked Ham** (page 124)? There is nothing quite like the sweet-salty goodness of a baked ham. The smell brings me right back to the days my mama and my grandmama were cooking for me. And the best thing about it is that there are always heaps and heaps of leftovers that you get to enjoy for days on end.

By choosing leaner cuts most often, by cooking in healthy ways using less oil, and by managing my portions, I've been able to keep meat very much a part of my diet. These small changes here and there add up to a healthier diet and a better me. I surely do hope these recipes can do the same for you.

Sausage and Bean Chili

I always serve this hearty chili with my Buttermilk Corn Muffins (page 304). The slightly sweet muffins are a nice complement to the hearty, porky chili. And they are the perfect vehicle for sopping up the chili that doesn't quite make it onto your spoon.

1. In a medium pot, heat the oil over medium-high heat. Add the onion and cook, stirring occasionally, until softened, 3 to 5 minutes. Add the garlic and cook for 30 seconds.

2. Meanwhile, in a medium nonstick skillet, brown the sausage over medium heat, breaking it up with a fork as it cooks, 3 to 5 minutes. Remove the sausage with a slotted spoon and add to the onion in the pot. Add the beans, tomatoes, beef broth, vinegar, cumin, chili powder, and cinnamon and bring to a boil. Reduce the heat to medium-low, cover, and cook, stirring occasionally, for 20 minutes. Season to taste with salt and pepper and dig in.

Serves 6

2 tablespoons vegetable oil

1 onion, chopped

2 garlic cloves, chopped

½ pound sweet Italian sausage, casings removed

2 cans (15 ounces each) white beans, like navy or great northern

1 can (14½ ounces) no-salt-added diced tomatoes, with their juice

¼ cup low-sodium beef broth

1 teaspoon red wine vinegar

1 teaspoon ground cumin

1 teaspoon hot chili powder

¼ teaspoon ground cinnamon

Salt and freshly ground black pepper to taste

Holiday Baked Ham

1 whole cured ham (10 pounds)

¾ cup sugar-free apricot
preserves

3 tablespoons light brown sugar

5 tablespoons brown
or Dijon mustard

1 teaspoon ground ginger

1 teaspoon freshly ground
black pepper

Invite a crowd over and get out your good china. Holiday ham is cause for celebration all on its own. And here's a secret that you'll be celebrating while your guests are digging in: While I used to glaze my ham with a full ¾ cup sugar, I now use only 3 tablespoons, along with tasty sugar-free preserves, in this case apricot. I promise you, no one at the table will be the wiser. I like to serve baked ham with extra brown mustard on the side for slathering over the salty, juicy slices.

1. Preheat the oven to 350°F. Cover a large roasting pan with aluminum foil and place a roasting rack in the pan.

2. Score the fat of the ham in a diamond pattern (see Note). Place the ham on the roasting rack. Bake for 2 hours.

3. Meanwhile, in a medium saucepan over medium heat, whisk together the preserves, brown sugar, mustard, ginger, and pepper. Continue whisking until melted, about 2 minutes. Remove from the heat and set aside.

4. Remove the ham from the oven and spread the glaze all over the ham. Return the ham to the oven and bake until the glaze is thick and slightly caramelized, about 30 minutes more.

5. Transfer the ham to a cutting board and let it rest for 15 minutes before slicing and serving.

Serves 12

KEEP SCORE

To score the skin of your ham, remove the thick outer rind, leaving behind about a ¼-inch-thick layer of fat. Using a very sharp knife, lightly slice into the fat to create a diamond pattern over the surface of the fat. The scoring will help to render the fat, making for a tasty, crispy outer layer.

*Best Braised Southern Greens (page 225)
enhance the Holiday Baked Ham.* ▶

Quick Brined Pork Chops

1/4 cup salt

1 tablespoon light brown sugar

4 bone-in center-cut
    pork chops (1 inch thick;
    about 1/2 pound each)

Freshly ground black pepper
    to taste

1/4 teaspoon garlic powder

1/2 teaspoon dried oregano

2 tablespoons canola oil

Now, brining is a surefire way to get yourself the most tender meat possible, but I don't always have the time on my hands to wait several hours for the brining liquid to work its magic. That's why I love this quick option. All you need to do is soak your chops in the brine for about 30 minutes and you will have the most tender, the most succulent, the most delicious pork chops you can imagine.

1. In a medium saucepan, make the brine by combining the salt, brown sugar, and 2 cups water. Stir over medium-high heat just until the salt and brown sugar have dissolved. Remove the pan from the heat and stir in a handful of ice to cool down the brine quickly. This should bring the brining solution up to about 2 1/2 cups.

2. Place the pork chops in a baking dish just large enough to fit them snugly and pour the cooled brine over so that they are completely submerged. Cover with plastic wrap and place in the refrigerator for 30 minutes. If there are any parts of the chops that are not fully covered by the brine, turn the chops halfway through the brining time.

3. Remove the chops from the brine and discard the brine. Pat the chops dry with a paper towel and lightly sprinkle them on both sides with pepper, the garlic powder, and oregano. In a large skillet, heat the oil over medium-high heat. Add the chops and cook, without moving, until a dark golden crust forms on the bottom of each, about 5 minutes. Flip the chops and cook for 5 minutes more. Remove from the heat and let rest while you prepare a fresh salad to serve alongside.

Serves 4

BRINING BASICS

To make a good strong brine, make sure you've added enough salt to the liquid. You'll know you've got enough salt in the mix when a raw egg will float in the solution.

Smothered Pork Chops

I've always made my smothered pork chops in the low country style with plenty of bell peppers and onions. Then one day I found a green cabbage rolling around in my fridge and inspiration struck. These chops are smothered in shredded cabbage and onion, then zinged up with a splash of cider vinegar. It's a little German twist on a Southern classic and a good way to work more vegetables into your diet.

1. Pat the pork chops dry with a paper towel. In a small bowl, stir together the sage, salt, and pepper. Rub the mixture all over the pork chops. Refrigerate, uncovered, for at least 2 hours.

2. Place the flour in a shallow bowl. Remove the pork chops from the fridge and dip them in the flour to coat.

3. In a large skillet, melt the butter over medium-high heat. Add the pork chops and cook, without moving, until the chops are well browned, about 3 minutes per side. Transfer the chops to a paper towel–lined plate to drain.

4. Reduce the heat to medium. Add the oil and onion to the skillet and cook until the onion is translucent, 5 to 7 minutes. Toss in the cabbage and cook until it just begins to wilt, about 5 minutes. Stir in the garlic and cook until fragrant, 1 minute. Push the vegetables to the side of the skillet. Return the pork chops to the skillet. Mound the vegetables on top of the pork chops. Pour in 1 cup water. Cover the skillet and cook the pork chops over medium-low heat until they are cooked to your liking, 15 to 20 minutes.

5. Remove the pork chops from the skillet and place them on a serving platter. Increase the heat to medium-high and cook the vegetable mixture until the liquid reduces to a saucelike consistency. Stir in the vinegar. Mound the vegetables on top of the pork chops and serve.

Serves 4

4 bone-in pork loin rib chops (1 inch thick; about ¾ pound each)

2 tablespoons finely chopped fresh sage

4 teaspoons salt

2 teaspoons freshly ground black pepper

3 tablespoons all-purpose flour

2 tablespoons (¼ stick) unsalted butter

1 tablespoon olive oil

1 large onion, thinly sliced

6 cups shredded green cabbage (about ½ head)

3 garlic cloves, finely chopped

2 teaspoons cider vinegar

Pan-Seared Pork Loin with Tomato Gravy

When I decided to turn over a new leaf with my eating habits, I worried about my creamy gravies. Would they become a thing of the past? Happily, the answer to that question is no. This tomato gravy is every bit as smooth and creamy as the heavy cream version, despite its being made with milk. I now pair my tomato gravy up with super-lean pork loin, ensuring that this tasty treat has a lasting place in my high-rotation meals.

2 pork tenderloins
   (about 1 pound each)

Salt and freshly ground
   black pepper

1 tablespoon olive oil

1 tablespoon unsalted butter

1 small onion, finely chopped

¼ cup all-purpose flour

1½ cups milk

½ cup low-sodium chicken broth

1 can (10 ounces) Ro*Tel
   or other spicy diced tomatoes

¼ cup chopped fresh parsley

1. Preheat the oven to 400°F. Line a rimmed baking sheet with aluminum foil.

2. Sprinkle the tenderloins all over with salt and pepper. In a large skillet, heat the oil over medium-high heat. Cook the tenderloins until browned all over, 5 to 7 minutes. Remove the tenderloins and place on the prepared baking sheet. Place the baking sheet in the oven and cook the tenderloins until they reach the doneness you like, about 15 minutes. Let them rest for 5 minutes before thickly slicing.

3. Meanwhile, add the butter to the skillet you cooked the tenderloins in and melt over medium heat. Add the onion and cook, stirring, until softened, about 5 minutes. Sprinkle the flour over the onion and cook, stirring, for 1 minute. Slowly whisk in the milk, then the chicken broth. Simmer the mixture until thickened, 2 to 3 minutes. Whisk in the tomatoes and season to taste with salt and pepper.

4. Remove the skillet from the heat and stir in the parsley. Spoon the gravy over the sliced pork and serve it up.

Serves 6 to 8

Spice-Rubbed Roasted Pork Tenderloin

PORK

3 tablespoons salt

¾ cup sugar

2 pork tenderloins
(about 1 pound each)

PAULA'S SPICE RUB

⅓ cup packed light brown sugar

1 tablespoon chili powder

1 teaspoon ground cumin

½ teaspoon freshly ground
black pepper

½ teaspoon ground coriander

½ teaspoon ground cinnamon

¼ teaspoon crushed
red pepper flakes

With the couple hours of brining and the couple hours of marinating, there is a little waiting time involved in this dish. But I promise you it is well worth the wait. The brining makes the pork just as tender as a pat of butter, while the spice rub layers on all sorts of goodness. I've used regular chili powder here, but if you're looking for something a little smokier, go on ahead and substitute ancho chili powder or chipotle.

1. To prepare the pork: In a large bowl, combine the salt and sugar. Add 2 cups of hot water and stir until the salt and sugar are dissolved. Add 2 cups of cold water and stir again to combine. Place the tenderloins in the brining liquid and cover (or, if you like, pour the brine into a large resealable plastic bag, add the tenderloins, and seal). Refrigerate the tenderloins for 2 to 3 hours.

2. Meanwhile, to make the spice rub: In a medium bowl, whisk together the brown sugar, chili powder, cumin, pepper, coriander, cinnamon, and red pepper flakes until combined.

3. Remove the pork from the brine, discard the brine, and pat the tenderloins dry with a paper towel. Sprinkle the spice rub all over the tenderloins. Cover and refrigerate for at least 2 hours or up to 6 hours.

4. Preheat the oven to 400°F. Line a rimmed baking sheet with aluminum foil.

5. Place the tenderloins on the prepared baking sheet and roast until their internal temperature reaches 145°F, 20 to 30 minutes. Let the tenderloins rest for 5 to 10 minutes before slicing and serving.

Serves 4

Grilled Pork Tenderloin with Pineapple Salsa

When we go out for Chinese food, you can bet on my ordering the classic sweet-and-sour pork with pineapple. This recipe is my Southern barbecue version of that Chinese classic. It's a great way to dress up a lean cut like tenderloin and uses a lot less sugar than the original version. And it's so refreshing on a warm summer evening.

1. In a large bowl, whisk together the soy sauce, 3 tablespoons of the sugar, 1½ tablespoons of the lime juice, garlic, and ginger. Add the pork and toss to coat all over. Cover with plastic wrap and refrigerate, turning occasionally, for at least 2 hours or up to overnight. Let the pork come to room temperature for 20 minutes before cooking it.

2. In a small bowl, toss together the pineapple, bell pepper, scallion, the remaining 1 teaspoon brown sugar, the remaining 1½ teaspoons lime juice, the salt, and cayenne.

3. Spray a grill grate with cooking spray and preheat the grill to medium-high heat. Remove the pork from the marinade, shaking off any excess. Place the pork on the grill and cook, covered, until the pork reaches an internal temperature of 155°F, about 20 minutes. Turn frequently. Let the pork rest on a cutting board for 10 minutes before slicing and serving topped with the pineapple salsa.

Serves 6

⅓ cup low-sodium soy sauce

3 tablespoons plus 1 teaspoon light brown sugar

1½ tablespoons plus 1½ teaspoons fresh lime juice

2 garlic cloves, finely chopped

2 teaspoons finely chopped fresh ginger

2 pork tenderloins (about 1 pound each)

1¾ cups chopped fresh pineapple

⅓ cup chopped red bell pepper

3 tablespoons sliced scallion (white and light green parts)

Pinch of salt, plus more to taste

Pinch of cayenne pepper

BE CAREFUL
Take care spraying the grill grate on your barbecue. I choose to spray it just before I start preheating. That way the open flame won't kick up on me.

Slow Cooker Ribs

4 pounds pork spareribs
(about 3 racks), back membranes
removed, trimmed of excess fat,
and cut into individual ribs

Freshly ground black pepper
to taste

½ cup fresh orange juice

½ cup low-sodium soy sauce

½ cup red wine vinegar

½ cup low-sodium chicken broth

½ cup regular or reduced-sugar
ketchup

2 tablespoons dark brown sugar

2 tablespoons Dijon mustard

1 tablespoon grated fresh ginger

1 tablespoon chili powder

1 teaspoon garlic powder

2 large strips orange peel

2 scallions (white and light
green parts), finely chopped,
for serving

If it's ribs in the South, you can bet it's pork spareribs! This slow cooker version is a no-fuss way to get falling-off-the-bone, lip-smacking, finger-lickin' ribs just like my daddy used to make. These ribs are sweet, salty, and tangy and go so nicely with fresh coleslaw and home-baked corn bread to round out the meal. Just be sure to have plenty of napkins on hand because things will get messy!

1. Season the ribs all over with pepper and place in a slow cooker. In a medium bowl, whisk together the orange juice, soy sauce, vinegar, chicken broth, ketchup, brown sugar, mustard, ginger, chili powder, garlic powder, and orange peel until combined. Pour the sauce over the ribs, cover the slow cooker, and cook on low for about 8 hours.

2. Remove the ribs from the slow cooker and skim off the excess fat from the top layer of the sauce. Strain the sauce and pour it into a saucepan. Boil for about 5 minutes, then pour some of the sauce over the ribs so that they are well coated. Sprinkle the ribs with the scallions and serve extra sauce on the side.

Serves 4

PARK SMART
My son Bobby taught me a neat trick for sneaking a little more exercise into the day. When he goes shopping, he parks his car in the spot farthest from the door. That way he adds more walking into his day. I've been doing it myself and it feels downright good.

Memphis Dry Rub Ribs

2 tablespoons paprika

1 tablespoon chili powder

1 teaspoon dark brown sugar

1½ teaspoons salt

1 teaspoon ground cumin

1 teaspoon freshly ground
black pepper

1 teaspoon cayenne pepper

4 pounds pork spareribs
(about 3 racks), back
membranes removed and
trimmed of excess fat

I've portion controlled my ribs by switching smaller spareribs for meatier baby back ribs. And I'm real careful to trim off the excess fat. You'll find half the amount of sugar in this rub than in my old Memphis Dry Rub. But other than that, this recipe stays pretty true to the original.

1. In a small bowl, combine the paprika, chili powder, brown sugar, salt, cumin, black pepper, and cayenne. Rub the mixture all over the ribs. Cover the ribs loosely with plastic wrap and refrigerate for 3 hours.

2. Preheat the oven to 325°F. Let the ribs come to room temperature for 30 minutes. Line a rimmed baking sheet with aluminum foil.

3. Place the ribs, membrane side down, on a wire rack set over the prepared baking sheet. Drizzle 3 tablespoons water into the bottom of the pan. Cover the pan tightly with foil and bake for 1½ hours. Uncover and continue cooking until the ribs are very tender and lightly browned, about 30 minutes more. Test for doneness by poking a fork between the bones. Let the racks stand for 10 minutes before cutting into individual ribs.

Serves 4

Chicken-Fried Steak with Cream Gravy

*Is it still a cream gravy if it hasn't got a lick of cream? Well, sure it is because it's still got the coat-the-back-of-the-spoon creaminess that makes these gravies so popular throughout the South. This is no uppity meal, but it **is** fit for a king.*

2 large egg whites

½ cup plus 1 tablespoon all-purpose flour

¾ teaspoon salt, plus more to taste

½ teaspoon freshly ground black pepper, plus more to taste

½ teaspoon garlic powder

4 lean cubed round steaks (4 ounces each)

3 tablespoons canola oil

3 tablespoons finely chopped onion or scallion

½ cup low-sodium chicken broth

¼ cup milk

1. In a shallow bowl or pie plate, whisk the egg whites with 2 teaspoons water. In a separate bowl or pie plate, whisk together ½ cup of the flour, the salt, pepper, and garlic powder. Dip the steaks, one at a time, into the egg whites, letting any excess drip off. Then dip the steaks into the flour mixture. Gently shake each steak to remove any excess.

2. In a large nonstick skillet, heat 2 tablespoons of the oil over medium-high heat. Add the steaks and cook until well browned, 3 to 4 minutes per side. Transfer to a paper towel–lined plate to drain.

3. Add the remaining 1 tablespoon oil to the skillet. Add the onion and cook over medium heat until soft, 3 to 5 minutes. Stir in the remaining 1 tablespoon flour and cook for 1 minute. Slowly whisk in the chicken broth and milk. Simmer until the gravy is thick and bubbly, about 2 minutes. Season to taste with salt and pepper. Serve the steaks with the gravy over the top.

Serves 4

CUBED STEAKS
Cubed steaks are great for quick-cooking meals like this. They are top round or top sirloin cuts that are tenderized like crazy by the butcher. The name "cubed" references the little square indentations the tenderizing creates on the surface of the meat.

Grillades and Grits

Grillades is a classic New Orleans slow-cooked beef dish that used to be served with rice. Through the years it came to be paired up with grits. And that's just the way I like it. This dish smells so mouthwateringly good while it's cooking, you'll hardly be able to wait for dinnertime.

1. To prepare the grillades: In a large skillet, heat the oil over medium-high heat. Season the meat all over with the House Seasoning. Working in batches, add the meat to the skillet and brown on both sides, 2 to 3 minutes total. Transfer to a plate.

2. Meanwhile, in a small bowl, whisk the cornstarch into the beef broth until dissolved.

3. Add the broth mixture to the skillet along with the tomatoes, scallions, Worcestershire sauce, balsamic vinegar, and oregano. Bring to a boil and cook, stirring, until thickened, about 3 minutes. Return the meat and any accumulated juices to the pan. Reduce the heat to medium-low, cover, and simmer gently until the meat is very tender, 1 to 1½ hours.

4. Meanwhile, prepare the grits: In a medium saucepan, bring the milk, salt, and water to a boil. Slowly whisk in the grits and cook, stirring frequently, for 15 to 20 minutes, until thickened. The grits are done when they have the consistency of smooth cream of wheat.

5. Ladle the grits into bowls and top with the grillades.

Serves 4

GRILLADES

2 tablespoons vegetable oil

1 pound beef bottom round, cut into 8 equal pieces and pounded to ¼-inch thickness

¾ teaspoon Paula Deen's House Seasoning (see page 6)

2 teaspoons cornstarch

½ cup low-sodium beef broth

1 can (14½ ounces) no-salt-added diced tomatoes

½ cup chopped scallions (white and light green parts)

1 teaspoon Worcestershire sauce

1 teaspoon balsamic vinegar

½ teaspoon dried oregano

GRITS

1¼ cups milk

½ teaspoon salt

1¼ cups water

½ cup stone-ground grits (not instant or quick cooking)

LEAN AND LONG
I use bottom round beef for my grillades because it's the leanest of the long-cook beef cuts. And it's every bit as flavorful as the more heavily marbled cuts.

Better-Than-Basic Meat Loaf

1 pound extra-lean ground beef

½ cup finely chopped
yellow onion

½ cup finely chopped
green bell pepper

1 large egg, lightly beaten

1 can (14½ ounces) no-salt-added
diced tomatoes, drained well

½ cup finely grated Parmesan
cheese

1 teaspoon salt,
plus more to taste

¼ teaspoon freshly ground
black pepper, plus more to taste

1 teaspoon olive oil

1 large Spanish or Vidalia onion,
sliced in half, then cut into
¼-inch slices

1½ tablespoons Dijon mustard

With meat loaf, more is almost always better. And this better-than-basic meat loaf surely has more flavor than most. The onion, bell pepper, and tomatoes give it a tasty base while the Parmesan adds richness. But the topping is the real kicker: a smothering of caramelized sweet onion and spicy Dijon mustard. No sir, this is not your everyday, run-of-the-mill meat loaf.

1. Preheat the oven to 375°F.

2. In a large bowl, combine the beef, yellow onion, bell pepper, egg, diced tomatoes, Parmesan, salt, and black pepper. Mix well with your hands. Place the mixture in a baking dish big enough to hold the meat loaf. Shape the meat mixture into a loaf about 8 by 3 inches. Bake for 30 minutes.

3. Meanwhile, in a large skillet, heat the oil over medium heat. Add the Spanish onion, season to taste with salt and pepper, and stir. Cook, covered, for 10 minutes, stirring once or twice, until the onions are very soft. Uncover and continue cooking, stirring frequently, until golden brown, about 15 minutes more.

4. Remove the meat loaf from the oven and spread the mustard over the top. Sprinkle over the caramelized onions and continue baking for 15 minutes more until the meat loaf is well browned and the internal temperature registers 155°F to 160°F on an instant-read thermometer.

Serves 4

TAKE THE TEMPERATURE
If you haven't got an instant-read thermometer already,
I highly recommend you invest in one. It takes the guesswork
out of knowing when your meat and chicken are done. I prefer
the digital type because I find it's just a little bit easier to read.

Hot French Green Bean and Potato Salad (page 40) complements Better-Than-Basic Meat Loaf. ▶

Slow Cooker Brisket

1 beef brisket (5½ pounds),
    trimmed of excess fat

2 tablespoons Paula Deen's
    House Seasoning
    (see page 6)

1 large onion, thickly sliced

3 garlic cloves,
    peeled and smashed

⅓ cup cider vinegar

¼ cup packed light brown sugar

¼ cup tomato paste

2 tablespoons Worcestershire
    sauce

1 cup low-sodium beef broth

It never ceases to amaze me that such an inexpensive, unassuming piece of meat like brisket can transform into a delectably tender, juicy dinner. And it's so darn easy to pull together. Just rub the meat with my special House Seasoning, let the meat marinate overnight, and the next morning, pop it into the slow cooker with some onion and a sweet and savory sauce. Then go out and get on with your day knowing that the brisket is bubbling away at home. You will smell that meat as soon as you walk back through the door. What a wonderful welcome home!

1. Sprinkle one side of the brisket with 1 tablespoon of the House Seasoning, rubbing it in well. Flip the brisket over and sprinkle with the remaining 1 tablespoon House Seasoning, rubbing it in well. Let the meat rest, covered with plastic wrap, in the refrigerator overnight.

2. Place the onion, garlic, and meat in a slow cooker.

3. In a small bowl, stir together the vinegar, brown sugar, tomato paste, and Worcestershire sauce. Add the beef broth and stir to combine. Pour the broth mixture over the meat and vegetables. Cover the slow cooker and cook on low for 8 to 9 hours.

4. Remove the brisket from the slow cooker and skim off the excess fat from the top layer of the sauce. Slice the brisket and serve topped with the onion and drizzled with the sauce. Pass any extra sauce on the side.

Serves 8 to 10

SLOW COOK FOR HEALTH

Slow cookers are an easy, economical, time-saving way to cook just about anything. On top of all that, slow cookers provide a supremely healthy way to prepare food. By cooking food at a low temperature over a long period of time, the ingredients retain more of their vitamins and nutrients. And you don't need a lot of oil for slow cooking, but it still produces moist, tender food. Perhaps your family should have a slow cooker in the house.

Better Burgers

Oh my, if you have ever tried one of my Butter Burgers, you know how downright delicious they are. Well, there are Butter Burgers and then there are Better Burgers. These are the burgers I enjoy more often, while I save the butter burgers for special occasions. Happily, better burgers are just as tasty as they are better for you. I make these patties with extra-lean ground beef and olive oil instead of butter to moisten them right up. These deeply flavorful burgers remind me of a good steak sandwich. Now, that's a burger I can stand behind.

2 pounds extra-lean ground beef

2 tablespoons olive oil

1 tablespoon Worcestershire sauce

1 tablespoon dried minced onion

Salt and freshly ground black pepper to taste

6 white or whole-wheat hamburger buns

6 tomato slices, for serving

6 lettuce leaves, for serving

1. In a large bowl, combine the beef, oil, Worcestershire sauce, minced onion, and salt and pepper to taste. Form into 6 patties.

2. Heat a large nonstick skillet over medium heat. Add the burgers to the pan and cook, turning once, until the burgers reach the doneness you like, about 7 minutes for medium-rare.

3. Sandwich the burgers inside the buns with the tomato and lettuce. And don't forget to pass the ketchup and mustard!

Serves 6

Cowboy Rib Eyes with Caramelized Mushrooms and Shallots

2 bone-in rib-eye steaks
  (1 pound each)

1 to 2 tablespoons Paula Deen's
  House Seasoning
  (see page 6)

2 tablespoons olive oil

1 large shallot, finely chopped

2 teaspoons fresh thyme

1 pound cremini mushrooms
  or mix of shiitake, cremini,
  and oyster mushrooms, sliced

1 tablespoon cream sherry

Salt and freshly ground
  black pepper to taste

I love a good rib-eye steak because the marbling gives it such extraordinary flavor. Along with that marbled flavor, though, comes added fat. So, these days, I treat myself to rib eye on special occasions. And this preparation certainly screams special. Caramelized mushrooms and shallots and fresh thyme are cooked down in a rich sherry sauce. This is one of my fancy dinners that I pull out when I really want to impress my guests.

1. Rub the steaks all over with the House Seasoning. Wrap in plastic wrap and refrigerate overnight.

2. Bring the steaks to room temperature for at least 1 hour before you are going to cook them. Spray a grill grate with cooking spray and preheat the grill to medium-high heat.

3. Meanwhile, in a large skillet, heat 1 tablespoon of the oil over medium heat. Add the shallot and thyme and cook, stirring, until the shallot is tender, 3 to 4 minutes. Using a slotted spoon, transfer the shallot and thyme to a small bowl. Then add half the mushrooms to the pan and cook, without stirring, until they begin to brown, about 6 minutes. Using a slotted spoon, transfer the mushrooms to the bowl with the shallot and thyme. Add the remaining 1 tablespoon oil and the remaining mushrooms to the pan. Cook, without stirring, until the mushrooms begin to brown, about 6 minutes. When they are brown, return the reserved mushroom mixture to the pan and toss well to combine. Add the sherry, stir to coat the mushrooms, and cook for 1 minute more. Season to taste with salt and pepper. Cover the skillet to keep the mushrooms warm while you grill the steaks.

4. Cook the steaks on the grill directly over the flames for 5 minutes per side. Then move the steaks off the direct heat to a cooler spot on the grill and cook for 3 to 5 minutes more, until the internal temperature reaches 120°F for medium-rare or 130°F for medium, depending on what you prefer. Let the meat rest for 5 to 10 minutes before slicing and serving with the caramelized mushrooms and shallot.

Serves 4

Skillet Shepherd's Pie

For me, the best part of a shepherd's pie is the delicious potato topping. This recipe puts a new spin on that topping by mixing white and sweet potatoes together. I don't know why these two potatoes aren't mixed together more often. I've found them to be a match made in heaven. The white potatoes lend their fluffiness to the mash while the sweet potatoes bring their deep sweet flavor. This is my new favorite way to enjoy mashed potatoes and it's better for you to boot!

1 pound russet potatoes, peeled and cut into 1-inch cubes

1 pound sweet potatoes, peeled and cut into 1-inch cubes

½ cup buttermilk

½ teaspoon ground nutmeg

Salt and freshly ground black pepper to taste

1 pound ground lamb

2 tablespoons vegetable oil

1 pound button mushrooms, quartered

1 cup chopped onions

1 cup chopped carrots

1 tablespoon cornstarch

1 cup low-sodium beef broth

2 tablespoons dry red wine

1 tablespoon tomato paste

1 tablespoon Worcestershire sauce

½ teaspoon dried thyme

¼ teaspoon garlic powder

1. Preheat the oven to 375°F.

2. Place the russet potatoes in a medium pot and place the sweet potatoes in a separate medium pot. Cover the potatoes in each pot with cold salted water. Bring to a boil over medium-high heat and cook until the potatoes are very tender, 9 to 10 minutes for the sweet potatoes and about 12 minutes for the russets. Drain well and combine the potatoes in one of the pots.

3. While the potatoes are still hot, using a potato masher, mash in the buttermilk, nutmeg, and salt and pepper to taste. Mash until the potatoes are the consistency you like. Set aside.

4. In a large ovenproof skillet, brown the lamb over medium-high heat. Remove with a slotted spoon and reserve. Drain the fat from the skillet. Heat the oil in the skillet and add the mushrooms, onions, and carrots and cook, stirring frequently, until the mushrooms are well browned and the carrots have begun to soften, about 10 minutes.

5. In a small bowl, whisk the cornstarch into the beef broth until dissolved. Add to the skillet along with the red wine, tomato paste, Worcestershire sauce, thyme, garlic powder, and the reserved lamb. Bring to a boil, stir, then turn off the heat. Top the lamb mixture with the potato mixture, using a spatula to spread the potatoes evenly over the top. Place in the oven and bake for 25 to 30 minutes, until golden and bubbly.

Serves 8

Cheeseburger Meat Loaf

1 pound lean ground beef

¼ pound lean ground pork

1 cup shredded Monterey Jack
  cheese

½ cup finely chopped onion

⅓ cup dried bread crumbs

2 large egg whites

2 tablespoons plus ⅓ cup regular
  or reduced-sugar ketchup

2 tablespoons mustard

1 teaspoon garlic powder

¾ teaspoon salt

¼ teaspoon freshly ground
  black pepper

I am so excited about this recipe, y'all. My classic Cheeseburger Meat Loaf has been in my recipe lineup for years. But, oh my goodness, did it need slimming down. I've cut the amount of meat I use and I've used a mix of lean beef and pork to give it extra richness. And I gave the sour cream the boot. It's still just as delicious. While there's still plenty of cheese mixed in, I've cut the cheesy sauce I used to slather the whole loaf in, but, if you like, feel free to smother it with some homemade caramelized onions.

1. Preheat the oven to 350°F. Lightly grease a baking rack with cooking spray and set it over a rimmed baking sheet lined with aluminum foil.

2. In a large bowl, combine the beef, pork, Monterey Jack, onion, bread crumbs, egg whites, 2 tablespoons of the ketchup, the mustard, garlic powder, salt, and pepper. Use your hands and make sure you mix the ingredients really well so they are thoroughly combined. Shape into a loaf about 9 by 5 inches.

3. Place the loaf on the prepared baking rack. Brush the outside of the meat loaf with the remaining ⅓ cup ketchup. Bake for 60 to 70 minutes, until the internal temperature registers 155°F to 160°F on an instant-read thermometer. Let the loaf cool for 10 minutes before slicing and serving.

Serves 8

Smothered Liver with Onions

We Southerners do love our chicken livers. But did you know we also love a good calf's liver dinner? This here is a classic dish that my mama used to make. And I was the one child at the table who never had a problem with it. Liver is packed full of protein so you can just about get your daily allowance right here in this one dish.

1. In a large skillet, heat 1 tablespoon of the oil over medium heat. Add the onion and cook, stirring, until tender, about 10 minutes. If the pan starts to dry out, add another tablespoon of oil.

2. Add the sage and a large pinch of salt and pepper to the onion. Stir in the honey and vinegar, then scoop the onion slices onto a serving platter and cover loosely with aluminum foil to keep warm.

3. Wipe out the skillet and add 1 tablespoon of the oil over medium-high heat. While the skillet heats, pat dry the liver with a paper towel and season to taste with salt and pepper. Add the liver slices to the pan, in batches if necessary, and cook for about 2 minutes per side. (Add more oil to the pan between batches if the pan starts to dry out.) The liver is done when it is golden on the outside but still pink on the inside. As the slices cook, place them on the serving platter on top of the onions. Garnish with parsley.

Serves 4

2 to 3 tablespoons olive oil, plus more as needed

1 large Vidalia or other sweet onion, thinly sliced

1 teaspoon chopped fresh sage

Salt and freshly ground black pepper to taste

1 teaspoon honey

½ teaspoon white wine vinegar

1 pound calf's liver, sliced ¼ inch thick

Chopped fresh parsley, for garnish

SMALLER PLATES
I used to own great big dinner plates that I'd serve piles and piles of food on. Now, I've bought myself a set of smaller plates. That way, when I serve myself my helping, I stop when the smaller plate is full. And because I've pretty much cut out second helpings, I end up eating less.

Roast Leg of Lamb with Mint

1 bone-in leg of lamb (7 pounds), trimmed of excess fat

1 cup loosely packed fresh mint leaves

2 tablespoons Dijon mustard

2 tablespoons olive oil

6 garlic cloves, coarsely chopped

Salt and freshly ground black pepper to taste

Some people like to serve mint sauce on the side with their leg of lamb. But I like to roast the lamb with a minty, mustardy rub all over it. Every bite of this delicious roast is exploding with the fresh zingy rub. And, whoa Mama, does the house smell divine while this meat is cooking away in the oven. It sets your mouth to watering from the get-go.

1. Remove the lamb from the refrigerator 30 minutes before cooking.

2. Preheat the oven to 450°F. Lightly grease a large roasting pan with cooking spray.

3. In a food processor or blender, puree the mint, mustard, oil, and garlic to form a coarse paste.

4. Season the lamb generously with salt and pepper and rub the mint paste all over. Place the lamb in the prepared pan, fat side up. Roast for 15 minutes, then reduce the heat to 350°F and roast until an instant-read thermometer inserted into the thickest part of the meat reaches 130°F, for medium-rare, about 90 minutes more. For medium doneness, the internal temperature should reach 140°F. Let the lamb rest for 15 minutes before carving.

Serves 8 to 10

AT THE TABLE, PLEASE

Eating a meal in front of the television is fine on Super Bowl Sunday, but I try not to make a habit of it. In my household, dinner is at the kitchen table, where the family can gather round and talk about the day. And that's a good practice because eating in front of the TV tends to make you eat more, even when you're no longer hungry. Besides, that time at the table with the ones you love is quality time I, for one, don't want to miss out on.

Celebrating with our eldest grandson, Jack. ▶

Chicken, Game Hens, and Turkey

I'm going to let you in on a little secret that we Southerners have always known: When it comes to meat, poultry just can't be beat. Whether it's Sunday supper, an easy workweek meal, or a fancy Friday-night dinner party, chances are if you're in the South, poultry will be the main event. That's good news for all of us out here looking to maintain a healthy, balanced diet, because eating chicken and other fowl is just about the best way to get in your daily protein.

Eating poultry because it's lean is important, but even more important is the taste. I never get tired of fowl because it is so versatile. You are in for a great meal whether you choose to roast it, as with *Roast Chicken Sunday Supper* (page 166), or grill it, as with *Greek Chicken Kebabs on the Grill* (page 174), or braise it, as I do in *Slow Cooker Lemon Rosemary Chicken* (page 165). The sky's the limit, and that is why every cookbook of mine contains a great big old poultry chapter. There are so many interesting things you can do with chicken, turkey, and other fowl I have to admit that I have trouble containing all my recipes in one chapter.

I've redesigned some of my classic poultry dishes that I just can't live without. I've managed to cut the fat in *The Lady & Sons Chicken Potpie* (page 159) and *Paula's Chicken and Dumplin's* (page 156) without losing out. You know they passed my taste test because I kept my name on them. Now, that's standing behind a recipe!

I suppose the most surprising redesign I've managed is on my fried chicken. I reckon I'm pretty well known at this point for my crispy, tender chicken, so I had to work extra hard to come up with a healthier version that would please my fans, my family, and myself. The result is my **Oven-Fried Chicken** (page 154), a recipe as tasty as it is healthy.

My mama used to say to me, "Paula, your spices need to be scared of you, not the other way around." And that is never truer than when you're working with poultry. I've found that a bird really sits up and sings when you load it up with all sorts of spices. In fact, I think that's a pretty good rule of thumb for eating lighter all around. When you cut down on fat, pump up the spices and you won't even notice the fat you've taken away. Just have a look at the **Louisiana Blackened Chicken Cutlets** (page 173). The Cajun spice mix on the chicken breast makes this lean cut so much more interesting, thanks to a healthy dose of thyme, oregano, garlic, and onion powder.

I've always enjoyed turkey meat, but I never really dove into all the different cuts that are available on the supermarket shelves. I mostly stuck with the turkey breast and the whole turkey for special-occasion dinners. But, my goodness, now I have also discovered just how tasty turkey cutlets and ground turkey are. I've even started cooking some of my classic beef dishes using ground turkey. I don't miss a lick of flavor cooking up **Southern Turkey Chili in a Biscuit Bowl** (page 180) with lean ground turkey instead of beef. And **Turkey Scallopini** (page 183) has become one of my favorite midweek meals; in the past I would have made it with veal.

There just seems to be no end to the ways I love to prepare poultry. And finding a way to make the preparations good for you is a snap when you're starting with these lean meats. Inexpensive, healthy, and tasty, poultry is tailor-made for the modern Southern diet.

Sesame Chicken Tenders

I say you're never too old to enjoy a good chicken tender. These grown-up tenders make for a delicious party appetizer. Best yet, I cook them in just 1½ tablespoons of peanut oil. They come out crisp on the outside and tender on the inside. The hoisin-soy dipping sauce is sweet and spicy and works perfectly with the sesame coating.

1. Position an oven rack in the upper third of the oven. Preheat the oven to 425°F.

2. To make the dipping sauce: In a small bowl, combine the hoisin, soy sauce, vinegar, garlic, and ginger. Stir well to combine.

3. To make the chicken tenders: In a small bowl, whisk together the egg white, sesame oil, salt, pepper, and garlic powder. The mixture should be a bit frothy. On a sheet of parchment paper, combine the sesame seeds and onion flakes. Dip the tenders into the egg white mixture, gently shaking off the excess, then roll the tenders in the sesame seed mixture.

4. In a large ovenproof skillet, heat the oil over medium heat. Drop a few sesame seeds into the pan, and when they begin to sizzle, add the tenders and cook until they are golden on the bottom, about 2 minutes (make sure not to burn the onion). Turn the chicken over, place the skillet in the oven, and cook for 8 minutes. Turn the pieces over again and cook for 2 minutes more. Serve with the hoisin dipping sauce.

Serves 4

DIPPING SAUCE

¼ cup hoisin sauce

¼ cup low-sodium soy sauce

1 tablespoon cider vinegar

1 small garlic clove, finely chopped

1 teaspoon finely grated fresh ginger

CHICKEN TENDERS

1 large egg white

½ teaspoon sesame oil

½ teaspoon salt

½ teaspoon freshly ground black pepper

½ teaspoon garlic powder

¾ cup sesame seeds

2 teaspoons dried onion flakes

12 chicken tenders (about 1½ pounds)

1½ tablespoons peanut oil

Oven-Fried Chicken

4 bone-in chicken thighs
(about ½ pound each)

½ cup buttermilk

1 tablespoon Dijon mustard

1 teaspoon hot sauce

1 garlic clove, finely chopped

¼ teaspoon salt,
plus more to taste

¼ teaspoon freshly ground black
pepper, plus more to taste

½ cup plain bread crumbs

I'm not going to pretend to you that I don't still love traditional fried chicken. Heavens, no, it is a part of my food history! But nowadays, I leave that to a special occasion. More often than not, I turn to this baked version. Let me tell you, it is absolutely delicious. I still marinate the meat in a spicy buttermilk bath so that it comes out juicy and tender on the inside. And the bread crumb crust lends it a crispy bite. Gone is the fat-laden skin and gone are the several inches of cooking oil (not to mention the mess). What's left is great flavor and great crunch.

1. Remove the skin from the chicken and discard. In a medium bowl, whisk together the buttermilk, mustard, hot sauce, and garlic. Season the chicken all over with salt and pepper, add the chicken to the buttermilk mixture, and marinate for 30 minutes.

2. Meanwhile, preheat the oven to 425°F. Grease a rimmed baking sheet with cooking spray.

3. In a wide shallow bowl, toss together the bread crumbs and ¼ teaspoon each of the salt and pepper. Remove the chicken from the marinade, letting any excess drip off, then dip the chicken in the bread crumbs to coat well. Place the chicken on the prepared baking sheet. Coat the chicken generously with cooking spray. Bake until the chicken is lightly browned and just cooked through, about 30 minutes.

Serves 4

HOMEMADE CRUMBS

I like to make my own bread crumbs these days by simply grinding up slices of sandwich bread in my food processor. You can remove the crusts if you like or just grind them up in the mix. I spread the crumbs out on a tray to dry for a bit, then I package them up in freezer-proof resealable plastic bags. I pop them in the freezer and they keep for many, many months. For a healthier bread crumb, use whole-wheat sandwich bread.

Try Grilled Corn with Parmesan and Mayonnaise
(page 242) when you serve Oven-Fried Chicken. ▶

Paula's Chicken and Dumplin's

Now why didn't I think of this before? Sweet potato drop dumplings in my chicken and dumplin's instead of plain flour dumplings. Not only is this new adaptation so much better for you, it is really, really tasty and brings a whole new level of interest to the dish. On top of that clever change, I use only lean white meat chicken. I'm pretty sure my Grandmama Paul would be downright proud of me for coming up with this.

CHICKEN

4 bone-in chicken breast halves (3 pounds)

1 chicken bouillon cube

2 celery stalks, chopped

1 onion, chopped

1 bay leaf

½ teaspoon Paula Deen's House Seasoning (see page 6)

1 can (10¾ ounces) low-fat condensed cream of celery or cream of chicken soup

¼ teaspoon freshly grated nutmeg

DUMPLINGS

1 cup all-purpose flour

1 tablespoon baking powder

¾ teaspoon salt, or to taste

¼ teaspoon dried sage

½ cup cooked, mashed sweet potato (from about 1 small sweet potato)

⅓ cup milk

1. To make the chicken: In a large pot, combine the chicken, bouillon cube, celery, onion, bay leaf, House Seasoning, and 8 cups water. Bring to a boil over medium-high heat. Reduce to a simmer and cook, covered, until the chicken is cooked through, about 20 minutes. Remove the chicken and set aside to cool. Reserve the cooking liquid. Add the can of soup and nutmeg to the pot and simmer gently over medium-low heat. When the chicken is cool enough to handle, pick the meat off the bones, discarding the bones and skin. Place the chicken meat in a medium bowl.

2. To make the dumplings: In a medium bowl, whisk together the flour, baking powder, salt, and sage. In a small bowl, whisk together the sweet potato and milk. Pour the sweet potato mixture into the flour mixture and stir until a soft dough forms. Bring the broth that you cooked the chicken in to a slow boil and drop in the dough by the tablespoonful. Reduce the heat, cover, and simmer for 15 minutes, until the dumplings are just cooked through. Return the chicken to the pot and simmer until heated through.

Serves 4

Chicken Divan

Comforting casseroles like chicken divan are big favorites of mine. Just as I had to rethink my plate, I also had to rethink my casseroles. I now fill my divan to the brim with loads of freshly steamed broccoli florets and then layer in some lean chicken breast. The cheesy sauce is spiced with just a touch of curry powder and lightened up with a hit of lemon juice. Then I top it all off with slightly sweet, nutty whole-wheat cracker crumbs. It's so good, y'all.

1. Preheat the oven to 350°F. Grease a 13 by 9-inch baking dish with cooking spray.

2. In a medium saucepan, add the chicken breasts and fill with enough water to cover the chicken by 1 inch. Bring to a boil over high heat. Reduce the heat and simmer, covered, for about 10 minutes, or until the chicken is just cooked through. Let the chicken sit in the poaching liquid until cool enough to handle, then shred the chicken using two forks or your hands.

3. In a deep skillet, melt the butter over medium heat. Add the onion and cook until soft, about 5 minutes. Add the flour and curry powder and cook, stirring, for about 1 minute. Gradually whisk in the milk, chicken broth, white wine, and lemon juice. Increase the heat to medium-high and bring to a boil to thicken. Remove from the heat and stir in the Cheddar.

4. In a large bowl, combine the chicken, broccoli, and Cheddar sauce, stirring until well combined. Season to taste with salt and pepper and give it another stir. Then pour the mixture into the prepared baking dish.

5. In a medium bowl, toss the crackers with the Parmesan. Scatter over the top of the baking dish. Give the cracker topping a healthy spray with the cooking spray. Bake for 25 to 30 minutes, until browned and bubbling.

Serves 6

3 boneless, skinless chicken breasts (½ pound each)

2 tablespoons (¼ stick) unsalted butter

1 small onion, chopped

¼ cup all-purpose flour

1 teaspoon curry powder

1 cup milk

½ cup low-sodium chicken broth

½ cup dry white wine

1 tablespoon fresh lemon juice

¾ cup shredded Cheddar cheese

5 cups broccoli florets (from 1 large head), steamed

Salt and freshly ground black pepper to taste

1½ cups crushed whole-wheat crackers, such as Ritz

½ cup grated Parmesan cheese

SPRAY OIL
If you haven't used the fantastic spray cooking oils on the supermarket shelves, I highly recommend you run out and get yourself some. They provide a great way to grease a pan using the minimum of oil. They come in all sorts of varieties too. I keep an olive oil and a vegetable oil spray in my kitchen at all times.

The Lady & Sons Chicken Potpie

Most times, cooking pieces of lean chicken breast in the oven for forty minutes would spell a dry dinner. But in my potpie, the chicken cooks nestled into a creamy sauce under the protective cover of homemade pastry. It comes out moist and bursting with flavor from the sauce it cooked in. This is good down-home cooking made just a little bit better for you.

1. To make the crust: In a large bowl, whisk together the flour and salt. Cut in the butter using two forks or your hands until the mixture forms coarse crumbs. Sprinkle in enough ice water until the mixture just comes together. Form the dough into a ball and flatten into a disk. Cover with plastic wrap and refrigerate until ready to use.

2. To make the filling: In a large nonstick skillet, heat the oil. Add the onion and carrot and cook until soft, 5 to 7 minutes. Stir in the flour and cook for 2 minutes. Slowly whisk in the chicken broth, milk, salt, garlic powder, and pepper. Add the potato. Simmer over medium-low heat until the potatoes are half tender and the sauce is slightly thickened, about 10 minutes. Whisk in the mustard. Stir in the chicken, peas, and parsley.

3. Preheat the oven to 425°F. On a lightly floured surface, roll the dough into a 10-inch circle.

4. Scrape the filling into a 9-inch pie plate. Drape the circle of dough over the filling, tucking the edges in around the rim of the plate. Cut a slit in the center of the crust.

5. Place the potpie on a rimmed baking sheet. Bake until the crust is golden brown and the filling is bubbling, about 40 minutes. Let cool for 10 minutes before serving.

Serves 8

CUT THE CRUST
Take note that this new potpie of mine features only a top crust. Cutting out the extra bottom crust helps me keep my carb and fat intake in check.

CRUST

1 cup all-purpose flour, plus more for dusting

¼ teaspoon salt

6 tablespoons (¾ stick) unsalted butter

2 to 4 tablespoons ice water, as needed

FILLING

2 tablespoons olive oil

⅔ cup chopped onion

⅔ cup chopped carrot

3 tablespoons all-purpose flour

1¾ cups low-sodium chicken broth

1 cup milk

1¼ teaspoons salt

1 teaspoon garlic powder

½ teaspoon freshly ground black pepper

⅔ cup peeled and chopped potato

1½ tablespoons Dijon mustard

1¾ cups cooked boneless, skinless chicken breast, cubed

¾ cup frozen peas

¼ cup finely chopped fresh parsley

Chicken Curry with Red Bell Pepper and Pineapple

1 tablespoon olive oil

1 onion, chopped

2 celery stalks, chopped

1 red bell pepper, chopped

1 cup coarsely chopped pineapple (drained if canned)

2 garlic cloves, chopped

2½ teaspoons curry powder

Salt and freshly ground black pepper to taste

½ cup low-sodium chicken or vegetable broth

1 can (13½ ounces) light unsweetened coconut milk

Zest and juice of 1 lime

3 boneless, skinless chicken breasts (½ pound each), cubed

⅓ cup raisins

Rice, for serving (optional)

Sliced scallions (dark green parts), for garnish

Toasted blanched almonds, for garnish

If you're like me and you prefer your sweet and savory tastes together in one dish, then I suggest you give this one a try. This super-easy chicken dish features sweet pineapple and raisins paired up with curry, coconut milk, and a nice bright dash of lime juice. And it all comes together in a single pot, so the washing up is a snap. I like to serve this one-pot meal over a heap of brown rice, with sliced scallions and almonds sprinkled over the top.

1. In a medium Dutch oven or heavy-bottomed soup pot, heat the oil over medium-high heat. Add the onion, celery, and bell pepper and cook until soft, 5 to 7 minutes. Add the pineapple, garlic, curry powder, and salt and pepper to taste. Cook, stirring, for 2 minutes.

2. Pour in the chicken broth, coconut milk, lime zest, and lime juice. Bring to a boil for 2 minutes, then reduce to a simmer. Simmer for 10 to 15 minutes. Add the chicken and raisins to the curry and simmer for 5 minutes, until the chicken is cooked through and the raisins are plump. Serve warm over rice (if using), topped with scallions and toasted almonds.

Serves 4

Roasted Chicken Breasts
with Orange and Parmesan

I have found many ways to add character to lean boneless chicken breasts over the years, but if I had my druthers, I'd just about always choose bone-in chicken over boneless. The bones add flavor to the meat and help keep it moist. And the orange, Parmesan, and rosemary in this dish make it special enough for company.

1. Preheat the oven to 425°F. Pat the chicken dry with paper towels.

2. In a large shallow bowl or pie plate, combine the Parmesan, orange zest, salt, and pepper and stir to combine. In another shallow bowl, whisk the egg whites with the oil until frothy. Dip the chicken into the egg whites, gently shaking off the excess, then coat with the Parmesan mixture.

3. Grease a flameproof and ovenproof roasting pan with cooking spray. Lay the parsley and rosemary sprigs in the pan and top with the chicken breasts, skin side up. Scatter the shallots around the chicken and bake for 40 to 45 minutes, until the chicken is cooked through. Transfer the chicken breasts, shallots, and herbs to a serving dish and add the white wine to the pan, scraping the bottom to release any brown bits stuck to the pan. Cook for 2 minutes, then add the orange juice and cook for 1 minute more.

4. Spoon the orange sauce over the chicken and shallots and serve. Garnish with the fresh parsley.

Serves 4

4 skin-on bone-in chicken breast halves (about ¾ pound each)

1 cup grated Parmesan cheese

1½ teaspoons finely grated orange zest

1 teaspoon salt

½ teaspoon freshly ground black pepper

2 large egg whites

1 teaspoon olive oil

4 fresh flat-leaf parsley sprigs, plus chopped fresh parsley, for garnish

3 fresh rosemary sprigs

3 large shallots, peeled

¼ cup dry white wine

Juice of 1 orange

EGG WHITE WASH
You'll notice I add a bit of oil to my egg wash here. Because I've skipped the yolks and use only egg whites, the teaspoon of oil is helpful for getting the coating to stick securely.

Lemon Chicken with Artichokes

1½ pounds boneless, skinless chicken breasts (about 3)

1 teaspoon salt

½ teaspoon freshly ground black pepper

¼ cup all-purpose flour

2 tablespoons olive oil

½ cup low-sodium chicken broth

1 tablespoon fresh lemon juice, plus more to taste

1 can (14 ounces) artichoke hearts, drained and coarsely chopped

2 teaspoons drained capers (optional)

1 tablespoon unsalted butter

Chopped fresh basil, for serving

Some days I like a creamy chicken dish and other days I crave something brighter like this fresh and zingy lemon and artichoke chicken. While it's light and refreshing it's also super satisfying. Make sure you serve it with bread or potatoes to sop up the delicious sauce.

1. Slice each chicken breast in half horizontally (you should now have about 6 thin pieces of chicken). In a shallow bowl or pie plate, whisk together the salt, pepper, and flour. Dip the chicken pieces in the seasoned flour to coat all over. Gently shake each piece to remove the excess.

2. In a large skillet, heat the oil over medium-high heat. Add the chicken, in batches if necessary, and cook without moving, until golden, 2 to 3 minutes. Flip and cook until no longer pink, 2 to 3 minutes more. Transfer the chicken to a plate and cover with aluminum foil to keep warm.

3. Add the chicken broth and lemon juice to the skillet and give the bottom of the skillet a good scrape to pick up any brown bits stuck to the bottom. Simmer until bubbling, 3 to 4 minutes. Stir in the artichokes and capers (if using) and cook for 1 minute. Swirl in the butter. Give the sauce a taste and add more lemon juice if you think it needs it. Spoon the sauce over the chicken and sprinkle with basil before serving.

Serves 4 to 6

SUPER SAUCE
When you make the sauce for this dish, be sure to give the bottom of the pan a good scraping after you pour in the broth. This will bring every inch of the pan-seared chicken flavor into your sauce and onto your plate.

Smothered Chicken

2 tablespoons fresh thyme leaves
or 2 teaspoons dried thyme

2 teaspoons salt,
plus extra to taste

½ teaspoon freshly ground black
pepper, plus more to taste

1 whole chicken (3½ to 4 pounds),
rinsed, patted dry, and cut into
8 pieces

2 tablespoons olive oil

2 large Spanish onions,
cut into ½-inch-thick slices

1 celery stalk, finely chopped

1 green bell pepper, thinly sliced

2 garlic cloves, peeled
and smashed

*Well now, I love near about anything if it's got a smothered topping.
And this chicken is certainly no exception. The chicken cooks in the
pot right along with Spanish onions, celery, green bell pepper, and
smashed garlic. Then the whole delicious mess is piled high on top
of the tender chicken.*

1. In a small bowl, combine the thyme, salt, and pepper.
   Sprinkle all over the chicken pieces.

2. In a large Dutch oven, heat the oil over medium-high heat.
   Add the chicken in batches, skin side down, and cook until
   golden brown, 7 to 8 minutes per side. Transfer the chicken
   to a plate.

3. Add the onions, celery, bell pepper, and garlic to the
   same pan and cook, stirring frequently, until softened,
   about 5 minutes. Season to taste with salt and pepper.
   Return the chicken to the pan, spoon the vegetable mixture
   over the chicken, and add ¼ cup water. Cover the pan,
   reduce the heat to low, and cook, stirring occasionally,
   until the chicken is fork tender and cooked through, about
   40 minutes. If at any time the pan looks dry, add a tablespoon
   or 2 of water. Toss out the garlic cloves before serving.

Serves 4

Slow Cooker
Lemon Rosemary Chicken

I tell you, my slow cooker sure does get a workout throughout the colder months. But I love its convenience during the warmer weather too. What is brighter than lemon chicken? This beautiful one-pot chicken drizzled in a light and creamy sauce is perfect in the spring and summer, served with a fresh green salad.

1. Place the onion slices in a slow cooker. Season the chicken with salt and pepper to taste and arrange on top of the onions. Add ¾ cup of the chicken broth, the white wine, lemon peel, lemon juice, rosemary, and garlic. Cover the pot and cook on low for 5 to 6 hours.

2. Remove the chicken from the slow cooker. Place the chicken on a warm platter and tent with aluminum foil. Strain the vegetables and the lemon zest to get the cooking liquid. Place the cooking liquid in a medium saucepan.

3. In a small bowl, whisk together the cornstarch and the remaining 2 tablespoons chicken broth. Add to the saucepan, bring to a boil over medium-high heat, and cook, stirring constantly, until thickened, about 2 minutes. Serve the chicken with the sauce poured over the top.

Serves 4

1 small onion, sliced

8 bone-in, skinless chicken thighs (about ½ pound each)

Salt and freshly ground black pepper to taste

¾ cup plus 2 tablespoons low-sodium chicken broth

¼ cup dry white wine

Large strips of lemon peel from 1 lemon

2 tablespoons fresh lemon juice

1 tablespoon chopped fresh rosemary

4 garlic cloves, chopped

2 tablespoons cornstarch

Roast Chicken Sunday Supper

¼ cup olive oil

1 lemon, thinly sliced

1 small bunch fresh thyme

1½ teaspoons salt,
plus more to taste

½ teaspoon black pepper,
plus more to taste

1 whole chicken (3½ to 4 pounds),
rinsed and patted dry

3 carrots, cut into 1½-inch chunks

2 turnips, quartered

1 large onion, cut into
1½-inch chunks

As in most Southern homes, Sunday supper is sacred in my family. So the meal I serve to my loved ones has got to be something special. And you can bet this meal is. I season my chicken with a fragrant lemon and thyme rub and marinate it overnight. A golden brown, juicy chicken cooked right on top of a bed of sweet, roasted vegetables is a homey kind of comfort. It's the kind of meal that throws a great big bear hug around you with each and every bite.

1. In a small bowl, combine the oil, lemon slices, thyme, salt, and pepper. Rub the mixture all over the skin of the chicken and the inside of the cavity, spreading it as evenly as possible so that the chicken will brown evenly. Cover tightly with aluminum foil and let it rest in the refrigerator overnight.

2. The next day, let the chicken come to room temperature for 30 minutes before cooking. Position an oven rack in the center of the oven and preheat the oven to 450°F.

3. Remove any lemon slices and thyme from the outside of the chicken and press them deep inside the chicken cavity. Scatter the carrots, turnips, and onion in the bottom of a large roasting pan. Pour enough water into the pan to just cover the bottom. Season the vegetables to taste with salt and pepper. Place the chicken, breast side up, on top of the bed of vegetables.

4. Place the pan on the oven rack and roast for 20 minutes. Baste the bird all over with its juices and continue roasting for 25 minutes more, basting two or three more times (if the chicken is not golden brown all over at this point, continue to cook for 10 minutes more).

5. Reduce the heat to 325°F. Finish roasting, without basting, until the thigh juices run clear when pierced with a knife, or until an instant-read thermometer inserted into the thigh registers 170°F, 20 to 25 minutes more.

6. Transfer the chicken to a cutting board to rest for 5 to 10 minutes before carving. Serve with the vegetables and pan juices.

Serves 4

Braised Chicken with Mushrooms and White Wine

1 whole chicken (3 to 4 pounds), rinsed, patted dry, and cut into 8 pieces

Salt and freshly ground black pepper to taste

1 teaspoon olive oil

2 turkey or regular bacon slices, cut into 1-inch pieces

1 onion, thinly sliced

1 apple, thinly sliced

2 garlic cloves, finely chopped

8 ounces button mushrooms, thinly sliced

½ cup dry white wine

3 or 4 fresh thyme sprigs

1 bay leaf

1 tablespoon unsalted butter

1 tablespoon cider vinegar, or to taste

Fresh flat-leaf parsley, chopped (optional)

Savannah is generally a warm-weather place, but on those nights when the weather turns chilly and all I feel like doing is curling up on the couch with a blanket, this is the dish I like to make. I reckon this is just about as much comfort food as it gets, chock-full of fall-off-the-bone chicken, earthy mushrooms, and smoky bacon. I give it a nice sweet note by cooking some thinly sliced apple with the onion. I like to use Golden Delicious, but really any old apple will do the trick.

1. Preheat the oven to 350°F. Generously season the chicken pieces with salt and pepper to taste and let them sit, covered, at room temperature for 30 minutes.

2. In a Dutch oven or heavy-bottomed pot, heat the oil over medium-high heat. Add the bacon to the pot and cook until crisp, about 5 minutes. Remove with a slotted spoon to a paper towel–lined bowl or plate to drain. Place the seasoned chicken, skin side down, in the pot, in batches, cooking until the skin is golden brown and crisp, about 4 minutes. Flip each piece and cook for another 1 to 2 minutes more. Remove the chicken pieces and place on a plate.

3. Add the onion, apple, and garlic to the pot. Cook, stirring, until softened, about 3 minutes. Add the mushrooms and cook, stirring, until they are a rich dark brown, about 7 minutes. Season to taste with salt and pepper. Add the white wine and stir to combine. Cook until the wine is reduced by half, 3 to 4 minutes. Return the chicken pieces and their juices to the pot. Top with the thyme and bay leaf.

4. Cover the pot and braise the chicken in the oven for 30 to 35 minutes, until the chicken is cooked through.

5. Arrange the chicken on a pretty serving platter and tent with aluminum foil to keep warm. Remove the bay leaf and thyme from the liquid and bring the liquid to a boil over medium-high heat. Reduce the heat and simmer for 10 to 15 minutes, until the sauce is reduced by half. Melt in the butter and add the vinegar. Season to taste with salt and pepper. Pour over the chicken pieces and garnish with chopped parsley (if using).

Serves 4

With my adorable grandbabies, Henry, Matthew, and John (left to right).

Cajun Stuffed Cornish Game Hens

2 tablespoons olive oil

1 cup chopped onion

1 cup chopped celery

1 Granny Smith apple, peeled and chopped (about 1 cup)

3 slices rye or whole-wheat bread (3 ounces), lightly toasted and cut into 1-inch pieces

2 tablespoons low-sodium chicken broth

Salt and freshly ground black pepper to taste

1½ teaspoons sweet paprika

¾ teaspoon dried thyme

¾ teaspoon ground cumin

¼ teaspoon ground cinnamon

⅛ teaspoon cayenne pepper

6 Cornish game hens (1½ pounds each), rinsed and patted dry

This is Cajun cooking with a little twist of my own thrown in. I've added apples to the stuffing and cinnamon to the spice rub. Because, after all, who doesn't love cinnamon with apples? I serve these elegant birds with wild rice and a mixed greens salad to round out the meal.

1. Preheat the oven to 400°F.

2. In a large skillet, heat the oil over medium-high heat. Add the onions and celery and cook, stirring occasionally, until soft, about 5 minutes. Add the apple and cook for 1 minute more. Remove from the heat, add the bread and chicken broth, and toss to combine. Season to taste with salt and black pepper.

3. In a small bowl, combine the paprika, thyme, cumin, cinnamon, and cayenne. Season the hens with salt and black pepper and rub all over with the paprika mixture.

4. Stuff the hens with the bread mixture and place in a large roasting pan. Roast the hens until the juices run clear when the hens are pierced with a knife in the thickest part of the thigh and an instant-read thermometer inserted into the stuffing registers 165°F, 40 to 50 minutes. Let hens rest for 5 minutes before serving.

Serves 6

RAGIN' RYE

Rye bread is chock-full of fiber, calcium, and protein. If you've had a diabetes diagnosis, your doctor may recommend this as the bread you should be eating. I also like it for its distinct caraway taste. That's certainly what makes this dish stand out in the crowd. But whole-wheat bread works well too, if that's what you prefer.

Chicken Breasts Stuffed with Ham and Provolone

Sometimes a simple chicken breast just won't do the trick, and you'll find yourself wanting just a little something more for your dinner. Filling a chicken breast with salty ham steak and melted provolone transforms this lean cut into a scrumptious bite, something you'd actually write home about. It tastes too good to be true!

1. Preheat the oven to 400°F.

2. Place the chicken breasts between two pieces of wax paper. Using the smooth side of a meat mallet or a rolling pin, pound the chicken breasts to ¼-inch thickness. Season to taste with salt and pepper and top each breast with 2 slices provolone and ¼ cup ham. Roll up the chicken breasts and secure with toothpicks or tie them with butcher's twine.

3. Brush the bottom of a 13 by 9-inch baking dish with 1 tablespoon of the butter. Place the rolled chicken breasts in the dish, seamside down, season each with more salt and pepper, and drizzle with the remaining 2 tablespoons butter. Bake until the internal temperature of the chicken reaches 165°F, 20 to 25 minutes. Place the chicken on a plate, reserving the pan juices, and tent the chicken with aluminum foil.

4. Pour the pan juices into a small saucepan, add the white wine, and simmer over medium-high heat for 3 minutes. Whisk in the chicken broth and mustard and simmer for 5 minutes more. Remove the pan from the heat and stir in the parsley, chives, and dill.

5. Remove the toothpicks or string from the chicken, slice into rounds, and pour the sauce over the chicken to serve.

Serves 4

4 boneless, skinless chicken breasts (½ pound each)

Salt and freshly ground pepper to taste

8 slices provolone cheese

1 cup finely chopped ham steak (about 8 ounces)

3 tablespoons unsalted butter, melted

½ cup dry white wine

1 cup low-sodium chicken broth

2 teaspoons whole-grain mustard

2 teaspoons chopped fresh parsley

2 teaspoons chopped fresh chives

2 teaspoons chopped fresh dill

Southwest Chicken Enchiladas

2 boneless, skinless chicken breasts (½ pound each)

1 garlic clove, peeled and smashed, plus
1 garlic clove, finely chopped

1 teaspoon black peppercorns

¾ cup shredded Cheddar cheese

¾ cup shredded Monterey Jack cheese

1 tablespoon canola or safflower oil

¾ cup finely chopped onion

1 tablespoon chili powder

1 teaspoon ground cumin

1 teaspoon dried oregano

1½ teaspoons salt

¼ teaspoon freshly ground black pepper

⅓ cup all-purpose flour

2 cups low-sodium chicken broth

¾ cup milk

1 can (4 ounces) chopped green chiles

4 low-carb whole-grain or regular flour tortillas (8 inches)

¾ cup thinly sliced scallions (white and light green parts)

4 teaspoons chopped fresh cilantro (optional)

These enchiladas bring me to cheesy heaven. They are so rich, creamy, spicy, and decadent that I almost can't believe they're as healthy as they are. Instead of frying the tortillas, I dip them in a little hot chicken broth to make them nice and pliable for rolling. And poaching chicken is one of the healthiest ways to prepare your meat, with the added benefit of making your lean chicken breast as juicy and tender as can be.

1. In a medium saucepan, combine the chicken with 2 cups water, the smashed garlic, and peppercorns. Partially cover with a lid and bring to a boil over medium-high heat. Boil for 1 minute. Remove the pan from the heat, cover completely, and let the chicken sit in the hot liquid for about 15 minutes, or until the chicken is no longer pink. Remove the chicken from the pan, and, using two forks or your hands, shred the chicken.

2. Preheat the oven to 375°F. Grease a 9-inch square baking dish with cooking spray.

3. In a medium bowl, combine the Cheddar and Monterey Jack.

4. In a large saucepan or skillet, heat the oil over medium heat. Add the onion and cook, stirring, until tender, 5 to 7 minutes. Add the chopped garlic and cook for 1 minute more. Add the chili powder, cumin, oregano, salt, and pepper and cook for 1 minute. Stir in the flour until it is well blended and cook for 1 minute more. Gradually whisk in 1½ cups of the chicken broth and the milk. Bring to a boil, then whisk and continue to cook until thickened, about 2 minutes. Remove the pan from the heat, add the green chiles and ¾ cup of the cheeses, and stir until the cheeses are melted. Combine 1½ cups of the cheese sauce with the shredded chicken and set aside. Reserve the remaining cheese sauce.

5. In a large nonstick skillet, heat the remaining ½ cup chicken broth. Dip the tortillas, one at a time, into the hot broth just until limp, about 4 seconds on each side. Working on a clean surface, spoon about one quarter of the chicken mixture down the center of each tortilla, sprinkle with 1 tablespoon of the

scallions and 1 teaspoon of the cilantro (if using). Roll up the tortillas and place them, seam side down, in the prepared baking dish.

6. Pour the remaining cheese sauce evenly over the tortillas. Sprinkle with the remaining ¾ cup cheese, cover the pan with aluminum foil, and bake for 20 minutes. Uncover and bake for 10 minutes more, until the cheese is golden brown and bubbly. Remove the baking dish from the oven and let the enchiladas stand for 5 minutes before serving. Garnish with the remaining scallions.

Serves 4

Louisiana Blackened Chicken Cutlets

Blackened catfish is a favorite Cajun specialty of mine. And now I've got another way to enjoy the signature spices of Louisiana. This chicken dish is loaded with flavor. What it's not loaded with is fat. I've cut the butter in this dish dramatically. I found that when you've got this much spicy goodness happening in a dish, you really don't miss the extra richness.

1. In a shallow bowl or pie plate, stir together the paprika, thyme, oregano, onion powder, garlic powder, salt, and pepper.

2. Combine the oil and butter in a medium bowl. Dip the chicken into the mixture, letting any excess drip off, then dip into the spice mixture to coat thoroughly.

3. Heat a large, preferably cast-iron, skillet over medium-high heat until very hot. Add half the chicken and cook, turning once, until cooked through, 3 to 4 minutes per side. Wipe out the pan and repeat with the remaining chicken. Serve with lemon wedges on the side.

Serves 4

¼ cup smoked paprika

1 tablespoon plus 1 teaspoon ground thyme

2 teaspoons dried oregano

2 teaspoons onion powder

1 teaspoon garlic powder

1 teaspoon salt

1 teaspoon freshly ground black pepper

2 tablespoons olive oil

2 tablespoons (¼ stick) unsalted butter, melted and cooled

8 boneless, skinless thin-cut chicken breasts (¼ pound each)

1 lemon, cut into wedges, for serving

Greek Chicken Kebabs on the Grill

KEBABS

⅓ cup olive oil

¼ cup white wine vinegar

Juice of 1 lemon

1 garlic clove, finely chopped

½ tablespoon dried oregano

1 tablespoon chopped
fresh parsley

2 pounds boneless, skinless
chicken thighs, cut into 1-inch
cubes (about 24 pieces)

1 pint cherry tomatoes

8 ounces cremini or white button
mushrooms

1 large zucchini, cut in half
lengthwise and cut into
1-inch pieces

4 metal or wooden skewers
(soaked for 20 minutes in water,
if using wooden skewers)

Salt and freshly ground
black pepper to taste

My son Bobby has been singing the praises of olive oil over butter for some time now. It seems that the Greeks have a way of cooking that can help you live longer, and the best part is they still use plenty of olive oil. So I decided to give it a try and darned if I didn't find that it was a delicious way to eat as well! These lemony, garlicky chicken kebabs topped with tangy yogurt sauce are so easy to prepare and make for a perfect meal on a warm summer night.

1. To make the kebabs: In a 1-cup measure, combine the oil, vinegar, lemon juice, garlic, oregano, and parsley and mix well. Place the chicken in a large resealable plastic bag and pour ½ cup of the marinade over the chicken. Seal the bag, shake gently to coat the chicken, and refrigerate for 1 hour.

2. Add the remaining ¼ cup marinade to another resealable plastic bag and add the tomatoes, mushrooms, and zucchini. Refrigerate for 1 hour.

3. Meanwhile, to make the lemon mint tzatziki: In a medium bowl, combine the yogurt, oil, cucumber, lemon juice, garlic, lemon zest, mint, and salt and white pepper to taste. Stir to combine well and refrigerate until ready to use.

4. Grease a grill grate by spraying it with cooking spray. Preheat the grill to medium-high.

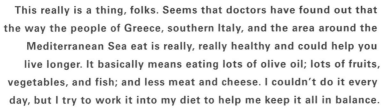

THE MEDITERRANEAN DIET

This really is a thing, folks. Seems that doctors have found out that the way the people of Greece, southern Italy, and the area around the Mediterranean Sea eat is really, really healthy and could help you live longer. It basically means eating lots of olive oil; lots of fruits, vegetables, and fish; and less meat and cheese. I couldn't do it every day, but I try to work it into my diet to help me keep it all in balance.

5. Drain the chicken and vegetables, discarding the marinade. Alternating chicken and vegetables, thread the skewers. Season to taste with salt and black pepper. Be sure to leave a little space between the chicken and vegetables so that the skewers cook evenly. Place the skewers on the grill and cook, turning frequently, until the chicken is cooked through, 18 to 20 minutes. Serve with the lemon mint tzatziki.

Serves 4 / Makes 1 cup tzatziki

LEMON MINT TZATZIKI

1 cup nonfat Greek yogurt

1 teaspoon olive oil

⅓ cup finely chopped cucumber

2 teaspoons fresh lemon juice

½ teaspoon finely chopped garlic

½ teaspoon finely grated lemon zest

1 tablespoon chopped fresh mint

Salt and white pepper to taste

Matthew's favorite chore at Ginny's house.

Pecan-Crusted Chicken Thighs

Even though these beauties are baked instead of fried, the nutty, crunchy coating helps to keep the chicken extra moist and juicy. Cooking at a high temperature ensures that the thighs cook from the outside in, so that the crust crisps up before the meat dries out. This is a finger-lickin' kind of meal if ever there was one.

1. Preheat the oven to 400°F. Lightly grease a rimmed baking sheet with cooking spray.

2. In a small bowl, combine the pecans, bread crumbs, salt, chili powder, and thyme.

3. Dip each chicken thigh into the beaten egg white mixture, letting any excess drip off. Dip into the pecan mixture and turn to coat evenly.

4. Place the chicken thighs on the prepared baking sheet. Drizzle with the oil. Bake until the chicken is cooked through and the coating is golden, about 25 minutes.

Serves 4

½ cup finely chopped pecans

3 tablespoons plain bread crumbs

¾ teaspoon salt

½ teaspoon chili powder

½ teaspoon dried thyme

4 bone-in, skinless chicken thighs (about ½ pound each), patted dry

1 egg white, lightly beaten with 1 teaspoon water

2 tablespoons olive oil

Lighter Chicken and Waffles

CHICKEN

2 cups cornflakes, crushed

3 teaspoons smoked paprika

½ teaspoon cayenne pepper

1 teaspoon salt

4 tablespoons (½ stick)
unsalted butter, melted

1 tablespoon olive oil

12 chicken tenders
(about 1½ pounds)

WAFFLES

2 cups all-purpose flour

1 tablespoon sugar

3 teaspoons baking powder

1 teaspoon salt

2 cups milk

5 tablespoons unsalted butter,
melted and cooled

2 large eggs

1 large egg white

This recipe boasts two of my favorite breakfast mainstays, cornflakes and waffles. I bring them together to create a hearty dinner based on a traditional soul food dish. I skip the fried chicken and lighten up this classic by substituting cornflakes-coated chicken tenders that are oven baked. The crunchy, savory chicken bites are out of this world paired up with the slightly sweet waffles.

1. To make the chicken: Preheat the oven to 400°F. Grease a rimmed baking sheet with cooking spray.

2. In a medium bowl, combine the cornflakes, paprika, cayenne, and salt. In a small bowl, combine the butter and olive oil.

3. Dip the chicken tenders into the butter mixture, letting any excess drip off, then dip into the cornflakes mixture to coat thoroughly. Place on the prepared baking sheet and bake for about 25 minutes, or until browned and cooked through.

4. Meanwhile, to make the waffles: In a large bowl, whisk together the flour, sugar, baking powder, and salt. In a medium bowl, whisk together the milk, butter, eggs, and egg white until combined. Using a rubber spatula, fold the milk mixture into the flour mixture just until combined.

5. Preheat a standard electric waffle iron according to the manufacturer's instructions. To make extra sure your waffles don't stick, give the waffle iron a spray with cooking spray.

6. Pour ½ cup batter into the waffle iron. Cook until golden brown and crispy on both sides, about 5 minutes. Repeat with remaining batter, keeping finished waffles warm in a 200°F oven.

7. Place 2 waffles on each plate and top with 3 chicken tenders each.

Makes 8 waffles / Serves 4

Turkey-Stuffed Bell Peppers

I used to make my stuffed bell peppers with white rice and ground beef. Now, I most often make them with bulgur and lean ground turkey. Talk about turning over a new leaf! I'd have never made the switch if I didn't find I liked the taste just as much. The bulgur helps to bulk up the stuffing while taking on all the great flavorings it's mixed with. And by using lean turkey meat, you won't wind up with a soggy, greasy bell pepper.

1 teaspoon olive oil

1 onion, finely chopped

1 garlic clove, finely chopped

½ teaspoon salt

⅛ teaspoon freshly ground black pepper

¾ pound turkey sausages, meat squeezed out of the casings

1 can (14½ ounces) no-salt-added plum tomatoes, roughly chopped with ½ to ¾ cup of their juice

¼ cup bulgur wheat

4 red, orange, or yellow bell peppers, cut in half lengthwise and stem, seeds, and membranes removed

½ cup grated Parmesan cheese

1. Preheat the oven to 400°F.

2. In a large skillet, heat the oil over medium-low heat. Add the onion and garlic and cook, stirring, for about 5 minutes, or until the onion is tender. Season with the salt and pepper. Add the turkey and cook, stirring to break up the meat, for about 4 minutes, or until the meat is brown. Add the tomatoes with their juice and the bulgur, cover the pan, and continue to cook for 5 minutes more.

3. Divide the turkey mixture among the bell pepper halves so that they are generously stuffed. Place the bell peppers in a roasting pan and add ¼ cup water to the pan. Lay a sheet of parchment paper over the bell peppers, cover the pan with aluminum foil, and bake for 20 minutes. Remove the foil and parchment paper, sprinkle the bell peppers with the Parmesan, and continue to cook, uncovered, until the bell peppers are tender and the cheese has browned, about 5 minutes.

Serves 4

A BETTER WHEAT

Bulgur wheat is a cereal grain that has so many health benefits, I'm not sure there's page enough to list them all. Most important, though, it's high in fiber and protein. Would you believe it actually contains more than double the fiber found in brown rice? It's low in calories and it's inexpensive. Best of all, it tastes great in many dishes, from salads to soups to stuffings like the one here.

BISCUIT BOWLS

2 cups Heart Smart Bisquick baking mix

⅔ cup milk

½ teaspoon cayenne pepper

All-purpose flour, for dusting

CHILI

2 tablespoons canola oil

1 pound ground turkey

1 onion, chopped

1 green bell pepper, chopped

1 tablespoon chili powder

2 teaspoons ground cumin

1 teaspoon salt

2 cans (14½ ounces each) no-salt-added diced tomatoes

½ cup low-sodium chicken broth

1 can (15 ounces) kidney beans, rinsed and drained

Kernels from 3 ears of corn (about 2 cups)

Shredded sharp Cheddar cheese

Low-fat Greek yogurt

Sliced scallions (white and light green parts)

Baked tortilla chips

Hot sauce

Southern Turkey Chili in a Biscuit Bowl

I just love these cute little biscuit bowls. They make this easy meal so special. Dressed up with all the fun fixings that a Southwestern feast demands, they positively call out for a celebration. There certainly is plenty to celebrate about this meal. I make my chili with lean ground turkey and protein-packed beans. And the biscuit bowls are prepared from a heart-healthy whole-wheat mix. It doesn't get much better than this, folks.

1. To make the biscuit bowls: Preheat the oven to 450°F. Invert a standard muffin pan and coat the underside with cooking spray.

2. In a medium bowl, stir together the baking mix, milk, and cayenne to make a stiff dough. Shape into a ball. Dust a work surface with a small handful of flour and knead the dough three or four times. Divide the dough into 6 pieces and, using a rolling pin or your hands, flatten each piece into a 6-inch round. Place 1 dough round over the backs of 6 muffin cups and press around the cup to form a bowl shape. Bake until lightly browned, about 8 minutes. Let cool slightly on the pan, then remove the biscuit bowls and set aside while you make the chili to fill them with.

3. To make the chili: In a Dutch oven, heat the oil over medium heat. Add the turkey and cook, breaking it up with a spoon, until most of the pink is gone, about 4 minutes. Add the onion and bell pepper and cook until the turkey is completely browned and the vegetables are tender. Add the chili powder, cumin, and salt and stir to coat the vegetables and meat. Stir in the tomatoes, chicken broth, and beans. Bring the mixture to a boil. Reduce to a simmer, cover, and cook for 25 minutes. Add the corn, cover again, and cook for 5 minutes. Uncover and cook for 5 minutes more.

4. To serve, spoon the hot chili into the biscuit bowls. Top with shredded Cheddar, yogurt, scallions, and tortilla chips. And be sure to pass around extra toppings and hot sauce at the table.

Serves 6

Juicy Turkey Burgers

¼ cup finely chopped onion
(from about 1 small onion)

1 large carrot, grated

1 tablespoon tomato paste

1½ teaspoons Dijon mustard

1 teaspoon Paula Deen's House
Seasoning (see page 6)

1 pound lean ground turkey

Whole-grain flatbread or pita,
for serving

Mustard or ketchup, for spreading

Tomato, lettuce, onion,
and avocado, for topping

My son Jamie taught me the cute trick of adding grated carrots to my burgers. They add a sweet richness that you'd really be missing out on if you used just ground turkey on its own. He's such a clever boy, that Jamie. Makes you wonder where he got his smarts from.

1. In a large bowl, combine the onion, carrot, tomato paste, mustard, and House Seasoning. Add the turkey and fold gently into the mixture. Using your hands, form into 4 equal-size patties, being careful not to overhandle.

2. Grease a grill pan or cast-iron skillet with cooking spray. Heat the pan over medium-high heat. Sear the burgers until browned, about 7 minutes on one side and 5 minutes on the other side.

3. Serve on whole-grain flatbread or pita and spread with mustard or ketchup. Top with tomato, lettuce, onion, avocado, or whatever else you like on your burger.

Serves 4

Turkey Scallopini

This light turkey dish is bright and zippy and fresh tasting. I like to eat it along with a few roasted new potatoes and a big ol' pile of green beans. Make sure your turkey cutlets are nice and thin or give them a good pounding with the smooth side of a meat mallet if you need to thin them out. This is a really quick-cooking dish, so be ready to slap it all on a plate and sit down to dinner in no time flat.

1. Place the flour in a shallow bowl. Pat the turkey dry and season all over with salt and pepper. Dredge half the turkey slices in the flour, shaking off the excess. In a large heavy skillet, heat 1 tablespoon of the oil over medium-high heat until hot but not smoking. Add the floured cutlets and cook until browned on both sides and just cooked through, 3 to 4 minutes. Transfer to a platter and tent with aluminum foil to keep warm. Dredge the remaining cutlets in the remaining flour. Heat another tablespoon of oil in the skillet and cook the remaining cutlets. Transfer to the platter with the other cutlets.

2. Add the remaining 1 tablespoon oil to the skillet with the garlic and cook over medium heat, until the garlic is fragrant, about 30 seconds. Add the chicken broth and the white wine, increase the heat to medium-high, and scrape the bottom of the pan to release any brown bits. Boil until the broth is reduced by about half, about 5 minutes. Stir in the lemon zest, lemon juice, capers, and parsley, and season to taste with salt and pepper. Reduce the heat to medium and return the cutlets with their juices to the skillet. Cook until heated through, about 1 minute. Serve drizzled with the lemony caper sauce.

⅓ cup whole-wheat or all-purpose flour

1½ pounds thinly sliced turkey cutlets (about ¼ inch thick)

Salt and freshly ground black pepper to taste

3 tablespoons olive oil

3 garlic cloves, finely chopped

½ cup low-sodium chicken broth

½ cup dry white wine

1 teaspoon finely grated lemon zest

2 tablespoons fresh lemon juice

2 tablespoons capers, rinsed and chopped

2 tablespoons chopped fresh parsley

Serves 4

QUICK COOK
Because this is such a quick-cooking dish,
it's tailor-made for lean turkey cutlets. Try not
to overcook them or they may dry out.

Braised Turkey Breast and Vegetables

Salt and freshly ground
black pepper to taste

1 boneless turkey breast
(2½ to 3 pounds), rinsed
and patted dry

1 tablespoon olive oil

¼ pound Canadian bacon,
chopped

2 onions, chopped

3 celery stalks, chopped

2 parsnips, chopped

1 large turnip, chopped

3 carrots, chopped

1 teaspoon fresh rosemary,
thyme, or sage, chopped

Chopped fresh parsley,
for garnish (optional)

Move over whole roasted turkey, there is a new bird in town and it's braised! If you haven't tried a braised turkey breast before, you are missing out on something really special. While a roasted turkey has a tendency to dry out in the oven, you will never have that problem with braised turkey breast. I tell you I have made this a hundred times and it always stays nice and juicy. I like to serve this with a whole load of winter vegetables, basically whatever I've got on hand. I also like to change up the herbs I use. That way it never tastes like the same dish twice.

1. Preheat the oven to 350°F.

2. Generously sprinkle salt and pepper all over the turkey. In a large skillet, heat the oil over medium-high heat. Add the turkey, breast meat side down, and cook until the skin is dark golden on all sides, 7 to 10 minutes. Using tongs, remove the turkey from the pan and set aside on a plate.

3. Cook the Canadian bacon in the fat remaining in the skillet until nearly crisp, about 3 minutes. Add the onions, celery, parsnips, turnip, carrots, and herbs and cook, stirring, until beginning to brown, 10 to 12 minutes. Season to taste with salt and pepper. Transfer the vegetables and bacon to a 13 by 9-inch casserole or baking dish. Set aside the skillet. Nestle the turkey breast, breast meat side up, in the middle of the vegetables, pouring in any liquid from the plate.

4. Off the heat, pour 2 cups water into the skillet you browned the turkey, bacon, and vegetables in. Use a wooden spoon to scrape up any brown bits on the bottom and mix into the water. Pour this liquid into the baking dish.

5. Roast the turkey for 45 minutes, remove from the oven, and baste with some of the pan juices. Return to the oven, continue to baste every 20 minutes, and roast until an instant-read thermometer inserted into the thickest part of the breast registers 150°F, 35 to 40 minutes more. Let the turkey rest for 10 minutes before slicing. Serve alongside the roasted vegetables and pan juices, garnished with parsley, if you like.

Serves 6

Chopped Turkey Barbecue

3 teaspoons olive oil

1 small onion, thinly sliced

2 garlic cloves, chopped

2 turkey or regular bacon slices,
chopped

1 can (6 ounces) pineapple juice

¼ cup balsamic or cider vinegar

¾ cup regular or reduced-sugar
ketchup

2 tablespoons Dijon mustard

1 tablespoon Worcestershire
sauce

1½ teaspoons sweet paprika

Pinch of cayenne pepper

Salt and freshly ground
black pepper to taste

2 boneless, skinless turkey
breasts (1½ to 1¾ pounds each)

Whole-wheat or regular
hamburger buns, for serving

Coleslaw and pickles,
for serving

This sweet and tangy barbecue is flavored by some of the usual suspects: Worcestershire sauce, mustard, and ketchup. But it's also got a couple unique flavorings that I think make it something really special. I sweeten it up with pineapple juice and balsamic vinegar. The balsamic also has the benefit of giving it a nice deep color. It's a hot mess on the plate, just like it ought to be, so break out the bibs and dig in!

1. Preheat the oven to 375°F.

2. In a medium saucepan, heat 1 teaspoon of the oil over medium-low heat. Add the onion and cook to a golden brown, about 5 minutes. Add water if the onion begins to brown too quickly or needs more moisture. Add the garlic and cook for 2 minutes. Remove the onion and garlic from the pan and reserve. Add 1 teaspoon of the remaining oil to the pan and raise the heat to medium-high. Add the bacon and cook until crisp, about 5 minutes.

3. Add the pineapple juice and vinegar to the bacon and cook until reduced by half, 5 to 7 minutes. Add ¼ cup water, the ketchup, mustard, Worcestershire sauce, paprika, cayenne, salt and pepper to taste, and the caramelized onion and garlic. Simmer for 7 to 10 minutes. Taste for seasonings and add more if you like.

4. Carefully pour the sauce into a blender and puree until smooth. Place the turkey breasts in a 13 by 9-inch casserole or baking dish. Slather the breasts with half the sauce, reserving the other half for later. Drizzle with the remaining 1 teaspoon oil.

LETTUCE WRAP

Anything my son Jamie used to put between two slices of bread he now likes to roll up in lettuce leaves. I was skeptical at first, but after seeing how much weight he was losing, I decided to give it a whirl. My goodness, is it tasty! Just one more way you can enjoy a recipe like this one.

Easy Coleslaw (page 32) is the perfect accompaniment to Chopped Turkey Barbecue.

5. Roast until the internal temperature of the turkey reaches 140°F on an instant-read thermometer, 45 minutes to 1 hour. Let the turkey rest for at least 10 minutes, then shred the meat using two forks or your hands. Add the remaining sauce to the shredded turkey and stir to coat thoroughly.

6. Serve the shredded meat warm or room temperature, sandwiched in buns with coleslaw and pickles on the side.

Makes 8 to 10 large sandwiches

7

Fish and Shellfish

I have my home of Savannah, Georgia, to thank for my deep love of seafood. And thankful I am; yes, sir. Because when you love fish, it's easy to eat right. The seafood we get in Savannah is so fresh it practically jumps onto your plate. That has been a big factor in opening me up to trying different types of fish. They all have their own individual tastes and textures and they all respond just a little bit differently to various cooking methods.

Two of my favorite fish have got to be salmon and red snapper. Salmon is buttery and rich and tastes so delicious cooked on a smoky grill. ***Grilled Salmon with Mustard Glaze*** (page 211) is such an easy way to prepare this wonderful fish. It needs nothing more than a slathering of sweet and spicy glaze and a few minutes on the grill to cook up to perfection. Red snapper I prefer baked in the oven. It's a mildly sweet fish that I like to flavor with fresh herbs and lemon slices. ***Parcel-Wrapped Red Snapper*** (page 206) may sound fancy, but it's really not. It's a foolproof way to cook fish that involves simply topping the fish with flavorings and wrapping it up in aluminum foil or parchment paper. The fish always comes out moist and perfectly flaky.

My true love in the seafood department is shrimp. Grilled, fried, boiled, or broiled, there is no preparation for shrimp that I don't swoon over. When Michael wants to butter me up, forget the flowers! All he has to do is bring home some freshly caught shrimp.

◄ *Crabbing on the Wilmington River with Patrick Dobbs,*
a.k.a. my number-one househusband.

A **Shrimp Po'boy** (page 194) is one of my favorite lunchtime treats. These days I most often make it with broiled shrimp instead of deep-fried. Broiling is a wonderful way to bring out the natural sweetness in foods. The shrimp will stay tender and soft on the inside with a nice outer crunch.

For special occasions, a good old **Low Country Boil** (page 198) is the way to go. Sausage and shrimp together is just this side of paradise, I tell you. This meal calls out for a crowd, so make sure you have plenty of friends and family over when you put out a boil.

What could be more delicate than a beautiful scallop? I love to sear them in a mix of butter and olive oil just until they have a browned crust on the outside and no more. They are tender and sweet and buttery and need so little to make them sit up and sing. **Seared Scallops on Barley Salad** (page 210) is a quick dish, served with a hearty salad, that I enjoy all summer long.

Seafood is the lifeblood of Savannah, and I have learned to appreciate the beauty of nearly everything the waterways here have to offer. And luckily, seafood fits into my lifestyle and suits my health needs so well. With seafood, simple preparations taste best, are the healthiest for you, and get you out of the kitchen and to the table quickly. Now, I ask you, what's not to love about that?

Beaufort Shrimp Pie

Ever since I discovered the beautiful town of Beaufort in South Carolina's Sea Islands, I've been in love with this traditional seafood pie. It is a celebration of the bounty of the sea that feeds that lovely community. But times change and so has my shrimp pie. Instead of bacon, my pie now features lots of good-for-you leafy spinach. And in place of bread crumbs, I fill the dish with that nutritional powerhouse quinoa. These modifications have brought about a new and improved pie that is (dare I say it?) even tastier today.

1. Preheat the oven to 350°F. Lightly grease an 8-inch square baking dish with cooking spray.

2. In a small saucepan, bring the water to a boil. Add the quinoa, reduce the heat to medium-low, cover, and simmer until the liquid is absorbed, about 15 minutes. Fluff the quinoa with a fork and scrape into the prepared baking dish. Layer the shrimp evenly on top of the quinoa.

3. Meanwhile, in a large skillet, heat the oil over medium-high heat. Add the onion and bell pepper and cook, stirring, until soft, about 5 minutes. Add the spinach and garlic and cook until the spinach is wilted, about 1 minute. Scatter the vegetables evenly over the shrimp in the baking dish.

4. In a medium bowl, whisk together the milk, eggs, lemon zest, ½ teaspoon salt (or to taste), and black pepper. Pour evenly over the casserole and bake until the filling is set, about 45 minutes.

Serves 4

1 cup water, lightly salted

½ cup quinoa, rinsed and drained

½ pound cooked medium shrimp, peeled and deveined

2 tablespoons olive oil

1 onion, chopped

1 large yellow or orange bell pepper, chopped

1 bag (5 ounces) washed baby spinach

1 large garlic clove, finely chopped

1 cup milk

2 large eggs, lightly beaten

1 teaspoon finely grated lemon zest

Salt and freshly ground black pepper to taste

BAG SPINACH

Spinach can be time-consuming to deal with, I know. It takes a great deal of washing to get the grit out. So I always use bagged washed baby spinach. It makes things so much easier. You could also use half a package of thawed, frozen chopped spinach if that's what is easiest for you.

Savannah Crab Cakes

1 pound crabmeat,
  picked over to remove
  bits of shell

¼ cup chopped red onion

¼ cup chopped fresh parsley

¼ cup regular or light sour cream

1 large egg

1 teaspoon Dijon mustard

1 teaspoon Worcestershire sauce

¾ teaspoon salt

⅛ teaspoon cayenne pepper

Juice of ½ lemon, plus extra
  lemon slices, for serving

2 dashes hot sauce (optional)

1 cup whole-wheat or regular
  panko bread crumbs

I'll be the first to admit it, everything worth knowing about crab cakes, I learned from my husband Michael. Now, here's my chance to teach him a thing or two. This baked crab cake is my new, healthier way to enjoy the Savannah treat I love so much. When I tried them out on Michael he was more than a little skeptical. But one bite showed him that these crab cakes are bursting with fresh crab flavor.

1. Preheat the oven to 400°F. Grease a rimmed baking sheet with cooking spray.

2. In a large bowl, mix together the crabmeat, red onion, parsley, sour cream, egg, mustard, Worcestershire sauce, salt, cayenne, lemon juice, hot sauce (if using), and ½ cup of the bread crumbs. Form the mixture into 6 even-size flat disks, each about 2½ inches in diameter.

3. Place the remaining ½ cup of bread crumbs in a shallow bowl or pie plate. Gently dip the crab cakes in the bread crumbs until well coated and place on the prepared baking sheet.

4. Bake until golden brown on the bottom, about 10 minutes. Gently flip the crab cakes and bake for 5 to 10 minutes more. Serve warm or at room temperature with lemon slices.

Makes 6 crab cakes / Serves 6

FRYING OPTION

If you'd like a crunchier crust, you can shallow fry the crab cakes in about 1 tablespoon oil for a minute or two, then finish them in a 400°F oven for about 10 minutes. You'll be adding a bit more fat to the plate, but you'll get more crunch with it.

Shrimp Po'boy

Whether it's catfish, oyster, or shrimp, a po'boy has got to be one of the world's finest sandwiches. The old Paula would have fried the shrimp and loaded up on the mayo in the dressing. Now I broil my shrimp and cut the mayo in the dressing with Greek yogurt. It's still an overstuffed sandwich, y'all. And it's still one of the finest.

DRESSING

⅓ cup Greek yogurt

⅓ cup regular or light mayonnaise

1 tablespoon regular or reduced-sugar ketchup

2 teaspoons fresh lemon juice

1 small garlic clove, chopped

4 dashes hot sauce, or to taste

Salt to taste

SANDWICH

1½ pounds medium shrimp, peeled and deveined

4 teaspoons olive oil

2 teaspoons sweet paprika

1½ teaspoons Paula Deen's House Seasoning (see page 6)

½ teaspoon dried thyme

½ teaspoon dried oregano

¼ teaspoon cayenne pepper, or to taste

4 French rolls (7 inches each)

2 large tomatoes, thinly sliced

12 dill pickle slices

2 cups shredded iceberg lettuce

1. To make the dressing: In a blender or small food processor, combine the yogurt, mayonnaise, ketchup, lemon juice, garlic, and hot sauce. Puree until smooth. Season with a touch of salt, if you like. Refrigerate until ready to use.

2. To make the sandwich: Preheat the broiler. Lightly grease a rimmed baking sheet with cooking spray.

3. In a medium bowl, toss the shrimp with the oil and add the paprika, House Seasoning, thyme, oregano, and cayenne. Toss until the shrimp are evenly coated. Place on the prepared baking sheet and broil, turning once, until cooked through, about 2 minutes per side.

4. Slice the rolls in half lengthwise and pull out most of the soft insides (you will remove about 1 cup of bread per roll, which you can use for making bread crumbs later). Place the rolls, cut sides up, on another baking sheet and toast lightly under the broiler.

5. Divide the shrimp among the bottom halves of the rolls and top with the tomato and pickle slices. Spread the top halves of the rolls with the dressing and fill with the lettuce. Sandwich together and serve with lots of napkins, y'all!

Serves 4

Shrimp and Greens

While the crushed red pepper flakes and the hot sauce in this recipe are totally optional, I highly recommend you add some spice. Because that's the way a good old Southern shrimp and greens dish is meant to be savored. I fondly recall many meals at my family's table with the hot sauce making the rounds. I'd wait patiently to start digging in until the bottle made its stop with me. Come to think of it, that may have been the only time I waited patiently at the dinner table! Well, it was worth the wait.

4 turkey or regular bacon slices, cut crosswise into ½-inch pieces

2 tablespoons (¼ stick) unsalted butter

1 onion, finely chopped

2 cups low-sodium vegetable broth

2½ bunches collard greens (2½ pounds), stems removed and leaves coarsely chopped

Salt and freshly ground black pepper to taste

1 can (28 ounces) no-salt-added plum tomatoes, drained, chopped, and drained again

1 tablespoon olive oil

1 pound large shrimp, peeled and deveined

Crushed red pepper flakes or hot sauce (optional)

1. In a large skillet, cook the bacon over medium-high heat until crisp, about 5 minutes. Drain the bacon on a paper towel–lined plate. Pour off all but 1 tablespoon of the fat from the skillet. Add the butter to the skillet and melt over medium heat. Add the onion and cook, stirring, until softened, about 5 minutes. Add the vegetable broth and greens and season with salt and pepper. Reduce the heat to low, cover, and cook for 20 minutes. Add the tomatoes and cook at a low simmer, uncovered, for 15 minutes more. Transfer the greens to a medium bowl. Wipe out the skillet.

2. Heat the oil in the same skillet over medium-high heat. Add the shrimp, season with salt and pepper, and cook until pink, 3 to 4 minutes.

3. Divide the greens among four bowls and top with the shrimp. Garnish with the reserved bacon. Sprinkle with the crushed red pepper flakes or hot sauce (if using).

Serves 4

GO GREEN
I can't overstate how good dark leafy greens are for you. They taste great too! If you can't find collards for this dish, you can use kale, mustard greens, or even spinach.

Shrimp and Grits

A plate of creamy grits topped with fresh juicy shrimp simply cannot be beat. I used to make this dish using heavy cream, but nowadays I use milk instead. That helps me cut a fair amount of fat from this dish without sacrificing the rich, smooth texture of the grits. I've also added some green in the form of asparagus. I'm always sneaking green vegetables into my dishes these days. But I cook the shrimp with all the great flavors I always have. If I'd made any big changes, believe me, I'd be hearing it from Michael. For the sake of marital peace, I decided to leave well enough alone.

1. In a medium saucepan, bring the water to a boil over medium-high heat. Slowly whisk in the grits and ¼ teaspoon of the salt. Whisk constantly for 1 minute. Reduce the heat, cover, and cook, lifting the lid to stir occasionally, for 15 to 20 minutes, until the grits are thick and creamy.

2. Meanwhile, in a large skillet, heat the oil over medium-high heat. Add the tasso and cook, stirring once, until crisp, 7 to 9 minutes. Add the leek, onion, bell pepper, and asparagus and cook, stirring until tender, about 5 minutes. Add the tomatoes and cook for 1 minute more. Add the shrimp and cook until pink, 3 to 4 minutes. Remove the shrimp from the pan, leaving the vegetable mixture, and set aside.

3. Add the white wine to the pan and cook for 30 seconds. Slowly add the milk and gently simmer for about 5 minutes. Season the vegetable mixture with the remaining ¼ teaspoon salt and the pepper.

4. Divide the grits among four plates. Place the shrimp over the grits. Pour the vegetable mixture over the grits and garnish with a scattering of scallion.

Serves 4

2 cups water

½ cup quick-cooking grits (not instant grits)

½ teaspoon salt

2 tablespoons olive oil

3 ounces tasso ham, cut into ¼-inch cubes

2 tablespoons thinly sliced leek (white part only)

2 tablespoons finely chopped onion

2 tablespoons finely chopped green bell pepper

⅓ pound asparagus (about 8 average spears), woody ends trimmed, cut into 1-inch pieces

2 small plum tomatoes, cut into ½-inch pieces

20 large shrimp (about ⅔ pound), peeled and deveined, tails intact

2 tablespoons dry white wine

½ cup milk

¼ teaspoon freshly ground black pepper

1 scallion (green part only), sliced, for garnish

Low Country Boil

Crab boil seasoning
  (Zatarain's for spicier Louisiana
  style or Old Bay for milder
  Maryland style)

8 small red potatoes

4 chicken andouille sausages,
  halved

3 ears of corn, cut into thirds

2 pounds large shrimp,
  with their shells

This meal hollers out for a party. It's a great excuse to have a crowd over. But a party doesn't have to be an excuse to blow your healthy diet. This all-new boil recipe is a leaner, meaner version of my classic recipe. It's got a few less potatoes and corn and I've switched out pork sausage for chicken sausage. But there's still enough shrimp in there to satisfy even your biggest shrimp lover. And it's just as full flavored as it's always been.

1. Fill a large pot with enough water to cover all the ingredients. Add 2 teaspoons crab boil seasoning for every quart of water and bring to a boil over medium-high heat.

2. Add the potatoes and sausages to the boiling water and cook over medium heat for 20 minutes. Add the corn and cook for 10 minutes more. Add the shrimp and cook for exactly 3 minutes. Drain and serve.

Serves 8

Crab-Stuffed Shrimp

*Crab and shrimp together is a heady combination, y'all. I just love it.
This dish is so rich and deluxe tasting, your family will think you hid
a stick of butter in there. But there's not even a lick, just olive oil.
Whether you tell them or not is up to you.*

1. Preheat the oven to 375°F. Lightly grease a rimmed baking
   sheet with cooking spray.

2. In a medium skillet, heat 2 tablespoons of the oil over
   medium heat. Add the onion and cook, stirring occasionally,
   until softened, about 5 minutes. Add the garlic and cook
   for 30 seconds. Add the flour and cook, stirring constantly,
   for 1 minute. Add the milk and sherry and cook, stirring
   constantly, until thickened (the mixture will have the
   consistency of condensed soup). Season to taste with
   cayenne, salt, and black pepper. Remove from the heat
   and fold in the crabmeat. Taste and adjust seasonings, if
   you think it needs it.

3. Split the shrimp down the bottom center to the tails, being
   careful not to cut all the way through. Stuff the shrimp
   with the crabmeat mixture. In a small bowl, combine the
   remaining 1 tablespoon oil and the paprika and brush the
   mixture over the shrimp and crabmeat. Place the shrimp
   on the prepared baking sheet and bake for 15 minutes, until
   the shrimp are cooked through.

4. Meanwhile, in a small bowl, combine the Parmesan, basil,
   and lemon zest. Divide the shrimp among four plates and
   sprinkle the cheese mixture over the top.

Serves 4

3 tablespoons olive oil

½ cup chopped onion

1 garlic clove, chopped

1 tablespoon all-purpose flour

½ cup milk

1 tablespoon sherry

Cayenne pepper to taste

Salt and freshly ground
   black pepper to taste

½ pound crabmeat, picked over
   to remove bits of shell

1 pound jumbo shrimp, peeled
   and deveined, tails intact

Pinch of sweet paprika

¼ cup grated Parmesan cheese

2 tablespoons chopped fresh basil

¼ teaspoon finely grated
   lemon zest

Crawfish Étouffée

2 tablespoons vegetable oil

2 tablespoons (¼ stick) unsalted butter

1 cup chopped onions

½ cup chopped celery

½ cup chopped green bell pepper

1 garlic clove, chopped

2 tablespoons all-purpose flour

2 cups low-sodium fish or chicken broth

1 tablespoon tomato paste

1 teaspoon Cajun seasoning

2 bay leaves

4 dashes hot sauce, or to taste

1 pound peeled crawfish tails, thawed if frozen

Salt and freshly ground black pepper to taste

3 cups cooked brown or white rice, for serving

¼ cup chopped scallions (dark green parts), for garnish

I may not be from Louisiana but Cajun cooking is near and dear to my heart. And I reckon étouffée is maybe its finest contribution to the food world. Sometimes I make this with shrimp, but when I can get my hands on crawfish, I go with this classic rendition. Get a pot of this going on the stove and y'all will bring the Big Easy straight to your kitchen.

1. In a large saucepan, heat the oil and butter over medium heat. Add the onions, celery, and bell pepper and cook, stirring occasionally, until very soft, about 10 minutes. Add the garlic and cook for 30 seconds. Add the flour and cook, stirring constantly, for 1 minute. Add the fish broth, tomato paste, Cajun seasoning, bay leaves, and hot sauce and cook, stirring, until slightly thickened, about 5 minutes. Add the crawfish and simmer gently, uncovered, for 10 minutes. Remove the bay leaves. Season with salt and black pepper to taste.

2. Serve the étouffée in shallow bowls over the rice and garnish with the scallions.

Serves 4

Baked
Coconut Shrimp

½ cup unsweetened
shredded coconut

½ cup whole-wheat or regular
panko bread crumbs

½ teaspoon salt

1 teaspoon onion powder

1 teaspoon garlic powder

½ to 1 teaspoon cayenne pepper,
or to taste

2 large egg whites, lightly beaten

½ teaspoon olive oil

24 large shrimp
(about ¾ pound), peeled
and deveined, tails intact,
and butterflied

Lemon wedges, for serving

*I love to make this dish when it's cold and rainy outside and
I need to be reminded that the warm weather will be back soon.
Coconut shrimp is like a little taste of summer on the tongue.
I bake the shrimp at a real high temperature. That way it
comes out nice and golden on the outside, but tender and
juicy on the inside.*

1. Preheat the oven to 450°F. Grease a rimmed baking sheet
   with cooking spray.

2. In a shallow bowl or pie plate, stir together the coconut,
   bread crumbs, salt, onion powder, garlic powder, and
   cayenne. In a medium bowl, beat the egg whites with
   the oil. Add the shrimp to the egg whites and toss to coat.
   Lift each shrimp from the egg whites, letting the excess
   drip off, and then coat in the coconut mixture, pressing
   to adhere. Place the shrimp on the prepared baking sheet
   in a single layer. Bake for 8 to 10 minutes, until the shrimp
   are golden on the outside and tender on the inside.
   Serve with lemon wedges.

Serves 4

EXERCISE AND DIET
**If you get out and exercise, you will look at food
differently, I tell you. When you take the time to work
on your body by getting it moving, you think twice
about blowing all that work on a big fattening meal.
And that's when you start to find balance in your life.**

Buttery Lemon Sole

When it comes to a fine fish like lemon sole, there's not much more you need than butter, lemon, and a bit of salt. Keeping it simple is the best way to enjoy it. And it's the easiest too.

1. In a shallow bowl or pie plate, whisk together the salt, pepper, and flour. Dip each fillet into the seasoned flour to coat all over. Gently shake each fillet to remove the excess.

2. Heat a large skillet over medium-high heat until hot. Add the butter and cook until bubbling. Add the fish. Cook, without moving, until the undersides are golden, about 2 minutes. Carefully flip the fillets and continue to cook until golden and opaque, about 2 minutes more. Serve immediately, topped with a squeeze of lemon and sprinkled with chives.

Serves 4

¾ teaspoon salt

½ teaspoon freshly ground black pepper

3 tablespoons all-purpose flour

4 lemon sole fillets (6 ounces each)

2 tablespoons (¼ stick) unsalted butter

Lemon wedges, for serving

Chopped fresh chives, for serving

Crab-Stuffed Lemon Sole

These cute lemon sole packets are perfect for a special dinner party. Whether you choose to put them out on the table right in the casserole dish they are cooked in or plated up with some pretty little dill sprigs to decorate, you will be sure to impress the pants off any guest who's lucky enough to sit down at your table.

1. Preheat the oven to 375°F. Line the bottom of a 13 by 9-inch baking dish with parchment paper. Lay the lemon slices on top of the paper.

2. In a small skillet, melt ½ tablespoon of the butter over medium-low heat. Add the onion and cook until soft, about 5 minutes. Add the garlic and cook for 1 minute more. Set aside to cool.

3. Season the fillets by sprinkling with the salt, pepper, and garlic powder.

4. In a large bowl, combine the crabmeat, the cooled onion mixture, the bread crumbs, half-and-half, and salt and pepper to taste. If you are using lemon sole fillets, lay 2 fillets together, overlapping slightly down the long end. Spoon ¼ cup of the crabmeat mixture down the center of each pair of fillets and roll lengthwise into a bundle. Secure the ends with toothpicks. Repeat with the remaining fillets. If you are using flounder fillets, stuff each single fillet as you would stuff the lemon sole.

5. Lay the bundles, seam side down, on top of the lemon slices in the prepared dish. Dot each fillet with a portion of the remaining 1 tablespoon butter, sprinkle with paprika, and top with a small sprig of fresh dill.

6. Bake the fillets until the fish is flaky, about 15 minutes for the lemon sole and 18 to 20 minutes for the flounder. To serve, spoon the pan juices over the fillets.

Serves 4

1 lemon, thinly sliced

1½ tablespoons unsalted butter

1 small onion, chopped

1 small garlic clove, finely chopped

8 lemon sole fillets
(2 ounces each)
or 4 flounder fillets
(6 ounces each)

Salt and freshly ground black pepper to taste

Garlic powder to taste

½ pound crabmeat, picked over to remove bits of shell

2 tablespoons whole-wheat or regular panko bread crumbs

⅓ cup half-and-half

Smoked paprika, for sprinkling

4 fresh dill sprigs

2 Yukon gold potatoes
(about 1 pound total), peeled

2 tablespoons (¼ stick) unsalted
butter, at room temperature

2 teaspoons finely chopped
fresh chives

2 teaspoons finely chopped
fresh parsley

2 teaspoons finely chopped
fresh basil

1 teaspoon chopped fresh thyme

½ teaspoon finely chopped garlic

½ teaspoon finely grated
lemon zest

Salt and freshly ground
black pepper to taste

4 red snapper fillets
(4 ounces each), skin removed

16 grape tomatoes,
sliced in half lengthwise

White wine, for sprinkling

KEEP A GARDEN
I always have herbs
growing in my yard. They
are very easy to tend to and
that way I never get caught
out when I need them for a
dish. Fresh herbs add flavor
and interest to your meals.
And when you pile on the
flavor, you can usually get
away with less fat.

Parcel-Wrapped Red Snapper

What a wonderful way this is to cook fish! By cooking a delicate whitefish like snapper in a little parcel filled with herbs and other seasonings, you give the fish a chance to suck up all the great flavors, without adding too much butter. And you wind up with the most insanely delicious, most mouthwateringly moist piece of fish for dinner. I like to put the parcels straight onto individual plates and have everyone open them up right there at the table.

1. Preheat the oven to 375°F.

2. In a medium saucepan, cover the potatoes with water and bring to a boil over medium-high heat. Reduce the heat and simmer for 8 to 10 minutes. The potatoes should be slightly resistant when pierced with a sharp knife. (They will finish cooking when they bake in the oven with the fish.) Drain the potatoes well and cut into about sixteen ½-inch slices.

3. Meanwhile, make the herb butter. In a small bowl, combine the butter, chives, parsley, basil, thyme, garlic, lemon zest, and salt and pepper to taste. Using a small rubber spatula or the back of a wooden spoon, mix until well combined.

4. Cut out four 15-inch square pieces of parchment paper. To prepare a parcel, lay 4 potato slices in the center of the square. Top with 1 fillet. Dot the fillet with ½ tablespoon of the herb butter. Scatter 8 tomato halves over the fillet and sprinkle with a small amount of white wine. Season the fish with salt and pepper. Fold the parchment paper up around the contents and seal securely. Repeat with the remaining ingredients and parchment pieces. Place the parcels on a rimmed baking sheet and bake for 20 minutes, until the fish is opaque and flakes easily.

Serves 4

Creamy Shrimp and Corn Casserole

I love sweet corn with shrimp, but add in creamy custard to boot and I go head over heels. I have cooked this casserole so many times now I reckon I could make it blindfolded. It comes together so quickly and always gets polished off just as fast.

1. Preheat the oven to 325°F. Grease a 2-quart baking dish with cooking spray.

2. In a medium saucepan, melt the butter over medium heat. Add the onion, bell pepper, and 1 cup of the corn and cook, stirring, until the onion is soft, about 5 minutes. Let the vegetables cool.

3. Meanwhile, in a blender or food processor, combine the remaining 1 cup corn, the flour, and 1 tablespoon of the evaporated milk. Puree until smooth.

4. In a large bowl, whisk together the eggs and egg whites. Stir in the remaining evaporated milk, the pureed corn mixture, the cooked and cooled vegetables, the Worcestershire sauce, Cheddar, salt, and black pepper.

5. Season the shrimp with salt and black pepper and place in the prepared baking dish. Pour the corn mixture over the shrimp. Bake until a knife inserted into the center comes out clean, 55 to 60 minutes. Serve immediately.

Serves 6

1 tablespoon unsalted butter

½ cup finely chopped onion

⅓ cup finely chopped
red bell pepper

2 cups fresh or frozen
corn kernels (if using frozen,
thaw before using)

2 tablespoons whole-wheat
or all-purpose flour

1 cup evaporated milk

3 large eggs

3 large egg whites

1 teaspoon Worcestershire sauce

¾ cup shredded sharp Cheddar
cheese

1 teaspoon salt, plus more
for seasoning the shrimp

½ teaspoon black pepper,
plus more for seasoning
the shrimp

24 large shrimp
(about ¾ pound),
peeled and deveined

Scallop, Pineapple, and Vegetable Skewers

3 tablespoons olive oil

1 tablespoon chopped fresh cilantro

1 tablespoon fresh lemon juice

Salt and freshly ground black pepper to taste

1 pound sea scallops

1 zucchini, cut into ½-inch slices

1 small red bell pepper, cut into 2-inch squares

8 pieces (1½ inches each) fresh pineapple (cut from about ½ small pineapple)

8 metal or wooden skewers (soaked for 20 minutes in water, if using wooden skewers)

Skewers are such a fun, casual way to eat during the warm summer months. I can thread just about anything on those little sticks and I'm pretty sure I'm going to love it. But buttery scallops and tangy pineapple are a particularly fine choice in my book— the naturally sweet flavors work really well together. These bright, colorful kebabs are a welcome addition to any outdoor barbecue.

1. In a blender or small food processor, puree the oil, cilantro, and lemon juice until smooth. Season to taste with salt and black pepper and divide into two small bowls.

2. Using two parallel skewers for each kebab, thread the scallops, zucchini, bell pepper, and pineapple alternately on the skewers. Using the cilantro oil in one of the bowls, brush the kebabs all over. Keep the rest of the cilantro oil separate to prevent cross-contamination with the raw seafood.

3. Spray the grill grate with cooking spray and preheat the grill to medium.

4 Place the kebabs on the grill and cook, turning once or twice, until the scallops are cooked through, about 10 minutes. Brush the kebabs with the remaining cilantro oil and serve.

Serves 4

SPIN CONTROL
Threading the scallops onto two parallel skewers prevents them from spinning when you turn them on the grill.

Seared Scallops on Barley Salad

1 cup pearl barley

2 cups water

¼ teaspoon salt,
  plus more to taste

1 small bunch arugula (8 ounces)
  or 1 bag (5 ounces), stemmed
  and chopped

1 pint (10 ounces) grape
  tomatoes, quartered
  (or cut in half if very small)

5 tablespoons olive oil

3 tablespoons fresh lemon juice

Freshly ground black pepper
  to taste

1½ pounds sea scallops

First time I made this dish, I thought it looked so pretty on the plate, I almost didn't want to eat it. Well, I got over that real fast. And good thing too, because it is too delicious for words. I like to make this when I'm having guests over for lunch. After all, a dish this pretty deserves the fancy china.

1. In a medium saucepan, combine the barley with the water and salt. Bring to a boil over high heat. Cover the pan, reduce the heat to low, and cook until the liquid is absorbed, about 40 minutes. Fluff the barley with a fork and scrape into a large bowl. Add the arugula and tomatoes to the bowl.

2. In a small bowl, whisk together 3 tablespoons of the oil, the lemon juice, and a pinch of salt and pepper. Pour over the barley salad and toss to combine. Add more salt and pepper if you think the salad needs it.

3. In a large nonstick skillet, heat the remaining 2 tablespoons oil over medium-high heat. Season the scallops with salt and pepper and cook for 1 to 2 minutes per side, until just cooked through (they should feel firm to the touch). Scoop the barley salad onto plates and top with the scallops.

Serves 6

Grilled Salmon with Mustard Glaze

This sweet, tangy glaze is the perfect complement to the buttery richness of the salmon. For all the great taste this dish brings to the table, you'd think it would take more time than it does. But it's done before you know it. Just a few flips on the grill and dinner is served.

1. Grease a grill grate by brushing it with oil. Preheat the grill to medium-high.

2. In a small bowl, combine the mustard, brown sugar, and lemon juice.

3. Brush the salmon all over with the oil and season with the salt and pepper. Place on the grill, skin side down, and cook, covered, until the underside is golden, about 3 minutes. Flip the salmon and grill, covered, until almost cooked through, about 3 minutes more. Flip the salmon again and spread the top of each fillet generously with the mustard glaze. Flip the salmon and grill, glaze side down, until caramelized, about 1 minute. Serve immediately.

Serves 4

2 tablespoons Dijon mustard

4 teaspoons light brown sugar

2 teaspoons fresh lemon juice

4 salmon fillets (6 ounces each), skin on

1½ tablespoons olive oil

¾ teaspoon salt

¾ teaspoon freshly ground black pepper

SALMON SKIN
While you don't have to eat the salmon skin (which is on the oily side), I do recommend you cook the salmon with the skin on. This way the fillet will stay intact on the grill, and the salmon stays nice and juicy.

Salmon Burgers with Sun-Dried Tomato Mayonnaise

¼ cup regular or light mayonnaise

1 tablespoon coarsely chopped oil-packed sun-dried tomatoes

1 teaspoon fresh lemon juice

2 dashes hot sauce

1½ pounds skinless salmon fillet, finely chopped

¼ cup whole-wheat or regular panko bread crumbs

1 tablespoon sweet pickle relish

1 tablespoon Dijon mustard

¾ teaspoon salt, or to taste

½ teaspoon freshly ground black pepper, or to taste

4 whole-wheat or regular hamburger buns, split

4 lettuce leaves, for serving

4 tomato slices, for serving

Salmon has such a full flavor that I like to serve it with a nice hit of sweetness. To that delicious end, I throw in a little bit of sweet relish to my salmon burger mix. And for good measure, I add chopped sun-dried tomatoes to my mayonnaise spread. A little goes a long way to cut the richness and lift this burger into sublime territory. Mix yourself up some crunchy slaw to serve alongside the burger or to pile high on top.

1. In a blender or food processor, puree the mayonnaise, sun-dried tomatoes, lemon juice, and hot sauce until nearly smooth (flecks of tomato will remain). Place in a small bowl and refrigerate until you're ready to use the tomato mayonnaise.

2. In a medium bowl, combine the salmon, bread crumbs, relish, mustard, salt, and pepper. Mix gently and shape into 4 patties.

3. Lightly grease a large nonstick skillet with cooking spray. Preheat over medium-high heat. Add the burgers, and cook for 3 minutes on each side for medium. If you would like them more well done, reduce the heat to medium so they do not burn.

4. Spread one of the cut sides of the buns with a little of the sun-dried tomato mayonnaise mixture. Place the burgers on the buns, top with the lettuce and tomatoes, and sandwich with the other bun halves.

Serves 4

Oven-Fried Catfish

4 skinless catfish fillets
(5 to 6 ounces each)

Salt and freshly ground
black pepper to taste

1 cup buttermilk

2 tablespoons hot sauce

¼ cup whole-wheat or
all-purpose flour

2 tablespoons cornmeal

2 teaspoons crab boil seasoning,
such as Old Bay

*Catfish is a classic Cajun ingredient. I love its slightly sweet
flavor and pretty much any preparation is a hit in my book.
I just make sure to always soak it in a buttermilk bath before
I start cooking it. The buttermilk helps to mellow out any strong
unwanted flavors that the fresh fish may carry.*

1. Season the fillets on both sides with salt and pepper.
   In an 8-inch square baking dish, stir together the buttermilk
   and hot sauce. Add the catfish fillets, making sure they're
   completely covered by the liquid. Cover the catfish with
   plastic wrap and let them sit in the fridge for 15 minutes.

2. Meanwhile, preheat the oven to 475°F. Grease a rimmed
   baking sheet with cooking spray. Place the baking sheet in
   the oven to preheat while you prep the remaining ingredients.

3. In a shallow bowl or pie plate, whisk together the flour,
   cornmeal, and crab boil seasoning. Remove the catfish from
   the buttermilk, letting any excess drip off. Dredge on both
   sides with the cornmeal mixture. Carefully remove the hot
   baking sheet from the oven and place the catfish on the
   sheet. Bake for 6 minutes, then carefully flip the catfish
   and continue cooking for 5 minutes more, or until cooked
   through and golden.

Serves 4

Orange-Glazed Tuna with Confetti Peppers

This dish not only tastes good, it looks darn good too. Be sure to use a mix of colored bell peppers and you will wind up with a dinner that's just as pretty as a picture.

1. Preheat the oven to 450°F. Line a rimmed baking sheet with aluminum foil and lightly grease with cooking spray.

2. In a small saucepan, combine the marmalade, ginger, soy sauce, sesame oil, and red pepper flakes. Bring to a boil over medium-high heat and cook until syrupy and thickened, about 5 minutes.

3. Season the tuna with salt and black pepper and place on the prepared baking sheet. Spoon half the orange glaze over the tops of the tuna and bake to the doneness you like, 6 minutes for medium-rare to 10 minutes for well-done.

4. Meanwhile, in a large skillet, heat the oil over medium-high heat. Add the bell peppers and House Seasoning and cook, stirring frequently, until the peppers are tender but still retain some snap, 4 to 5 minutes. Turn off the heat and stir in the lime juice.

5. Serve the tuna on a bed of the bell peppers with the additional glaze spooned over the top.

Serves 4

⅓ cup reduced-sugar orange marmalade

1 teaspoon finely chopped fresh ginger

1 teaspoon low-sodium soy sauce

1 teaspoon sesame oil

Pinch of crushed red pepper flakes

4 tuna steaks (6 ounces each)

Salt and freshly ground black pepper to taste

2 tablespoons olive oil

3 cups finely chopped bell peppers, any combination of red, green, yellow, and orange

½ teaspoon Paula Deen's House Seasoning (see page 6)

1 tablespoon fresh lime juice

CONCENTRATED SWEETNESS
Because the marmalade in this recipe is cooked down and thickened, the sweetness will concentrate and become more intense. So even though I use reduced-sugar marmalade, I still get tons of sticky sweet taste to satisfy me.

Pesto-Marinated Cod

In the summertime, my basil plants grow like weeds. When I see them starting to get a little out of control, I snip them right back and use the leaves I've collected to make up some pesto. I toss that pesto through pasta, slather it on bread, or use it to make a simple fish like cod sit up and sing. Delicious.

2 garlic cloves, coarsely chopped

2 tablespoons pine nuts

2 cups fresh basil leaves

⅔ cup fresh parsley leaves

1 tablespoon grated Parmesan cheese

2 tablespoons olive oil

Salt and freshly ground black pepper to taste

4 cod fillets (6 ounces each)

Sliced lemons, for serving

1. In a food processor or a blender, pulse the garlic, pine nuts, basil, parsley, and Parmesan until a thick paste has formed and the garlic and pine nuts are finely chopped. Scrape down the sides of the bowl with a rubber spatula and pulse again. With the processor running, add the oil in a thin stream and puree until combined. Scrape down the sides of the bowl and season to taste with salt and pepper.

2. Slather the fillets with the pesto and let them marinate in the fridge for at least 1 hour and up to 4 hours.

3. Preheat the oven to 400°F. Bring the fillets to room temperature. Place the fillets in a baking dish and roast for 15 minutes, or until the fish is no longer opaque and flakes easily. Serve with sliced lemons.

Serves 4

PRESTO PESTO

If you don't have the time (or the basil) to make your own pesto, you can use purchased pesto to make this dish. It works just great.

Pan-Seared Grouper
with Mango Salsa

MANGO SALSA

½ small red onion, finely chopped

1 ripe mango, peeled, pitted,
  and chopped

1 small jalapeño pepper, seeded
  and finely chopped

2 tablespoons fresh cilantro
  or basil, chopped

2 tablespoons fresh lime juice

½ teaspoon honey or agave
  (optional)

1 small ripe avocado, peeled,
  pitted, and chopped

Salt and freshly ground
  black pepper to taste

GROUPER

4 grouper fillets (6 ounces each)

Garlic powder, for sprinkling

Chili powder, for sprinkling

Salt and black pepper to taste

1 teaspoon olive oil

Oh my, but this is a tasty dish. This mango salsa would be delicious on just about anything, I reckon. But spooned on top of a firm, moist, and lightly spiced piece of grouper, it is out of this world. Go ahead and make up the salsa ahead of time so that the flavors have a chance to really come together. It's sweet, tangy, and just a little bit spicy. Kind of like me!

1. To make the mango salsa: In a medium bowl, combine the red onion, mango, jalapeño, cilantro, lime juice, and honey (if using; see note below). Stir well to combine. Add the avocado and gently toss. Season to taste with salt and black pepper and set aside at room temperature. The salsa gets better and better with time, so feel free to let it sit a good long while.

2. To make the grouper: Heat a large skillet over medium heat. Sprinkle the fish with the garlic powder, chili powder, and salt and black pepper. Add the oil to the pan and once hot, add the fillets and cook for 3 minutes. Flip the fillets and cook until just opaque, 3 to 4 minutes more. Place the fillets on a large serving platter or on individual plates and serve with the mango salsa.

Serves 4

SWEET TASTE

If your mango is very sweet and ripe, you may not need to add the honey or agave. Taste the salsa before adding the honey or agave to see if it's sweet enough for you.

Trout with Brown Butter and Pecans

I can't think of one thing that doesn't taste better with brown butter and pecans. But a mild fish like rainbow trout is made something really special when served this way. It's like dressing it up in its Sunday best.

1. In a shallow bowl or pie plate, whisk together the flour, cayenne, ½ teaspoon of the salt, and ¼ teaspoon of the black pepper. Dip the fillets into the flour mixture to coat all over. Gently shake the fillets to remove any excess.

2. In a large heavy skillet, heat the oil over medium heat. Add the trout, skin side down, and cook until the skin is golden brown, about 4 minutes. Flip the fillets and cook until just cooked through, 1 to 2 minutes more. Transfer to a plate with a slotted spatula and keep warm, loosely covered with aluminum foil.

3. Wipe the skillet clean with a paper towel and melt the butter over medium heat. Add the pecans, the remaining ¼ teaspoon salt, and the pinch of black pepper, stirring occasionally, until the mixture is golden brown, about 2 minutes. Stir in the lemon juice and parsley and spoon the sauce over the trout.

Serves 4

¼ cup whole-wheat or all-purpose flour

¼ teaspoon cayenne pepper

¾ teaspoon salt

¼ teaspoon plus a pinch of freshly ground black pepper

4 rainbow trout fillets (6 to 8 ounces each), skin on

2 tablespoons olive oil

2 tablespoons (¼ stick) unsalted butter

⅓ cup pecans, chopped

2 tablespoons fresh lemon juice

⅓ cup chopped fresh parsley

Broiled Tilapia
with Sesame and Soy

1 teaspoon grated fresh ginger

1 tablespoon sesame oil

⅓ cup low-sodium soy sauce

1 teaspoon finely chopped garlic

3 tablespoons fresh orange juice

4 tilapia fillets
  (5 to 6 ounces each)

1 to 2 teaspoons sesame seeds,
  for serving

1 scallion (white and light green
  parts), thinly sliced, for serving

I feel like tilapia just popped up out of nowhere in the last few years. One day it just appeared in my local fish market and I figured I'd give it a try. Well, honey, it quickly became my go-to whitefish. It is so versatile I can do near about anything with it and I find it's satisfying and delicious. This preparation has an Asian influence that marries the sweet and salty flavors I love so dearly. Because the fish is broiled, the sweet orange juice caramelizes on the fish. It is so darn good.

1. In a shallow bowl or pie plate, whisk together the ginger, sesame oil, soy sauce, garlic, and orange juice. Add the tilapia, turning to coat all over with the marinade. Cover and let it sit at room temperature for 15 minutes.

2. Position an oven rack 5 to 6 inches from the heat. Preheat the broiler to high.

3. Remove the fillets from the marinade and place on a rimmed baking sheet. Broil the fish for 5 minutes per side, until flaky and opaque. Serve sprinkled with the sesame seeds and scallion.

Serves 4

Baked Mackerel with Sweet Bell Peppers and Red Wine Vinegar

I find firm, meaty, and good-for-you mackerel is the kind of fish that stands up well next to strong flavors. And that's exactly what you'll find in this recipe. Sweet bell peppers, fragrant oregano, and zinging red wine vinegar are a power-packed combo that could overpower a less assertive fish. But here, they work so well together.

1. Preheat the oven to 375°F. Line a rimmed baking sheet with aluminum foil.

2. Season the mackerel with the cumin, chili powder, 1 teaspoon of the salt, and the pepper. Brush the fish with 4 teaspoons of the oil. Transfer to the prepared baking sheet and bake until the fish is opaque and flakes easily when pressed with a fork, about 10 minutes.

3. Meanwhile, heat a large nonstick skillet over high heat until hot. Add the remaining 2 teaspoons oil and the bell peppers. Cook, tossing occasionally, until the bell peppers are tender and golden, about 10 minutes. Season with the oregano and the remaining ½ teaspoon salt and more pepper if you like. Cook for 30 seconds. Pour in the vinegar, toss with the bell peppers, and remove from heat. Serve the mackerel topped with the bell peppers.

Serves 4

1½ pounds mackerel fillet, cut into 4 equal portions

1 teaspoon ground cumin

½ teaspoon chili powder

1½ teaspoons salt

¼ teaspoon freshly ground black pepper, plus more to taste

6 teaspoons olive oil

3 medium red or yellow bell peppers, cut into ¼-inch strips

1½ teaspoons chopped fresh oregano or ½ teaspoon dried

2 teaspoons red wine vinegar

8

Vegetables and Side Dishes

One day, not too far back, I looked down at my dinner and realized that I had it all wrong. My plate was jam-packed full with a big old hunk of meat loaf, a hearty helping of mac and cheese, and a tiny portion of green beans cooked in bacon fat. Everything I had been hearing about eating right clicked into place, and I realized right then and there that I needed to rethink my plate. And so a new phase in my life began. I set about doubling the green foods I prepare, sticking with a smaller portion of meat, and either skipping the carbs altogether or relegating them to a supporting role. Of all the lifestyle changes I have made in the past year or so, this has had the most impact.

Because of this change, I needed some new and interesting ways to dress up my veggies. First and foremost, I have got to love what I'm eating. Steamed green beans and tomato salad are fine now and again, but if I was going to stick to a better-for-me diet, I was going to have to add interest to the greener side of life. And that's where this chapter comes into the story. I think this is the most interesting vegetable and sides chapter I have ever put together. Each page is jumping with fresh ways to make you want to eat the veggies on the plate first. Why, there's so much character in this chapter, I almost hesitate to call these recipes sides.

I've always loved a good cobbler. Fruit and sugar with a biscuit topping offers a lot to love. So I thought, why not create a cobbler that is filled with vegetables? My *Veggie Cobbler* (page 252) is a great way to get a whole variety of vegetables in without even realizing you are doing something so good for your body. This clever recipe features eggplant, zucchini, and squash, all tucked in under a cheesy, buttery-tasting biscuit topping. Serve it as a side dish or an entrée for vegetarians.

For an elegant dinner party, where things can really spin out of control on the calorie front, I like to serve **Zucchini Boats with Tomato, Rice, and Olives** (page 248). The zucchinis are the boats and I stuff them with tomatoes, rice (brown or white), and olives. They make for a fabulous presentation on the plate, and because they catch your eye, you can't help but dig into them first.

Of course, the delicious classics remain. I'd be lost without **Best Braised Southern Greens** (page 225), **Tomato Pie** (page 226), or **Stewed Okra and Tomatoes** (page 235). These Southern classics are not only an important part of my diet, they're an important part of my identity. I grew up on these dishes. All I needed to do was tailor them for my new lifestyle, nipping away at some of the fat. It was surprisingly easy because I was starting out with such good-for-you ingredients.

Wherever possible, I choose sweet potatoes over regular potatoes now. Sweet potatoes' low glycemic index makes them much better for you. And they taste so darn good too! **Mashed Sweet Potatoes with Bourbon** (page 230) helps me miss regular potatoes just a little bit less. My classic sweet potato balls are still in my diet; they've just been reborn as **Nutty Sweet Potato Balls** (page 229), minus the giant marshmallow and a whole load of sugar.

I'm never going back to the old plate I used to pile high because I'm enjoying this way of eating just too much. I'm rediscovering old mainstays and uncovering a few new favorites along the way.

Best Braised Southern Greens

The pot liquor in this braised collards dish is so rich, smoky, and delicious that I drank so much the first time I made it that I almost forgot about the greens! Oh, but you do not want to forget these luscious, silky greens. They pick up the smoky flavor from the turkey wing and the bacon and are made awesomely delicious with a good shot of hot sauce and a healthy dash of my House Seasoning. What I don't use anymore in my greens is a whole stick of butter! In fact, there's not even a tablespoon in this here recipe and I don't even miss it. Now, how 'bout that?

1. In a large pot, cook the bacon over medium heat until crisp, about 5 minutes. If you are using turkey bacon, grease the pot with cooking spray before cooking the bacon. Add the onion and stir for 30 seconds, until fragrant.

2. Add the turkey wing, House Seasoning, hot sauce, and 6 cups water. Bring to a boil, then reduce the heat to medium-low and simmer, uncovered, for 15 minutes. Add the greens, cover, and simmer, stirring occasionally, for 45 minutes. Before serving, taste the greens and the pot liquor and add a pinch more House Seasoning, if you'd like.

Serves 6

2 turkey or regular bacon slices, chopped

1 large Vidalia or other sweet onion, chopped

1 smoked turkey wing (¼ pound)

2 teaspoons Paula Deen's House Seasoning (see page 6)

1 teaspoon hot sauce

2 bunches collard greens (2 pounds), stems removed and leaves coarsely chopped

SMOKY FLAVOR
I used to always use ham hocks to get great smoky flavor into my recipes. More often than not these days, I use smoked turkey wings or necks. They impart the smokiness I want without the extra fat.

Tomato Pie

All-purpose flour

1 batch Paula's New Flaky
    Piecrust (see page 325)
    or 1 9-inch unbaked
    prepared piecrust

3 ripe beefsteak tomatoes

Salt and freshly ground
    black pepper to taste

10 fresh basil leaves, chopped

½ cup chopped scallions
    (white and light green parts)

½ cup shredded mozzarella
    cheese

½ cup shredded Cheddar cheese

½ cup regular or light sour cream

¼ cup regular or light mayonnaise

Because I've cut the cheese in my tomato pie in half, I find the sweetness of the tomatoes really shines through. The pie is still creamy and cheesy, but I find it's a whole lot brighter because the tomatoes are now the real stars of the show.

1. Preheat the oven to 350°F.

2. Dust a work surface with a small handful of flour. Roll the dough into a 12-inch round about ¼ inch thick. Use it to line a 9-inch pie plate, folding over the excess edges of the dough and crimping them if you like. Chill in the refrigerator for 30 minutes or up to overnight (cover lightly with plastic wrap if chilling for more than 2 hours). If you are using a prepared piecrust, skip this step.

3. Slice the tomatoes in half lengthwise and core them. Squeeze out any seeds and liquid. Thinly slice the tomatoes and place them in a colander in the sink. Sprinkle with salt and let them drain for 10 minutes. Once drained, pat the slices gently with paper towels.

4. Layer the tomato slices, basil, and scallions in the prepared piecrust and season to taste with salt and pepper. In a medium bowl, combine the mozzarella, Cheddar, sour cream, and mayonnaise. Spread the cheese mixture in an even layer on top of the tomatoes and bake for 30 to 35 minutes, until lightly browned. Let the pie cool slightly and cut into slices. Serve warm or at room temperature.

Serves 8

New No. 7 Yams

It may be a little confusing, but we Southerners like to call our sweet potatoes yams. So when you're fixing to pull together my New No. 7 Yams, it's actually sweet potatoes you'll be needing. This dish rivals my Ol' No. 7 Yams, I tell you. The cinnamon, nutmeg, orange, and bourbon that made the old version so delicious are still here in my new adaptation. What's not there is two-thirds of the sugar and half the fat. I cooked these for Michael recently and he gave them his seal of approval. They are still that good.

4 large sweet potatoes
  (about 2½ pounds)

⅓ cup packed light brown sugar

⅓ cup bourbon

⅓ cup water

2 tablespoons (¼ stick)
  unsalted butter

1 cinnamon stick

¼ teaspoon freshly grated
  nutmeg

1 long strip orange peel

1. Preheat the oven to 400°F.

2. Cut a slit in the sweet potatoes and place on a rimmed baking sheet. Bake the potatoes for 1 hour, until they are soft to the touch.

3. Remove from the oven and let the sweet potatoes cool slightly before removing the skin. Reduce the oven temperature to 350°F.

4. Meanwhile, in a saucepan, combine the brown sugar, bourbon, water, butter, cinnamon stick, nutmeg, and orange peel. Bring to a boil, then reduce the heat and simmer until the sauce is reduced by half, 15 to 20 minutes.

5. Slice the potatoes ½ inch thick and layer them into a medium casserole dish or a square 9-inch baking dish. Throw out the orange peel, pour the syrup over the potatoes, and return to the oven to bake until bubbly, about 30 minutes.

Serves 8

MAKE AHEAD
For no-fuss entertaining, I like to cook the sweet potatoes the night before. Then I just have to slice them up on the day and toss them in the oven with all those festive flavors.

Nutty Sweet Potato Balls

Not to toot my own horn, but my sweet potato balls have reached a sort of legendary status in my family. So when I told them that I was going to have to rethink this dish, you'd have thought Christmas had been cancelled the way they went on. When I unveiled my new creation, a collective sigh was exhaled. The sweet potato balls are still sweet, though I cut down on the sugar, and now that sweetness is balanced with a crunchy, nutty coating and a surprise toasted pecan in the center.

1. Preheat the oven to 400°F.

2. Place the sweet potatoes in a medium baking dish and bake until they are soft to the touch, about 1 hour. Reduce the oven temperature to 375°F and line a rimmed baking sheet with aluminum foil. Spray the foil with cooking spray. (The potatoes can be baked the day before and kept covered in the fridge with their skins on.)

3. When the sweet potatoes are cool enough to handle, peel them. Place them in a large bowl and mash well. Stir in the brown sugar, flour, orange zest, orange juice, and nutmeg.

4. Place all but 16 pecans in a food processor and pulse until they are mostly finely chopped but still contain some larger chunks. In a medium bowl, toss the chopped pecans with the coconut and cinnamon.

5. Using lightly greased hands, form the sweet potato mixture into 16 evenly sized balls, each about 2 inches in diameter. Insert a whole pecan into each ball, roll the ball between your palms to smooth the surface again, and then roll the balls in the chopped pecan mixture. Place on the prepared baking sheet. Bake until browned, 15 to 20 minutes.

Makes 16 balls / Serves 8

4 large sweet potatoes (about 2½ pounds)

⅓ cup packed light brown sugar

2 tablespoons all-purpose flour

1 teaspoon finely grated orange zest

1 tablespoon fresh orange juice

½ teaspoon freshly grated nutmeg

1½ cups pecans, lightly toasted

3 tablespoons sweetened shredded coconut

1 teaspoon ground cinnamon

◀ Gus is thinking, "Why the heck am I not driving?" VEGETABLES AND SIDE DISHES

Mashed Sweet Potatoes with Bourbon

4 large sweet potatoes (about 2½ pounds), peeled and cut into 1½-inch pieces

2 tablespoons (¼ stick) unsalted butter

1 tablespoon maple syrup

2 tablespoons bourbon

Finely grated zest and juice of 1 orange

½ teaspoon ground cinnamon

Salt and freshly ground black pepper to taste

There's nothing quite like a good hit of booze to liven up a plate of food. Sure, there's a lot to love about mashed sweet potatoes made even sweeter with the help of maple syrup and orange juice. But there's oh so much more to love in mashed potatoes that offer a kick of bourbon. Honey, this dish is most certainly for the grown-ups!

1. In a large pot, cover the potatoes with cold salted water. Bring to a boil over medium-high heat and cook until the potatoes are very tender, 10 to 12 minutes. Drain the potatoes well.

2. Return the potatoes to the hot pot and add the butter, maple syrup, bourbon, orange zest, orange juice, and cinnamon. Using a potato masher or a hand-held mixer, beat the potato mixture at medium-low speed until the mash is the consistency you like. Season to taste with salt and pepper, mound into a pretty serving bowl, and serve hot.

Serves 4 to 6

Twice-Baked Potatoes with Variations

Your eyes are not deceiving you. Gone is the entire stick of butter I used to put in my baked potatoes. But the potato, well that just had to stay. There is so much that can be done with the humble potato. And this recipe is a testament to that fact. Whatever you can think of, it will probably taste good in there. Every type of cheese, vegetable, meat, or seafood can be stuffed back into that potato along with the creamy mashed insides. Follow these simple baking directions and let your imagination go hog wild.

1. Preheat the oven to 425°F.

2. Prick the potatoes lightly in several places with a fork. Wrap each potato in aluminum foil. Place on a small rimmed baking sheet and bake for 1 hour, until tender. Remove the potatoes from the sheet and lightly grease the baking sheet with cooking spray. Reduce the oven temperature to 350°F.

3. Carefully, as the potatoes will be hot, remove the foil. Slice off the top one third of each potato lengthwise, and discard. Gently scoop out the insides of the potatoes with a spoon (leaving enough so the potato skin will stay intact and not tear) and place in a medium bowl.

4. Stir in the butter, ¼ cup of the Cheddar, the cream cheese, sour cream, and scallions. Mash with a fork to combine and season with salt and pepper. Gently stuff the mixture back into the potato skins, being careful not to break them. Place the potatoes on the prepared baking sheet and top with the remaining ¼ cup Cheddar. Bake until the potato tops are browned and the inside is heated through, about 30 minutes.

Serves 4

4 large baking potatoes (about 3 pounds)

1 tablespoon unsalted butter

½ cup shredded Cheddar cheese

¼ cup (2 ounces) low-fat cream cheese (Neufchâtel), at room temperature

¼ cup regular or light sour cream

2 scallions (white and light green parts), thinly sliced

Salt and freshly ground black pepper to taste

For a spicy potato:
Substitute Monterey Jack cheese for the Cheddar cheese and add ¼ cup chopped (and drained) pickled jalapeño peppers.

For a crunchier potato:
Add 2 slices cooked and crumbled turkey or regular bacon to the filling. Top the potatoes with ¼ cup whole-wheat or regular panko bread crumbs and a drizzle of olive oil before baking.

For a main-dish potato:
Add 1 pound cooked and chopped shrimp to the filling.

For a meaty potato:
Add 1 cup chopped ham to the filling. Substitute grated Parmesan or Gruyère for the Cheddar cheese.

Oven-Fried Green Tomatoes

½ cup buttermilk

1 large egg

⅔ cup fine cornmeal

½ teaspoon salt

⅛ teaspoon cayenne pepper

2 large green tomatoes, sliced into ¼-inch-thick rounds

I reckon I'd have to give up my citizenship in the South if I ever fully gave up on fried green tomatoes. So I still indulge in them every now and again. But more often than not, these new ones are the green tomatoes I enjoy. My Grandmama Paul always went in for a cornmeal crust on her fried green tomatoes, but I always liked mine with a flour coating. For these oven-baked tomatoes, I went back to Grandmama Paul's way and decided to coat them with cornmeal. And that worked a treat. They are crispy crunchy on the outside and tangy and juicy on the inside.

1. Preheat the oven to 425°F. Line a large rimmed baking sheet with parchment paper.

2. In a shallow bowl or pie plate, whisk together the buttermilk and egg. In a separate bowl or pie plate, whisk together the cornmeal, salt, and cayenne. Dip each tomato slice into the buttermilk, letting any excess drip off. Then dip the slices into the cornmeal mixture, turning to coat evenly and pressing to adhere. Gently shake each slice to remove any excess.

3. Arrange the slices on the prepared baking sheet. Coat the top of the slices with cooking spray. Bake for 10 minutes, then flip to the other side of the slices and coat with cooking spray. Bake for 10 minutes more and flip again. Bake for 5 minutes more until lightly browned. Serve piping hot.

Serves 4

Crispy Baked Eggplant with Parmesan

1 large eggplant
  (about 1½ pounds)

Salt

1½ cups all-purpose flour

3 large eggs

Tabasco sauce to taste

1 cup grated Parmesan cheese

1 cup plain bread crumbs

Now tell me, is there anything better than a Parmesan crust? I just love the way a crunchy coating wraps around the tender baked vegetable inside. And eggplant is at its creamy best when it's baked, making for the perfect contrast between coating and filling.

1. Preheat the oven to 425°F. Lightly grease two rimmed baking sheets with cooking spray.

2. Slice the eggplant into ¼-inch thick slices. Place the eggplant in a colander set in the sink and generously season with salt. Let the eggplant sit for 15 minutes.

3. In a shallow bowl, pour in the flour. In another shallow bowl, whisk together the eggs and a couple shakes of Tabasco, depending on how spicy you like it. In a third shallow bowl, whisk together the Parmesan and bread crumbs until combined.

4. Pat the eggplant slices dry. Dip each slice into the flour and then the egg mixture. Let any excess egg drip off and dredge the slices in the Parmesan mixture until both sides are well coated. Place the eggplant on the prepared baking sheets.

5. Lightly spray the top of each eggplant slice with cooking spray. Bake for 25 minutes, until crispy and golden brown.

Serves 4

ACT FAST
Bring this veggie side to the table just as quickly as you can. That way the crust will stay as crisp as possible.

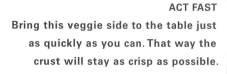

Stewed Okra and Tomatoes

I like okra fried, pickled, and roasted. But I love okra when it's stewed with tomatoes. This is a low country classic, and I swear it can't be beat. Be sure to cook the okra good and long so that it helps to thicken the tomato sauce it sits in. And make sure you've got some biscuits or corn bread on hand to sop up every last drop on your plate.

1. In a medium skillet, heat the oil over medium heat. Add the onion and bell pepper and cook until softened, 7 to 10 minutes. Stir in the garlic and cook for 1 minute.

2. Stir in the tomatoes, okra, chicken broth, and salt. Simmer gently until most of the liquid has evaporated and the okra is very tender, 30 to 40 minutes. If the liquid evaporates too quickly, add water ¼ cup at a time, as needed. Season with hot sauce and serve.

Serves 4

1 tablespoon canola oil

½ cup chopped onion

¼ cup chopped green bell pepper

2 garlic cloves, finely chopped

1 can (14½ ounces) no-salt-added diced tomatoes

¼ pound fresh okra, cut into ½-inch-thick slices

⅔ cup low-sodium chicken or vegetable broth

½ teaspoon salt

Hot sauce to taste

HOW DOES IT DO THAT?
So many people ask me about okra. And the question I get the most is: How does it thicken up a sauce? Well, that thickening power is thanks to the gooey substance around the seeds that's made up of protein, carbs, and fiber. I like to think of it as veggie cornstarch. That's what makes okra so special in stews like this and in one of New Orleans's most famous dishes, gumbo.

The Lady's New Succotash

Among the ham hock, the bouillon, and the seasoned salt, this recipe used to contain a mountain of sodium. Well, I cut that right back. And you know what? This is still one of my favorite sides at dinnertime. It's a colorful medley of veggies, cooked down with a smoky turkey wing and a shot of hot sauce.

1. In a medium saucepan, combine the turkey wing, House Seasoning, and 4 cups water. Bring to a boil over medium-high heat. Reduce the heat to medium-low and simmer, covered, for 1 hour. Remove the turkey wing and reserve.

2. Add the beans and hot sauce to the turkey broth and bring to a boil over medium-high heat. Reduce the heat to medium-low, cover, and simmer until the beans are tender, about 15 minutes. Remove the beans with a slotted spoon and reserve the broth.

3. Meanwhile, when the turkey wing is cool enough to handle, pick the meat off the bone, discarding the bone and skin. Chop the turkey meat.

4. In a large skillet, combine the drained beans, corn, okra, oil, turkey meat, and 1½ cups of the broth. Bring to a simmer over medium heat, then reduce the heat to medium-low and cook, covered, for 15 minutes. Add the tomatoes, parsley, and more House Seasoning if you think the succotash needs it. Cook until the tomatoes are hot. Serve with more hot sauce, if you like.

Serves 10

1 piece smoked turkey wing (½ pound)

½ teaspoon Paula Deen's House Seasoning (see page 6), plus more to taste

1 package (16 ounces) frozen lima beans or butter beans

¼ teaspoon hot sauce, plus more for serving

1 package (16 ounces) frozen corn

2 cups sliced okra, fresh or frozen

2 tablespoons olive oil

4 tomatoes, cut into chunks

⅓ cup chopped fresh parsley

Hot-Roasted Okra

1 pound fresh okra,
stem ends trimmed

2 to 3 teaspoons olive oil

Salt and freshly ground
black pepper to taste

Fried okra is truly heaven sent! But, honey, I can't eat it every day. That's why I developed this hot-roasted okra recipe. By cooking the okra at a high temperature in the oven, it gets nice and crispy on the outside while staying tender on the inside. I love to snack on these whenever I've got fresh okra in the fridge.

1. Preheat the oven to 450°F. Line a rimmed baking sheet with parchment paper. Be sure that the baking sheet is large enough to hold the okra in one layer.

2. In a large bowl, toss the okra with the oil and salt and pepper to taste to coat well. Using a slotted spoon, transfer the okra to the prepared baking sheet. Roast for 15 to 20 minutes, shaking the pan once or twice to prevent the okra from sticking, until the okra is browned and tender.

Serves 4

Mediterranean Cauliflower Casserole

It turns out casseroles don't always have to be creamy. Who knew? This casserole features the flavors of Greece: salty kalamata olives, sweet tomatoes, and a touch of feta cheese to top it all off. Can you guess who loves his cauliflower this way? Yep, it's none other than my boy Bobby.

1 head cauliflower (2 pounds), cut into florets

2 tablespoons olive oil

1 onion, chopped

1 garlic clove, chopped

1 can (14½ ounces) no-salt-added diced tomatoes

½ cup kalamata or other black olives, pitted and coarsely chopped

Salt and freshly ground black pepper to taste

4 ounces feta cheese, crumbled

1. Position an oven rack in the upper third of the oven. Preheat the oven to 450°F. Lightly grease a 2- to 3-quart baking dish with cooking spray.

2. In a medium pot of boiling, salted water, cook the cauliflower until just tender, about 5 minutes. Drain well.

3. In a large skillet, heat the oil over medium-high heat. Add the onion and cook until soft, about 5 minutes. Add the garlic and cook for 30 seconds. Reduce the heat to medium, add the tomatoes, and let them bubble away, stirring frequently, until the sauce is thickened, 8 to 10 minutes. Stir in the olives and season lightly with salt (the feta will add saltiness) and generously with pepper.

4. Scrape the cauliflower into the prepared baking dish, cover with the tomato sauce, and scatter the feta over the top. Bake until browned and bubbly, about 20 minutes.

Serves 8

Creamy Peas and Ham

4 tablespoons mild goat cheese
or low-fat cream cheese
(Neufchâtel)

¼ cup milk

1 teaspoon dried minced onion

1 package (10 ounces)
frozen peas, thawed

2 ounces ham, cut into ¼-inch
chunks (about ⅓ cup)

Salt and freshly ground
black pepper to taste

My goodness, this is a creamy concoction. I love it so. A little bit goes a long way, so think moderation when you're dishing this out. As I always say, it's about moderation, not deprivation.

In a medium saucepan over medium heat, bring the goat cheese, milk, and dried onion to a simmer and cook, stirring, until the cheese is completely melted. Add the peas and ham and cook, stirring, for 3 minutes, until heated through. Season to taste with salt and pepper. To thicken up the sauce a bit, let it stand for 3 minutes before serving.

Serves 4

Grilled Corn
with Parmesan
and Mayonnaise

6 ears of corn

3 tablespoons grated Parmesan
cheese

3 tablespoons regular
or light mayonnaise

*In the summer I enjoy this easy grilled corn dish as often as I can.
In the winter, I use the broiler to re-create the char-grilled flavor.
I like to sit this side next to a juicy steak or some tangy barbecue
chicken. Sometimes it's the simplest things in life that taste the best.*

1. Grease a grill grate by brushing it with oil. Preheat the grill
   to medium-high.

2. Remove the husks and silk from the corn. Place the corn
   on the grill and cook, covered, for 10 to 15 minutes, turning
   occasionally, until tender.

3. Meanwhile, whisk together the Parmesan and mayonnaise.

4. Remove the corn from the grill and spread each ear evenly
   with the Parmesan mixture. Serve just as soon as possible.

Serves 6

DON'T FORGET THE BROILER
There's no need to give up on grilled food during
the cold winter months. If you can't use your grill,
the broiler will get you pretty close. You may miss
some of the smoky flavor from the grill, but you'll get
the same style of high-heat cooking that you get outside.

Brussels Sprouts and Bacon

Is there any more perfect pairing than sprouts and bacon? That is a match made in heaven, I tell you! When cooked just right, the sprouts bring a mild cabbage flavor to the dish and the bacon brings the salty, porky highlights. And done right means no overcooking the Brussels sprouts, y'all. It can't be said enough, an overcooked sprout is gray and bitter and you do not want to serve that at your table. So keep a close eye on sprouts when they're on the boil, get them out as soon as you can pierce them with a fork, and you'll be good to go.

1 pound Brussels sprouts

1 teaspoon olive oil

1 turkey or regular bacon slice, chopped

Salt and freshly ground black pepper to taste

1. Halve each Brussels sprout and remove any tough stems or outer leaves. Bring a large pot of salted water to a boil. Add the sprouts and bring the water back to a gentle boil. Test a sprout after 3 to 4 minutes, depending on size, for tenderness. It should be easily pierced with a fork or paring knife. If it's still raw, continue boiling, checking every minute. The sprouts should not be overcooked.

2. In a medium saucepan, heat the oil over medium-high heat. Add the bacon and cook until crisp, about 5 minutes. Add the cooked Brussels sprouts to the pan and continue to cook until browned on the outside, 3 to 5 minutes. Season to taste with salt and pepper and serve.

Serves 4

BROADEN YOUR HORIZONS
I make it a point to try new vegetables when I come across them. And I am so happy for it. I usually end up discovering my next food obsession. If you have a memory of gray Brussels sprouts from your childhood as so many do, I highly recommend giving them another try. You may just get hooked!

Baked Beans

I simply cannot live without baked beans. And now I don't have to!
Making them from scratch like this means I control the sugar,
the carbs, and the sodium.

1. Preheat the oven to 350°F. Grease a 1-quart baking dish
   with cooking spray.

2. In a medium skillet, cook the bacon over medium heat until
   crisp, about 5 minutes. If you are using turkey bacon, grease
   the skillet with cooking spray before cooking the bacon.
   Drain the bacon on a paper towel–lined plate.

3. Drain off and discard the fat from the skillet and set the pan
   over medium heat. Add the oil and onion and cook, stirring,
   until soft, about 5 minutes. Remove from the heat. Stir in the
   drained bacon, the beans, ketchup, syrup, yellow mustard,
   dry mustard, and pepper to taste.

4. Spoon the bean mixture into the prepared baking dish.
   Cover loosely with aluminum foil and bake until the edges
   are bubbly and the filling is hot, about 25 minutes.

Serves 4

3 turkey or regular bacon slices,
  chopped

1 tablespoon olive oil

1 onion, finely chopped

1 can (15 ounces) navy beans,
  rinsed, ¼ cup bean liquid
  reserved

3 tablespoons regular or
  reduced-sugar ketchup

2 tablespoons maple syrup

1 tablespoon yellow or
  Dijon mustard

1 teaspoon dry mustard

Freshly ground black pepper
  to taste

FREEZE IT
Opening up a can was a little easier when I was craving the
taste of baked beans, but it was just not good for me. To make
things a little easier on me, I usually make double or even
triple batches of my homemade baked beans. Then I freeze
them in small containers to take out whenever I get a
hankering. They'll keep in the freezer for up to 6 months.

Sautéed Turnips and Greens

2 bunches turnips
(about 1½ pounds),
greens attached

1 teaspoon olive oil

1 slice turkey or regular bacon,
cut into 1-inch pieces

Pinch of crushed red
pepper flakes

White wine vinegar to taste

Salt and freshly ground
black pepper to taste

Sweet turnips, salty bacon, tangy vinegar, and a pinch of spicy red pepper flakes come together to make this dish a down-home classic. In the wintertime, I don't think there's a week that goes by when I don't have a pot of turnips and greens cooking up for dinner. If you happen to be one of those turnip skeptics, give this dish a try and I guarantee you'll soon be singing the praises of this humble root.

1. Trim the roots of the turnips and remove the greens at the stem. Thoroughly wash the turnips. If the turnips are not similar sizes, quarter or halve them to make them a consistent size. Remove the stems from the leaves and discard. Place the leaves in a large bowl of cold water. Use your hands to swish around the greens so all the dirt is dislodged and falls to the bottom of the bowl. You may need to repeat this step with fresh water a couple of times until the greens are completely grit free.

2. In a large saucepan, heat the oil over medium heat. Cook the bacon until crisp, about 5 minutes. Add the turnips and cook, stirring, for 5 minutes.

3. Add the greens, ⅓ cup water, and red pepper flakes to the pan. Bring to a simmer and cover with a lid. Simmer for 10 minutes, or until the turnips are tender and easily pierced with a knife. Uncover and simmer 5 to 10 minutes more, or until the water is evaporated. Add the vinegar to taste. Season to taste with salt and black pepper and serve.

Serves 4

New-Fashioned Green Bean Casserole

If y'all recall, I used to top this casserole with a full cup of Cheddar and an entire can of French-fried onions. Well, gone is the Cheddar and gone are the fried onions. In their place, I sprinkle over some lovely smoked almonds. And the smoky, salty nuts take this humble dish to new heights.

1. Preheat the oven to 350°F. Lightly grease a 2-quart baking dish with cooking spray.

2. In a large skillet, heat the oil over medium-high heat. Add the mushrooms and onion and cook, stirring frequently, until the mushrooms have released their liquid and the liquid has evaporated, about 5 minutes. If you are using sherry, add it now and let it bubble away completely, about 30 seconds. Add the green beans, soup, milk, and House Seasoning to taste.

3. Scrape into the prepared dish and bake for 20 minutes. Top with the almonds and bake for 10 minutes more, until the casserole is bubbly and the almonds are fragrant.

Serves 6

2 tablespoons vegetable oil

8 ounces button mushrooms, trimmed and sliced

½ cup chopped onion

1 tablespoon sherry (optional)

1 pound green beans, trimmed, cooked, and drained

1 can (10¾ ounces) low-fat or regular condensed cream of mushroom soup

⅓ cup milk

Paula Deen's House Seasoning to taste (see page 6)

⅓ cup smoked almonds, chopped

Zucchini Boats
with Tomato, Rice, and Olives

2 medium zucchini,
  sliced in half lengthwise

Olive oil, for brushing

1 cup part-skim mozzarella
  cheese

¾ cup cooked brown or white rice

2 tablespoons tomato sauce

2 tablespoons chopped
  black olives

2 tablespoons chopped fresh basil

½ teaspoon Paula Deen's House
  Seasoning (see page 6)

2 dashes hot sauce, or to taste

These zucchini boats look so pretty sitting next to your main meal. They have a way of dressing up the plate that makes you think it's a special occasion. But here's the secret: They are so easy to prepare. Whenever I've got some leftover rice in the fridge, I make these little beauties. And when I set them out on the table, I just wait for the applause.

1. Preheat the oven to 400°F.

2. Brush the cut sides of the zucchini with the oil and place, cut side down, on a rimmed baking sheet. Bake for 15 minutes, until tender. Using a teaspoon, gently scoop the flesh from the zucchini into a medium bowl, being real careful to leave the shells intact. Lower the oven temperature to 350°F.

3. To the zucchini flesh, add ¾ cup of the mozzarella, the rice, tomato sauce, olives, basil, House Seasoning, and hot sauce and mix well. Fill the zucchini shells with the mixture and top with the remaining ¼ cup mozzarella. Bake until the cheese is melted and the stuffing is heated through, 10 to 12 minutes.

Serves 4

MORE OPTIONS
Don't limit yourself to zucchini boats. There's a great big world of veggies out there. I change this recipe up by using summer squash or baby eggplants.

Green Beans Almondine

Cooking vegetables only until they're crisp helps to keep my veggies vitamin rich. These green beans stay bright green and snappy, then I toss them with butter, almonds, and shallots just until they are coated and glistening.

1. In a large pot of boiling salted water, cook the beans until just tender, 3 to 5 minutes. Drain well.

2. In a large skillet, melt the butter over medium heat. Add the almonds and toast until pale golden, about 2 minutes. Add the shallot and cook until translucent, about 1 minute. Toss in the beans and cook until warmed through. Season the beans with the salt and pepper and serve.

Serves 4

1 pound green beans, trimmed

1 tablespoon unsalted butter

⅓ cup slivered almonds

1 shallot, thinly sliced

½ teaspoon salt

Freshly ground black pepper to taste

◀ **1** *Jamie, Bobby, and me with our newest baby, Paula Deen's Family Kitchen, at The Island in Pigeon Forge, Tennessee.*
2 *So thankful for family and friends celebrating opening night: Aunt Peggy, center stage, right where she belongs, with friends Phil and Susan "Bubbles" Green.*
3 *My brother Bubba's best gift to me, my niece Corrie.*

FILLING

2 tablespoons olive oil

1 small eggplant, cut into ¾-inch chunks (about 4 cups)

1 zucchini, cut into ¾-inch chunks (about 1½ cups)

1 yellow squash, cut into ¾-inch chunks (about 1½ cups)

1 small onion, chopped

1 red bell pepper, cut into ¾-inch chunks (about ¾ cup)

3 garlic cloves, finely chopped

1 teaspoon salt

½ teaspoon freshly ground black pepper

1 can (14½ ounces) no-salt-added diced tomatoes

1 can (8 ounces) tomato sauce

2 teaspoons Italian seasoning

BISCUIT TOPPING

1 cup all-purpose flour

½ cup grated Parmesan cheese

1½ teaspoons baking powder

¼ teaspoon salt

3 tablespoons cold unsalted butter, cut into small bits

1 large egg, lightly beaten

⅓ cup milk

Veggie Cobbler

Your typical cobbler is the marriage of a sweet fruit filling with a flaky biscuit topping. I thought it was high time veggies got in on that action. What's not to love about a sautéed eggplant, zucchini, squash, onion, and bell pepper filling topped with a cheesy biscuit topping? And if you like, feel free to substitute half whole-wheat flour for white in the biscuit topping.

1. Preheat the oven to 375°F. Lightly grease a 2-quart baking dish with cooking spray.

2. To make the filling: In a large skillet, heat 1 tablespoon of the oil over medium-high heat. Add half the eggplant, zucchini, squash, onion, bell pepper, and garlic. Cook until the vegetables are lightly browned, about 5 minutes. Transfer to a bowl. Add the remaining 1 tablespoon oil and the remaining vegetables to the skillet. Cook until lightly browned, about 5 minutes.

3. Return the first batch of vegetables to the skillet with the second half of the vegetables and season with salt and black pepper. Stir in the diced tomatoes, tomato sauce, and Italian seasoning. Reduce the heat to medium-low. Cover the skillet and cook until the vegetables are crisp-tender, about 10 minutes.

4. Meanwhile, to make the biscuit topping: In a large bowl, whisk together the flour, Parmesan, baking powder, and salt. Cut in the butter with a fork or your hands until the mixture resembles coarse meal. Stir in the egg and milk until just combined.

5. Scrape the vegetable mixture into the prepared baking dish. Drop the biscuit dough by large spoonfuls over the vegetables. There will be spaces in between the biscuits. Bake until the biscuits are golden brown and the vegetables are bubbling, 20 to 25 minutes. Let the cobbler cool for about 10 minutes before serving.

Serves 8

Southern Potatoes Gratiné

Here's a crazy fun fact I think you'll enjoy. Did you know that Velveeta is actually lower in calories and fat per serving than Cheddar cheese? Well, my goodness, did that surprise me. And I took full advantage of that knowledge by using it here in my gratiné. It's so smooth and melty, I just couldn't resist the opportunity to use it in one of my veggie casseroles.

2 pounds russet or Idaho potatoes
(about 3 medium potatoes),
scrubbed

1 cup chopped scallions
(white and light green parts)

¾ cup milk

½ cup low-sodium chicken broth

1 tablespoon all-purpose flour

2 teaspoons Cajun seasoning

Salt to taste

4 ounces Velveeta,
cut into ½-inch cubes

¼ teaspoon sweet paprika

1. Preheat the oven to 375°F.

2. Slice the potatoes lengthwise into quarters, then cut crosswise into ¼-inch pieces.

3. In a 12 by 8-inch broiler-proof baking dish, toss the potatoes and the scallions together. In a small bowl, whisk together the milk, chicken broth, flour, and Cajun seasoning and add some salt, if you think it needs it. Pour the milk mixture over the potatoes, cover the dish with aluminum foil, and bake for 30 minutes, until the potatoes are tender.

4. Position an oven rack 4 to 6 inches from the heat. Preheat the broiler to high.

5. Remove the foil from the baking dish and top the potatoes with the Velveeta and paprika. Broil for 2 to 3 minutes, until browned and bubbly.

Serves 8

Sautéed Lima Beans and Vidalia Onions

3 tablespoons olive oil

1 turkey or regular bacon slice, chopped

1 large Vidalia onion (1 pound), thinly sliced

1 teaspoon Paula Deen's House Seasoning (see page 6), plus more to taste

1 package (16 ounces) frozen lima beans

Oh my, but this is comfort food at its finest! This dish boasts creamy beans, sweet caramelized Vidalia onions, and salty bacon to boot. Now I call that a whole lot to love.

1. In a large skillet with a lid, heat the oil over medium-high heat. Add the bacon and cook until colored, 1 to 2 minutes. Add the onions, stirring to coat with the oil. Reduce the heat to low, cover, and cook, stirring occasionally, until the onions are almost meltingly soft, about 30 minutes. Season to taste with the House Seasoning.

2. Meanwhile, in a medium saucepan, bring 3 cups of water and the 1 teaspoon House Seasoning to a boil. Add the lima beans and cook until tender, about 15 minutes. Drain the beans, reserving 1 tablespoon of the cooking water.

3. When the onions have finished cooking, add the lima beans and the reserved cooking water. Raise the heat to high and cook, stirring, for 5 minutes, until the onions are golden.

Serves 6

DRINK IT IN
I drink so much more water these days than I used to drink. That's because I found out water is one of the best gifts you can give your body. And when I remember to drink water throughout the day, I'm less tempted to snack between meals, so it actually controls my appetite.

Crispy Broiled Broccoli

There's nothing quite like broiling to bring out the natural sweetness of broccoli. The high heat causes the broccoli to caramelize and crisp up. All you need to do is toss the broccoli in a little olive oil and give it a sprinkling of seasoning and you have yourself a dish that's really something special.

1 pound broccoli

2 tablespoons olive oil

½ teaspoon sweet paprika

½ teaspoon salt

¼ teaspoon freshly ground black pepper

1. Separate the thick stems from the florets. Thinly slice the florets and stems into ¼-inch-thick slabs. Spread the broccoli on a large rimmed baking sheet. Toss with the oil, paprika, salt, and pepper.

2. Position an oven rack 4 to 6 inches from the heat. Preheat the broiler to high.

3. Place the baking sheet in the oven and broil for 3 minutes. Toss the broccoli and return to the oven until the broccoli is tender and lightly charred in places, about 3 minutes. Watch carefully to see that it does not burn. Serve hot or at room temperature.

Serves 4

9

Breakfast and Brunch

I'm sure you've heard it before: Breakfast is the most important meal of the day. And I couldn't agree more. I have always been a big believer in starting the day out with a healthy, hearty breakfast. Now with my type 2 diabetes diagnosis, breakfast has taken on even more importance in helping me keep my body running smoothly.

The first meal of the day is the fuel you need to get you going and keep you going until bedtime. Well, sure, there's coffee, but that will only get you so far. For real energy that will power you up for the long haul, listen to Paula and get yourself started with a good, healthy breakfast each and every morning.

Some mornings are busier than others and it can be a challenge to fix yourself up something tasty and healthy. For these days, I've got a few tricks up my sleeves that I'm going to pass on to you. Do you know how filling and delicious a smoothie can be? No? Well, neither did I. Until my dear, dear boy Bobby taught his mama a thing or two. Now I whip up smoothies all the time. They are delicious, sweet and creamy concoctions that give me all sorts of energy to get going. My *Fruity Yogurt Smoothie* (page 284) comes to you thanks to Bobby. It's got bananas, berries, yogurt, basically all your best breakfast ingredients pureed up into a handy shake that is out of this world. Add a little almond or peanut butter and you've got something really substantial to get you through to lunch.

I've also become a big believer in creating little packages for my eggs. That way, if I absolutely have to, I can take them with me out the door. Whether it be a **Breakfast Burrito** (page 277) or the **Ultimate Egg Sandwich** (page 271), these little parcels of protein are a great way to fit in a healthy meal in the morning.

One of the absolute best breakfasts you can fix yourself is oatmeal. Because I never can leave well enough alone, a plain old bowl of oats just won't cut it for me most mornings. So I went ahead and dreamed up sweet and luscious **Creamy Cinnamon Oatmeal Bake** (page 281). This is an oatmeal breakfast I think you can really look forward to.

Now, I've got to watch my carbs and especially sweetened carbs like prepackaged granola bars. That's why I like to make my own granola. On the weekends, I make up batches of loose granola and granola bars so that I have them handy during the busy workweek. **Cinnamon Apple Granola with Cranberries and Walnuts** (page 286) is a great example. It's basically another way of preparing oats with a little apple juice and honey to sweeten the deal. I love this granola with some creamy Greek yogurt dolloped on top. And all my grandkids, but especially little Henry Reed, love it with fresh strawberries and a drizzle of some more delicious honey.

Most of the time these are my breakfast choices and I'm just the picture of health. But every once in a while, I do like to splurge a little, especially if I'm having folks round for brunch. On those occasions, breakfast means treats like **All-New French Toast Casserole** (page 280), which still manages to be healthful because I sweeten it using only one tablespoon of maple syrup. With all the great taste the cinnamon, nutmeg, vanilla, and pecans add to the plate, the French toast really didn't need any more sweetening up.

Another brunch favorite features a former "everyday" food that I now call a "sometimes" food: grits. Sad for a Southerner to say, but with my diabetes diagnosis I learned that I really needed to moderate my intake of grits. So I save my famous **Eggs Baked with Grits and Ham** (page 264) for company. They say absence makes the heart grow fonder, and I've found that I appreciate this Southern grain even more, now that I don't have it every day.

All in all, I've made out pretty well with the changes to my breakfast menu. I've had to put some distance between me and a few old favorites, but I've also discovered so many new and exciting foods that I might never have stumbled upon had I not gone through this experience. And best of all, these new breakfast foods are making me feel so much better. I have more energy and I've never been stronger in my life. It's a pretty fantastic incentive to get up each morning and start the day out right.

Apple Pie Muesli

Apple pie in the morning! That sounds like my kind of start to the day. Fortunately, this little recipe provides all the great flavor of apple pie in a more healthful setting. I stir together oats, cinnamon, pecans, and a touch of brown sugar, and mix through fresh apple and yogurt.

1. In a medium bowl, combine the oats, brown sugar, cinnamon, pecans, and salt. Add the yogurt and apple and stir to combine. Refrigerate, covered, for at least 2 hours or up to overnight.

2. Serve sprinkled with more brown sugar and topped with a dollop of yogurt.

1 cup old-fashioned rolled oats

2 teaspoons brown sugar, plus more to taste

¾ teaspoon ground cinnamon

½ cup chopped pecans

Pinch of salt

1 cup low-fat Greek yogurt, plus more for serving

1 large apple, grated

Serves 2

Dutch Pancake with Applesauce

3 large eggs, lightly beaten

½ cup milk

½ cup all-purpose flour

¼ teaspoon freshly grated nutmeg

Pinch of salt

3 tablespoons unsalted butter

Confectioners' sugar, for sprinkling

Homemade Ginger Applesauce (see page 343), or store bought

I absolutely love Dutch pancakes, not only because they taste so good, but because they are a snap to make in the morning. You'll sometimes hear them called German pancakes or Dutch baby pancakes, but they're all basically the same thing—a simple popover baked in a skillet. All you do is mix up the batter, pour it into the pan, and bake until it puffs and browns. No hanging over the stove and flipping necessary. While I used to sweeten my Dutch pancakes with two entire cans of apple pie filling, I now sweeten them with a dusting of confectioners' sugar and some of my homemade applesauce on the side.

1. Preheat the oven to 425°F.

2. In a medium bowl, combine the eggs, milk, flour, nutmeg, and salt. Whisk lightly, leaving the batter a little lumpy.

3. In a 10-inch ovenproof skillet, melt the butter. When the pan is hot and the butter is fully melted, pour in the batter. Bake for 15 minutes, until the pancake is golden brown.

4. Remove the pancake from the oven and quickly sprinkle lightly with confectioners' sugar. Return to the oven for 2 minutes. Serve warm with applesauce and more confectioners' sugar, if you like.

Serves 2 to 4

TOO HOT TO HANDLE
If you haven't got yourself a skillet with an ovenproof handle, simply cover the handle with some aluminum foil and you should be fine. The foil will protect the handle from scorching.

Eggs Baked with Grits and Ham

½ teaspoon unsalted butter

¾ cup milk

½ cup water

¼ cup quick-cooking grits
  (not instant grits)

¼ teaspoon salt,
  plus more to taste

¼ cup chopped ham

4 extra-large eggs

Freshly ground black pepper
  to taste

4 teaspoons freshly grated
  Parmesan cheese

While this is certainly not a breakfast I make for myself every day, when I'm feeling like a little treat, there is nothing that tops eggs and grits in the morning. That combo right there is a shining example of a Southern breakfast. I've cut the butter way, way down to help make this a little bit healthier. But, oh my stars, this is still a decadently delicious dish to start your day out with.

1. Position an oven rack in the upper third of the oven. Preheat the oven to 350°F. Lightly grease four 6-ounce ramekins or baking dishes with the butter.

2. In a small saucepan, bring the milk and water to a boil over medium-high heat. Slowly whisk in the grits and salt. Whisk constantly for 30 seconds. Reduce the heat to medium and cook, stirring frequently, for 5 minutes, until the grits are thick and creamy (they will still be a bit on the loose side but will continue to thicken in the oven). Stir in the ham.

3. Divide the grits among the prepared ramekins and top each with 1 egg. Season the eggs with salt and pepper and sprinkle the Parmesan over the tops. Bake until the whites are just set, 12 to 15 minutes.

Serves 4

CARBS AND PROTEIN
It's real important to me that I couple my carb intake with proteins so that my blood sugar levels don't spike. So combining ham and eggs with grits not only makes for good eating, it makes good sense as well.

Savannah Omelet with Shrimp, Cherry Tomatoes, and Scallions

The city of Savannah and pretty pink shrimp go hand in hand, folks. Whenever I enjoy sweet, plump shrimp, I take a moment to thank my lucky stars I found my way to Savannah.

1. In a large nonstick skillet, heat the oil over medium-high heat. Add the scallions and cook until tender and slightly golden, 2 to 3 minutes. Add the shrimp and tomatoes and sprinkle with ¼ teaspoon of the salt and ¼ teaspoon of the pepper. Cook, tossing occasionally, until the shrimp are just cooked through, about 3 minutes. Scrape the shrimp mixture into a medium bowl.

2. In another medium bowl, whisk together the egg whites, eggs, and the remaining ¼ teaspoon salt and ¼ teaspoon pepper until frothy.

3. Using a paper towel, wipe out the skillet you cooked the shrimp in and return it to medium-low heat. Lightly grease the skillet with cooking spray. Pour in the egg mixture and tilt the skillet to coat the pan evenly with the eggs. Stir gently for 1 minute, then pat the eggs into an even layer over the bottom of the skillet. Sprinkle the shrimp-tomato mixture over one half of the omelet. When the underside of the omelet is barely golden, fold the unfilled side over the filling. Slide the omelet onto a plate. Cut in half and serve each half sprinkled with Tabasco.

Serves 2

2 teaspoons olive oil

3 scallions (white and light green parts), thinly sliced

¼ pound large shrimp, peeled, deveined, and cut in half horizontally

½ cup cherry tomatoes, cut in half horizontally

½ teaspoon salt

½ teaspoon freshly ground black pepper

6 large egg whites

2 large eggs

Tabasco or other hot sauce, for serving

Frittata with Mushrooms and Spinach

The texture of this fluffy frittata is like biting into a cloud. And a mighty tasty one at that! That's thanks to the egg whites lightening things up. Perfect morning food like this gives you the energy to get going on your day without weighing you down and making you feel too full.

1. Preheat the oven to 400°F.

2. In a large bowl, whisk together the eggs, egg whites, milk, ¼ cup of the Parmesan, the salt, black pepper, and red pepper flakes.

3. Heat the oil in a large ovenproof skillet over medium-high heat. Add half the mushrooms and cook until slightly softened. Add the remaining mushrooms and cook until tender and lightly crisped, about 5 minutes. Stir in the garlic and cook for 30 seconds. Add the spinach, a handful at a time, and cook until wilted, about 1 or 2 minutes.

4. Pour the egg mixture into the skillet. Cook until the bottom and sides of the frittata are lightly set, 2 to 3 minutes. Sprinkle the top of the frittata with the remaining ¼ cup Parmesan. Bake until puffed and golden, 15 to 20 minutes.

6 large eggs

3 large egg whites

⅓ cup milk

½ cup grated Parmesan cheese

½ teaspoon salt

¼ teaspoon freshly ground black pepper

Pinch of crushed red pepper flakes

1 tablespoon olive oil

6 ounces mixed mushrooms, such as cremini and shiitake, thinly sliced

2 garlic cloves, finely chopped

3 cups packed baby spinach leaves

Serves 6

SHAKE AND SLIDE
You need to be careful removing a frittata from the pan that it cooks in. What I like to do is give the pan a little shake once I take it out of the oven, just to ensure that the frittata is not sticking to the bottom. Then I tip the pan at an angle so that I can gently slide the frittata onto a plate. From there I slice and serve.

Ham and Spinach Whole-Wheat Toasties

1 tablespoon olive oil

4 cups packed baby spinach

¼ teaspoon garlic powder

Salt and freshly ground
black pepper to taste

1 tablespoon fresh lemon juice

8 slices whole-wheat bread,
lightly toasted

8 tablespoons grated Parmesan
cheese

4 slices low-sodium deli ham

These simple sandwiches are a healthy, satisfying way to start the day. But if you feel you need a little something more, they taste fantastic with a fried egg thrown into the mix. Or, if you fancy a vegetarian sandwich, go on ahead and use avocado in place of ham.

1. Position an oven rack in the middle of the oven. Preheat the broiler to high.

2. In a skillet, heat the oil over medium heat. Add the spinach and garlic powder and stir until wilted, about 1 or 2 minutes. Season the spinach to taste with salt and pepper and stir in the lemon juice.

3. Place 4 slices of the toast on a baking sheet and top with 1 tablespoon each of Parmesan, spreading out the cheese to cover the toast. Divide the spinach among the toast slices and top each with 1 slice of ham. Top with the remaining Parmesan, spreading it out over the ham.

4. Spray the sandwiches with cooking spray and place in the oven for about 2 minutes to melt the cheese. Flip the sandwiches and spray with more cooking spray. Cook about 2 more minutes until all the cheese is melted.

Serves 4

Eggs Florentine

Now, how smart is this? Instead of a traditional butter-packed hollandaise, this recipe of mine features a heart-healthy hollandaise based on avocado. It is so creamy and delicious I don't even think to make a traditional hollandaise anymore. This is a great breakfast for my fellow diabetics. It's packed with protein, features vitamin-rich spinach, and is served on a whole-wheat English muffin.

1. Using a spoon, scoop the avocado flesh into a medium bowl. Add the sour cream, mustard, buttermilk, lemon juice, paprika, and cayenne. Using a fork, whip until well combined. If you want the sauce thinner, add cold water, 1 tablespoon at a time. Set aside.

2. In a large skillet, heat the oil over medium-high heat. Add the spinach and cook for 2 minutes, until wilted, tossing frequently in the hot oil. Season to taste with salt and black pepper. Cover to keep warm.

3. Fill a small shallow saucepan with 2 inches of water and the vinegar and bring to a simmer. Break 1 of the eggs into a small cup and slide the egg into the water, stirring the water very gently with a spoon. Repeat immediately with 3 of the other eggs and cook until the whites are firm, about 3 minutes. Remove the eggs with a slotted spoon and drain them on paper towels. Repeat with the remaining 4 eggs.

4. Place 2 muffin halves on each of four individual serving plates and top each muffin half with some of the spinach, followed by 1 poached egg. Top the eggs with the avocado hollandaise and a sprinkle of paprika.

Serves 4

2 ripe avocados, halved and pitted

2 tablespoons regular or light sour cream

4 teaspoons Dijon mustard

4 teaspoons buttermilk

2 teaspoons fresh lemon juice

2 teaspoons sweet paprika, plus more for sprinkling

1 to 2 teaspoons cayenne pepper

1 tablespoon olive oil

8 cups packed baby spinach leaves

Salt and freshly ground black pepper to taste

1 tablespoon distilled white vinegar

8 large eggs

4 whole-wheat or regular English muffins, toasted

AWESOME AVOCADO
Avocados are not only wildly delicious, they are also fantastically good for you. They are a great source of fiber, potassium, and vitamin C, to name just a few benefits. And while avocados are a source of fat, it's the good fat, so they don't add to your cholesterol levels.

Creamy Scrambled Eggs with Tomatoes

2 small plum tomatoes

Salt and freshly ground
    black pepper to taste

5 large eggs

2 tablespoons (1 ounce) low-fat
    cream cheese (Neufchâtel),
    cut into small bits

2 teaspoons unsalted butter

1 scallion (white and light green
    parts), thinly sliced

These eggs are so rich and creamy you'd think they had a cup of heavy cream in them. But they don't! Just a dollop of low-fat cream cheese and some plum tomatoes make for super-moist scrambled eggs.

1. Cut the tomatoes in half lengthwise and seed them. Chop the tomatoes and toss them with some salt and pepper. Let the tomatoes sit in a small bowl to marinate.

2. Crack the eggs into a medium bowl. Lightly whisk the bits of cream cheese into the eggs. Drain the tomatoes and fold them into the eggs. Add a generous pinch of salt and pepper.

3. In a medium skillet, melt the butter over medium heat. Add the scallion and cook, stirring, until soft, 2 to 3 minutes.

4. Add the egg mixture to the pan and lightly scramble the eggs until softly cooked. Add a little more pepper and dig in.

Serves 2

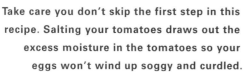

DRAW IT OUT
Take care you don't skip the first step in this recipe. Salting your tomatoes draws out the excess moisture in the tomatoes so your eggs won't wind up soggy and curdled.

Ultimate Egg Sandwich

Nothing beats a hearty egg sandwich in the morning. It fills me up and stays with me long into the morning, so I don't end up with the dreaded late-morning "snackies."

1. Grease a medium skillet with cooking spray. Add the bacon and cook over medium heat until crisp, about 5 minutes. Drain the bacon on a paper towel–lined plate and wipe out the skillet.

2. In a small bowl, use a fork to mash the avocado. Stir in the parsley and scallion and season to taste with salt and pepper. Spread the avocado mixture onto one side of each toast slice.

3. Grease the bacon skillet with cooking spray and heat the skillet over medium heat. Add the eggs and fry them on one side for 2 to 3 minutes. Crack the yolks and flip the eggs to cook until the yolks are just set. Place each egg on top of the avocado-spread toast. Top each egg with 3 bacon slices and 2 tomato slices. Top with another piece of toast and serve immediately.

Makes 4 sandwiches

6 turkey or regular bacon slices, cut in half

1 ripe avocado, halved, peeled, and pitted

2 teaspoons finely chopped fresh flat-leaf parsley

2 teaspoons finely chopped scallion (white and light green parts)

Salt and freshly ground black pepper to taste

8 slices soft whole-grain bread, toasted

4 large eggs

8 thick tomato slices

CHANGE IT UP
Don't limit yourself to whole-grain toast for this ultimate sandwich. I also like to use bagel flats or whole-wheat English muffins. And I'm a big fan of rye toast. Rye is a super-healthy choice in the morning as it won't spike your blood sugar levels, has tons of fiber and protein, and packs a real punch in the flavor department.

Asparagus "Quiche"

1 pound asparagus,
 woody ends trimmed

2 shallots, quartered

2 tablespoons olive oil

2 teaspoons salt

1 teaspoon freshly ground
 black pepper

4 large eggs

2 large egg whites

1 cup milk

¼ cup all-purpose flour, sifted

1 tablespoon chopped fresh
 tarragon

1 cup shredded Swiss cheese

Brunch in the Deen household always features a savory egg pie. And this crustless version of the quiche has become my new favorite. I like to make this in the springtime when thin, tender asparagus is so abundant. I pair up the asparagus with some fresh tarragon and Swiss cheese. At my gatherings, one of these tasty quiches never seems to be enough, so be prepared to make a few.

1. Preheat the oven to 425°F. Grease a 9-inch pie plate with cooking spray.

2. Place the asparagus and shallots on a rimmed baking sheet and toss with the oil. Sprinkle with 1 teaspoon of the salt and ½ teaspoon of the pepper. If you've got thin asparagus, roast them along with the shallots for 10 to 12 minutes, until tender and beginning to brown. If the asparagus are thick, roast them for 15 to 20 minutes. Remove from the oven, reduce the oven temperature to 350°F, cut the asparagus into 1-inch lengths, and coarsely chop the shallots.

3. Meanwhile, in a large bowl, whisk together the eggs, egg whites, and milk until combined, then gradually whisk in the flour. Fold in the tarragon, Swiss cheese, and the remaining 1 teaspoon salt and ½ teaspoon pepper.

4. Spread the asparagus and shallots over the bottom of the prepared dish and carefully pour over the egg mixture. Bake for 30 to 35 minutes, until puffed up and golden and just set in the middle. Let the quiche cool for at least 10 minutes on the counter, then slice and enjoy.

Makes one 9-inch quiche / Serves 6 to 8

Fruity Yogurt Smoothies (page 284) make a festive pairing with Asparagus "Quiche." ▶

Sausage, Mushroom, and Egg Bake

2 tablespoons olive oil

4 chicken or pork breakfast sausages (about ¾ pound), casings removed

8 ounces cremini or white button mushrooms, trimmed and sliced

6 large eggs, lightly beaten

1 cup milk

½ cup shredded Cheddar cheese

½ cup shredded Monterey Jack cheese

1 teaspoon dry mustard

¼ teaspoon dried sage

¼ teaspoon cayenne pepper

Salt and freshly ground black pepper to taste

When I'm having friends over for brunch, I cook a couple of these egg bakes the night before. Then I pop them in the oven to reheat on the day, and just like that, brunch is served. I've been able to cut down on the amount of sausage in my egg bakes by adding in a hearty vegetable to bulk them up. In this case I chose mushrooms, which taste great with the cheesy egg filling.

1. Preheat the oven to 350°F. Grease a 1½- to 2-quart baking dish with cooking spray.

2. In a large skillet, heat 1 tablespoon of the oil over medium-high heat. Add the sausage meat and stir, breaking it up with a spoon, until almost cooked through, about 5 minutes. Drain the sausage meat on a paper towel–lined plate.

3. Heat the remaining 1 tablespoon oil in the same skillet and add the mushrooms, stirring to coat with the oil in the pan. Cook, without stirring, for 5 minutes, until the mushrooms begin to brown. Remove the mushrooms from the skillet and let them cool slightly.

4. In a large bowl, combine the eggs, milk, Cheddar, Monterey Jack, dry mustard, sage, and cayenne, and season to taste with salt and black pepper.

5. In the bottom of the prepared baking dish, stir together the sausage and mushrooms. Pour the egg mixture over the top. Bake until the eggs are set and the top is golden brown, about 35 minutes.

Serves 6

Breakfast Pizza

I have found that a farm-fresh fried egg on top of just about anything makes it that much better. And pizza is no exception. Combining the classic flavors of pizza with the classic ingredients of breakfast is a bit of a stroke of genius, I have to say.

1. Preheat the oven to 400°F. Grease a large rimmed baking sheet with cooking spray.

2. Unroll the dough and place on the prepared baking sheet. Pat the dough out to about a 13 by 9-inch rectangle. Crimp the edges up about ¼ inch to create a crust. Bake the dough according to the package directions.

3. Meanwhile, in a medium skillet, cook the bacon over medium heat until crisp, about 5 minutes. If you are using turkey bacon, grease the skillet with cooking spray before cooking the bacon. Drain the bacon on a paper towel–lined plate and wipe out the skillet.

4. Spread the prebaked crust with the ricotta, then the tomato sauce. Sprinkle over the spinach and Parmesan. Top with the bacon slices and return the pizza to the oven for 6 to 10 minutes, until the crust is browned to your liking.

5. Meanwhile, add the oil to the wiped-out skillet and place over medium heat. When the oil is hot, add the eggs and fry them sunny-side up for 2 to 3 minutes, until the whites are set but the yolks are still runny.

6. Top the pizza with the fried eggs and sprinkle with the basil. Cut into 4 rectangles and serve.

Serves 4

1 can (13.8 ounces) whole-grain pizza dough, such as Pillsbury Artisan

4 turkey or regular bacon slices

¾ cup part-skim ricotta cheese

½ cup jarred tomato sauce

1 cup packed baby spinach

⅓ cup grated Parmesan cheese

1 tablespoon olive oil

4 large eggs

2 tablespoons chopped fresh basil

Breakfast Burrito

I love how this spicy breakfast wrap wakes me up in the morning. I usually use last night's leftover rice warmed up in the microwave. My son Jamie loves these burritos for morning tailgates before football games. To make them easily portable, he wraps them up in aluminum foil packages while they're still warm.

1. Preheat the oven to 250°F.

2. Place the tortillas in the oven until warm but still pliable, 5 to 10 minutes.

3. Meanwhile, in a medium skillet, cook the sausage over medium heat, breaking it up with a spoon, until it's cooked through. Add the rice and stir to combine well. Scrape the mixture into a medium bowl and wipe out the skillet.

4. In another medium bowl, whisk together the eggs, milk, scallions, and cilantro. Season to taste with salt and pepper.

5. Heat the oil over high heat in the wiped-out skillet. When hot, add the egg mixture and lightly scramble the eggs until softly cooked. Scrape into a separate medium bowl.

6. Fill each tortilla with one quarter of the pepper Jack. Top with one quarter of the sausage mixture and one quarter of the scrambled eggs. Sprinkle over one quarter each of the avocado and tomato. Fold over opposite ends of the tortillas and roll up the tortillas to create a closed package. Serve with sour cream and salsa, if you like.

Serves 4

4 whole-wheat burrito-size tortillas

8 ounces (½ package) bulk regular or light breakfast sausage meat, such as Jimmy Dean

1 cup cooked brown or white rice, warmed

6 large eggs

¼ cup milk

2 scallions (white and light green parts), thinly sliced

2 tablespoons chopped fresh cilantro

Salt and freshly ground black pepper to taste

1 tablespoon safflower or canola oil

¾ cup shredded pepper Jack cheese

½ ripe avocado, halved, peeled, pitted, and chopped

½ tomato, chopped

Regular or light sour cream (optional), for serving

Jarred salsa (optional), for serving

Four-Grain Waffles with Dried Cherry–Pineapple Sauce

WAFFLES

2 large eggs

½ cup old-fashioned rolled oats

1 cup all-purpose flour

1 cup whole-wheat flour

½ cup fine cornmeal

1 tablespoon baking powder

1 teaspoon salt

2 cups milk

1 teaspoon honey

3 tablespoons canola
  or safflower oil

I make these lovely four-grain waffles with just a hint of honey for sweetness. Then I like to top them with a rich, naturally sweet dried cherry–pineapple sauce, though a little maple syrup instead is nice too. This meal is sure to get them up and running to the breakfast table in the morning. And be quick, ya hear, because these waffles are best eaten right out of the iron, when they're at their crispiest and fluffiest.

1. To make the waffles: Separate the egg yolks and egg whites into two bowls. In the bowl of an electric mixer fitted with the whisk attachment, or using a hand-held mixer, whisk the egg whites until medium peaks form. The whites should be stiff enough to hang off the end of the whisk attachment but still a bit soft.

2. In a food processor, grind the oats into a fine flour. Pour the oat flour into a medium bowl and whisk in the all-purpose flour, whole-wheat flour, cornmeal, baking powder, and salt. In a separate medium bowl, whisk together the egg yolks, milk, honey, and oil. Using a rubber spatula, fold the milk mixture into the flour mixture until combined and smooth. Then gently fold in the egg whites. Don't worry if some of the egg whites are not completely incorporated into the batter.

3. Preheat a standard electric waffle iron according to the manufacturer's instructions. To make extra sure your waffles don't stick, give the surface a spray with cooking spray.

4. Pour ½ cup of batter into the waffle iron. Cook until golden brown and crispy on both sides, about 5 minutes.

5. To make the sauce: In a small saucepan over medium heat, combine the pineapple juice and cherries and simmer for 2 minutes. Add the pineapple and salt and simmer for 5 minutes more. Remove from the heat and stir in the nutmeg.

6. Cut the waffles in half and serve drizzled with the dried cherry–pineapple sauce. Pass extra sauce at the table.

Makes 6 large waffles / Serves 12

DRIED CHERRY–PINEAPPLE SAUCE

1⅓ cups pineapple juice

⅔ cup dried cherries

2 cups diced fresh or canned pineapple packed in water, drained if canned

Pinch of salt

½ teaspoon freshly grated nutmeg

WAFFLES 101
Don't be tempted to peek at your waffles as they are cooking away in the waffle iron. Keep that lid good and closed until the waffles are ready. Most waffle irons feature a little light that changes color when the waffles are done. And for extra assurance that the waffles don't stick, be sure to give the waffle iron a light greasing with cooking spray between every one or two waffles.

All-New French Toast Casserole

½ loaf French bread (8 ounces)

¼ teaspoon ground nutmeg

¼ teaspoon ground cinnamon

½ tablespoon pure vanilla extract

1 tablespoon maple syrup, plus more for serving

1½ cups milk

4 large eggs

½ cup chopped pecans

I like to have this casserole baking away in the oven when I've got guests coming by for brunch. The smell of the nutmeg, cinnamon, and maple is like a warm hug as they walk through the door. I prep it all up the night before so that all I've got to do on the day is pop it in the oven. I used to make this one-dish breakfast with double the amount of eggs and a couple cups of half-and-half. This version certainly lightens things up.

1. Grease an 8-inch square baking dish with cooking spray. Slice the bread into twenty ½-inch-thick slices. Arrange the slices in the prepared dish in 3 rows, overlapping the slices slightly.

2. In a large bowl, combine the nutmeg, cinnamon, vanilla, maple syrup, milk, and eggs, and whisk until blended but not too bubbly. Pour the mixture over the bread slices, making sure all the bread is covered evenly with the egg mixture. Spoon some of the mixture in between the slices. Cover with plastic wrap and refrigerate for at least 2 hours and preferably overnight.

3. When you are ready to cook the casserole, preheat the oven to 350°F.

4. Remove the casserole from the fridge and press the slices down into the liquid to make sure the bread absorbs as much as it can. Evenly sprinkle the pecans over the casserole and bake until puffed and lightly golden, about 30 minutes. Serve warm with extra maple syrup.

Serves 6 to 8

Creamy Cinnamon Oatmeal Bake

Anytime you can work oatmeal into your morning meal, it's a good idea to do so. It's one of the best ways to start off your day. And this creamy bake boasts three more super foods to get you going: dried blueberries, apple, and almonds. My stars, that's a lot of healthful ingredients! But if I had one word to describe this dish, it would be "luscious." The egg gives it the texture of velvet. It may be good for you, but it sure doesn't taste like it would be.

1. Preheat the oven to 350°F. Lightly grease a 9-inch square baking dish with cooking spray.

2. In a medium bowl, whisk together the milk, egg, maple syrup, vanilla, cinnamon, and salt. Stir in the oats, apple, and blueberries. Pour into the prepared dish and bake for 20 minutes. Top with the almonds and continue to bake until most of the liquid has been absorbed, 15 to 20 minutes more.

Serves 6 to 8

3½ cups milk

1 large egg, lightly beaten

⅓ cup maple syrup

1 teaspoon pure vanilla extract

1 teaspoon ground cinnamon

Pinch of salt

2 cups old-fashioned rolled oats

1 apple, peeled, cored, and chopped

⅓ cup dried blueberries or raisins or other dried fruit

¼ cup slivered almonds

COFFEE TALK
I love a steaming cup of coffee in the morning. The smell of it brewing in the kitchen makes me want to jump right out of bed. I have learned, though, to wait to have my coffee either with my breakfast or just after. The acidity in coffee can be a bit rough on your stomach first thing in the morning, so it's best to have it with food. More often than not, I take my coffee black or with just a splash of low-fat milk. Heavy cream and half-and-half add lots of unnecessary fat and calories to your morning cup of joe, and I'd rather save those calories for other meals during my day.

Buttermilk Cornmeal Pancakes

While I do enjoy a traditional flour pancake, the Southerner in me has a hard time going past cornmeal in the morning. That's why I developed these slightly sweet, corny pancakes. They are a proud Southern breakfast for a proud Southern woman.

¾ cup fine cornmeal

½ cup all-purpose flour

¼ cup whole-wheat flour

2 teaspoons sugar

½ teaspoon baking powder

½ teaspoon baking soda

¼ teaspoon salt

1¼ cups buttermilk

1 large egg, lightly beaten

2 tablespoons vegetable oil

1. In a large bowl, whisk together the cornmeal, all-purpose flour, whole-wheat flour, sugar, baking powder, baking soda, and salt. In a medium bowl, whisk together the buttermilk, egg, and oil. Gently whisk the buttermilk mixture into the flour mixture until combined.

2. Grease a large nonstick skillet with cooking spray and place it over medium-high heat. Working in batches, ladle the batter into the skillet, about ¼ cup per pancake. Cook without moving until the bottom is golden and most of the bubbles on the surface of the pancake have subsided, about 2 minutes. Gently flip and cook the other side until golden brown, about 2 minutes more. Transfer the cooked pancakes to a platter and place in a 200°F oven to keep warm. Repeat with the remaining batter.

Serves 4

Fruity, Crunchy Yogurt Parfait

1 cup regular or low-fat
   Greek yogurt

2 teaspoons honey

1½ cups fresh fruit, such as
   berries, melon, or citrus

1 cup Cinnamon Apple Granola
   with Cranberries and Walnuts
   (see page 286), or store bought

*This is a fancy little breakfast if I ever did see one. But luckily
it is simple to prepare. I make this for Michael on a special day,
like Valentine's Day or our anniversary. Sometimes I make it with
my homemade granola and sometimes I use low-sugar store-bought
granola. Other times I've been known to use Grape-Nuts cereal
instead. They all taste darn good.*

Scoop ¼ cup of the yogurt into each of two tall parfait glasses
or bowls. Drizzle ½ teaspoon honey into each glass, followed
by one quarter of the fruit, then ¼ cup of the granola. Repeat
with another layer of yogurt, honey, fruit, and granola in each
of the glasses. Serve with long spoons.

Serves 2

Fruity Yogurt Smoothie

½ cup low-fat or regular
   Greek yogurt

1 banana, peeled and chopped

½ cup fresh or frozen
   mixed berries

1 teaspoon honey,
   plus more to taste

2 ice cubes

*I have to send a big old thank-you out to my boy Bobby for this
recipe. I never knew that a fruit smoothie could taste so good and
satisfy me for so long. A glass of this smoothie is enough to keep me
going right through to lunch. Nicely done, sonny boy. You've gone
and taught your mama a thing or two.*

Place the yogurt, banana, berries, honey, and ice cubes
in a blender. Blend for about 30 seconds, until smooth and
creamy. I enjoy this smoothie ice cold.

Serves 1

BULK IT UP

**When I need a little more oomph in my smoothie, I add
a couple tablespoons of almond or peanut butter when
I blend up this concoction. It tastes so good and it
gives me the extra energy I'm looking for.**

Cinnamon Apple Granola
with Cranberries and Walnuts

3 cups old-fashioned rolled oats

1 cup walnuts, coarsely chopped

1 cup pumpkin or sunflower seeds

1½ teaspoons ground cinnamon

¼ teaspoon freshly grated
nutmeg

¾ teaspoon salt

¼ cup safflower oil

¼ cup honey

2 tablespoons apple juice

1 cup dried cranberries

The aroma of this granola baking is like smelling fall in the air—although, truth be told, I enjoy this granola all throughout the year. Cinnamon, nutmeg, apple juice, and walnuts all come together to create a comforting treat that will perk up any stomach in the morning. I like to top this low-sugar granola with Greek yogurt and pour in just a little milk. Delicious!

1. Preheat the oven to 300°F. Line a rimmed baking sheet with parchment paper.

2. In a large bowl, mix together the oats, walnuts, pumpkin seeds, cinnamon, nutmeg, and salt. In a medium bowl, whisk together the oil, honey, and apple juice. Add the honey mixture to the oat mixture and stir to combine well.

3. Spread the granola onto the prepared baking sheet in one layer. Bake for 45 minutes, stirring every 10 minutes or so, or until golden brown. Let the granola cool before mixing in the dried cranberries.

Makes 4 cups granola / Serves 16

Granola Bars

I make these granola bars so that I have an on-the-go breakfast option, but I wind up enjoying them any time of the day that I'm craving a nibble. They're a great healthy snack option whenever you feel your body needs an energy boost. And because they also make for an excellent after-school treat for the little ones, I package them up and drop them by Brooke and Jamie's house whenever I'm in the neighborhood.

1 large egg white

⅔ cup creamy regular or natural peanut butter

1 teaspoon pure vanilla extract

½ teaspoon ground cinnamon

½ teaspoon salt

⅓ cup packed light brown sugar

3 tablespoons honey

8 tablespoons (1 stick) unsalted butter, melted

3 cups old-fashioned rolled oats

½ cup chopped pecans

¼ cup dried cranberries

1. Preheat the oven to 350°F. Grease a 13 by 9-inch baking dish with cooking spray. Line the dish with parchment paper, allowing the excess paper to hang over the long sides. Lightly spray the parchment paper with cooking spray.

2. In a large bowl, whisk the egg white until frothy. Stir in the peanut butter, vanilla, cinnamon, salt, brown sugar, and honey. Add the butter, oats, pecans, and cranberries and stir well to combine.

3. Spread the mixture evenly into the prepared baking dish, pressing lightly to form an even layer. Bake for 40 to 45 minutes, until the top is a dark golden brown. Remove from the oven and let the granola cool for at least 1½ hours. When it is cool, cut the granola into 16 even-size bars.

Makes 16 bars

BUYER BEWARE
Granola bars sound like a super-healthy food, but they can be loaded with sugar when you buy them at the supermarket. That's why I like to make my own homemade bars. Even the natural brands at the supermarket can be really high in sugar, so if you are buying your bars, make sure you read the labels carefully.

10

Breads, Quick Breads, and Biscuits

I have always loved to bake biscuits and breads. They are as much a part of my DNA as they are a part of my diet. You see, baking in the South is not just about sustenance, it's about family tradition and bonding in the kitchen. So it was ever so important to me to develop a host of new bread and biscuit recipes that I'd feel good about handing down to the next generation.

I'll just go on and say it: Whole-wheat flour has become my friend. It features in almost half the recipes in this chapter. How I like to use whole-wheat flour is I like to combine it with all-purpose. That way, I can get a lighter texture than I would have achieved with just the whole wheat. Using this method, I was able to create the light and fluffy **Everyday Whole-Wheat Biscuits** (page 296) and the pillowy **Soft Whole-Wheat Sandwich Bread** (page 302). Without cutting these recipes with the white flour, they would have had an entirely different—and not different in a good way—texture.

Because I need to protect my body from blood sugar spikes, when I do go in for a baked good that's made with refined flour, I like to add some protein to it. The protein helps to slow down my body from absorbing the carbs and creating sugar from them. I am more than happy to add protein by slathering peanut butter on top of **Chocolate Chip–Zucchini Nut Bread** (page 309). You don't have to ask me

◀ *You know that saying "Misery loves company."*
Well, my good friend Donna Foltz makes exercising fun.

twice if I'd like some ham with my **Buttery Buttermilk Biscuits** (page 295). And thanks to Cheddar cheese, my **Cheesy Rosemary Beer Bread** (page 310) comes with its own source of protein baked right inside.

Portion control is key with breads and biscuits. I still enjoy a good sandwich, but more often than not, I take mine open-faced. They say that one slice of bread is a serving and that's how I build my sandwiches these days. I place a hearty slice on the bottom and top it with lean, low-sodium meats, a little cheese, and lots and lots of veggies. I may look a little funny eating my sandwich with a knife and fork, but I'm no less satisfied.

It really doesn't get much more Southern than corn bread and biscuits. I think Southerners are so clever for devising a million ways to bake corn bread. For a quickie version that's designed to sop up delicious sauces and gravies, **Skillet Corn Bread** (page 294) is the way to go. If you're hankering for corn bread *and* biscuit, **Black Pepper and Cornmeal Biscuits** (page 297) brings these two classics together. These biscuits are light and flaky and filled with awesome cornmeal flavor.

Hush puppies, spoon bread, buttermilk biscuits: This chapter reads like the history of Southern cooking. But the changes in these recipes are the real news. Everything Mama and Grandmama Paul taught me about baking can still be found in these pages, along with a little modern wisdom that makes these favorites work for me today.

Southern Spoon Bread

This custardy spoon bread is made just a little bit lighter because I whisk my egg whites to lovely soft peaks before folding them through. I recommend you grab a spoon and dig in quickly because this bread has a habit of disappearing.

½ cup yellow cornmeal

1 cup water

2 tablespoons (¼ stick) unsalted butter

½ cup milk

1½ teaspoons baking powder

½ teaspoon salt

2 large eggs, separated

1. Preheat the oven to 375°F. Grease a 1- to 1½-quart casserole dish with cooking spray.

2. In a small saucepan, stir together the cornmeal and water. Bring to a simmer over medium heat. Cook, stirring constantly, for 5 minutes, until the cornmeal is thickened.

3. Scrape into a medium bowl and stir in the butter, milk, baking powder, and salt. In a small bowl, lightly beat the egg yolks. Add a few tablespoons of the hot cornmeal mixture to the egg yolks, stirring briskly. Then add the yolks to the bowl with the rest of the cornmeal and stir to combine.

4. In the bowl of an electric mixer fitted with the whisk attachment, or using a hand-held mixer, whisk the egg whites until soft peaks form. Using a rubber spatula, gently fold the egg whites into the cornmeal mixture. Pour into the prepared casserole dish. Bake for 25 to 30 minutes, until set and golden. Serve this spoon bread hot!

Serves 4

HELPING HAND

If you are trying to lose a few pounds, find yourself a buddy to help you meet your goals. That support goes a long way. I know, because my family helped me in my journey to be a fitter me. And along the way, we *all* lost weight. Don't try to go it alone!

Baked Pimiento Hush Puppies

⅔ cup fine cornmeal

⅓ cup all-purpose flour

1 teaspoon baking powder

¾ teaspoon salt

⅛ teaspoon freshly ground
  black pepper

Pinch of cayenne pepper
  (optional)

½ cup buttermilk

1 large egg, lightly beaten

¼ cup chopped onion

½ cup shredded Cheddar cheese

1 jar (4 ounces) sliced pimientos,
  drained and chopped

What do you get when you combine sweet cornmeal, spicy cayenne, and rich Cheddar cheese with tangy pimientos? Why, you get the formula for the perfect hush puppy. And because I bake these up in mini muffin pans instead of frying them in the deep fryer, they are so much healthier and just about mess free. I serve hush puppies with almost anything, from eggs to fish to barbecue. Or you can just enjoy them on their own—maybe even slathered with a little more pimiento cheese on top.

1. Preheat the oven to 450°F. Lightly grease a 12-cup and a 6-cup mini muffin pan with cooking spray.

2. In a medium bowl, mix together the cornmeal, flour, baking powder, salt, black pepper, and cayenne (if using). In another medium bowl, whisk together the buttermilk and egg. Add the buttermilk mixture to the cornmeal mixture and fold to combine. Fold in the onion, Cheddar, and pimientos.

3. Drop the batter by the tablespoonful evenly into the muffin cups. Bake for 10 to 12 minutes, until the hush puppies are firm to the touch and the edges are golden brown. Serve the hush puppies warm.

Makes 18 hush puppies

Skillet Corn Bread

2 cups fine stone-ground
cornmeal

⅔ cup whole-wheat or
all-purpose flour

2 teaspoons baking powder

½ teaspoon baking soda

1 teaspoon salt

2 large eggs, lightly beaten

2 cups buttermilk

3 tablespoons unsalted butter

I never thought it was possible to make a good skillet corn bread without lard. Well, how wrong was I! I now make it with just three tablespoons of butter and it is absolutely scrumptious. Isn't it amazing how you're never too old to learn a thing or two?

1. Preheat the oven to 400°F. Place a 10-inch cast-iron skillet (or other heavy-bottomed ovenproof skillet) in the oven while the oven preheats.

2. In a large bowl, whisk together the cornmeal, flour, baking powder, baking soda, and salt. In a medium bowl, whisk together the eggs and buttermilk. Add the buttermilk mixture to the cornmeal mixture, stirring just until combined. Be careful not to overmix.

3. Carefully remove the skillet from the oven and add the butter. Swirl the skillet to lightly coat with the melted butter, then pour any extra butter into the batter and mix it in. Pour the batter into the hot skillet and bake for about 30 minutes, or until the top is lightly golden and a toothpick inserted into the center comes out clean. Serve from the skillet.

Serves 8 to 10

Buttery Buttermilk Biscuits

Here are my famous buttery buttermilk biscuits, minus half the butter. I promise, they are every bit as light, flaky, and scrumptious as the old ones. And the butter flavor is still front and center. But you can feel a whole lot better about consuming one (or two) of these now that I've cut the fat.

2½ cups all-purpose flour,
   plus more for dusting

1 tablespoon baking powder

¾ teaspoon baking soda

¾ teaspoon salt

4 tablespoons (½ stick)
   cold unsalted butter,
   cut into small bits

1¼ cups buttermilk,
   plus more for brushing

1 teaspoon honey

1. Preheat the oven to 425°F. Line a rimmed baking sheet with parchment paper.

2. In a large bowl, whisk together the flour, baking powder, baking soda, and salt. Cut in the butter with a fork or your hands until the mixture resembles coarse meal. Stir in the buttermilk and honey until just combined.

3. Turn the dough out onto a lightly floured surface. Pat the dough into a rectangle about ¾ inch thick. Using a 2-inch round biscuit cutter, cut the dough into biscuits. Gather the scraps and pat out the dough again (do this only once). You should be able to get 12 biscuits from the dough.

4. Generously brush the tops of the biscuits with the extra buttermilk and place the biscuits on the prepared baking sheet. Bake for 12 to 15 minutes, until golden and firm to the touch.

Makes about 12 biscuits

REWARD YOURSELF

Biscuits are a great love of mine. It's important not to cut the foods you really love out of your diet entirely. First and foremost, you've got to enjoy life! Either cut the portion sizes of your favorite fatty foods or tweak the recipes a little, as I've done here.

Everyday Whole-Wheat Biscuits

1¼ cups all-purpose flour

1¼ cups whole-wheat flour

1 tablespoon baking powder

¾ teaspoon baking soda

1 teaspoon salt

4 tablespoons (½ stick)
cold unsalted butter,
cut into small bits

1¼ cups buttermilk, plus more
for brushing

1 teaspoon honey

My biscuit lineup now features a whole-wheat biscuit. Because these are the biscuits I eat most often these days, I decided to call them my "everyday" biscuits. I suggest you eat these biscuits while they're still warm—that's when they're at their absolute best.

1. Preheat the oven to 425°F. Line a rimmed baking sheet with parchment paper.

2. In a large bowl, whisk together the all-purpose flour, whole-wheat flour, baking powder, baking soda, and salt. Cut in the butter with a fork or your hands until the mixture resembles coarse meal. Stir in the buttermilk and honey until just combined.

3. Turn the dough out onto a piece of wax or parchment paper. Pat the dough into a rectangle about ¾ inch thick. Using a 2-inch round biscuit cutter, cut out the biscuits. Gather the scraps and pat out the dough again (do this only once) to cut out more biscuits. You should be able to get 12 biscuits from the dough.

4. Generously brush the tops of the biscuits with the extra buttermilk and place the biscuits on the prepared baking sheet. Bake for 12 to 15 minutes, until golden and firm to the touch.

Makes about 12 biscuits

Black Pepper and Cornmeal Biscuits

I just love these spicy cornmeal biscuits. They're a bit of a different kind of biscuit, a little more like a cornmeal muffin than a light, flaky biscuit. They won't rise, so don't be concerned when yours don't. But they taste awfully good and are real handy for sopping up gravies and sauces.

1. Preheat the oven to 450°F. Line a rimmed baking sheet with parchment paper.

2. In a large bowl, whisk together the flour, cornmeal, baking powder, baking soda, salt, and pepper. Cut in the butter with a fork or your hands until the mixture resembles coarse meal. Stir in the buttermilk until just combined. Place the dough on a sheet of plastic wrap and press it into a flat disk. Wrap well and refrigerate for 20 minutes.

3. Turn the dough out onto a lightly floured surface. Pat the dough into a rectangle about ¾ inch thick. Using a 2-inch round biscuit cutter, cut the dough into biscuits. Gather the scraps and pat out again (do this only once). You should be able to get 12 biscuits from the dough.

4. Generously brush the tops of the biscuits with the extra buttermilk and place the biscuits on the prepared baking sheet. Bake for 9 to 11 minutes, until golden and firm to the touch.

Makes about 12 biscuits

1½ cups all-purpose flour, plus more for dusting

1 cup fine cornmeal

1 tablespoon baking powder

¾ teaspoon baking soda

¾ teaspoon salt

1 teaspoon coarse black pepper

4 tablespoons (½ stick) cold unsalted butter, cut into small bits

1¼ cups buttermilk, plus more for brushing

Pumpkin Scones

2 cups all-purpose flour,
  plus more for dusting

⅓ cup packed dark brown sugar

2 teaspoons pumpkin pie spice

1 teaspoon baking powder

½ teaspoon baking soda

½ teaspoon salt

6 tablespoons (¾ stick)
  cold unsalted butter,
  cut into small bits

⅓ cup buttermilk,
  plus more as needed

⅔ cup canned unsweetened
  pumpkin

2 teaspoons pure vanilla extract

⅓ cup chopped toasted pecans

2 teaspoons heavy cream

I always say, dry scones are the devil's handiwork! So for this recipe I was a little concerned about cutting out the sour cream I usually use. But I found that buttermilk did the trick just fine. And the canned pumpkin here also helped to ensure a moist, rich result. Be sure you don't handle the dough too much and these scones will wind up just as tender as can be. Their beautiful texture, coupled with the surprising crunch of pecans throughout, make for a special treat.

1. Preheat the oven to 400°F. Line a large rimmed baking sheet with parchment paper.

2. In a large bowl, whisk together the flour, brown sugar, pumpkin pie spice, baking powder, baking soda, and salt. Cut in the butter with a fork or your hands until the mixture resembles coarse meal.

3. In a medium bowl, whisk together the buttermilk, pumpkin, and vanilla. Stir the buttermilk mixture into the flour mixture. When you can't stir anymore, gently knead the mixture together with your hands until it forms a dough. If it seems too dry, add some more buttermilk, 1 tablespoon at a time, until it is moist enough to work with. The dough should be moist, but not sticky. Knead in the pecans.

4. Turn the dough out onto a lightly floured surface. Pat into a ½-inch-thick circle. Cut the dough into 8 equal wedges. Place the wedges on the prepared baking sheet. Brush the tops lightly with the cream. Bake until golden and firm, about 20 minutes. Cool the scones for 10 minutes before serving.

Serves 8

MINI WORKOUT
I tell you, baking is like a workout in and of itself. All that stirring, cutting in, and kneading can really get your heart rate going. So put your back into it and earn yourself a reward.

Irish Soda Bread

2 cups all-purpose flour,
  plus more for dusting

2 cups whole-wheat flour

½ cup old-fashioned rolled oats

1½ teaspoons baking soda

1 teaspoon salt

2 cups buttermilk

Bread making does not get any easier than this. All the magic happens in one great big bowl. Just stir the ingredients together, knead with your hands, plop the dough on a greased baking sheet, and bake. If you're feeling adventurous, add in some fun extras like currants or nuts.

1. Preheat the oven to 400°F. Lightly grease a rimmed baking sheet with cooking spray.

2. In a large bowl, whisk together the all-purpose flour, whole-wheat flour, oats, baking soda, and salt. Add the buttermilk and stir until incorporated. Right there in the bowl, use floured hands to knead the dough a couple times to form a 7-inch round loaf (it will be very sticky, so make sure you flour your hands). Place the loaf on the prepared baking sheet. Using a sharp knife, make an X about ½ inch deep across the top of the loaf.

3. Bake for 40 minutes, until a toothpick inserted into the center of the loaf comes out clean or when the loaf sounds hollow when tapped on its bottom. Remove the loaf from the pan and let it cool completely on a wire rack before slicing.

Makes one 8-inch loaf / Serves 8

Cheddar and Caraway Soft Bread Sticks

I just love a good cheesy bread stick. There's even more to love when you add in flavorful caraway seeds. The seeds really set this bread stick apart from the rest.

1. Preheat the oven to 400°F. Line two rimmed baking sheets with parchment paper.

2. On a lightly floured surface, roll the dough into a 13 by 18-inch rectangle. Brush the dough evenly with the butter and sprinkle with the Cheddar, caraway seeds, salt, and pepper. Lightly roll over the surface with the rolling pin once more to make sure the cheese and seeds stick to the melted butter. Slice into 12 even strips, each about 1¼ by 13 inches, trimming the sides or ends, if you need to. Cut each in half horizontally to make 24 bread sticks.

3. Gently place the bread sticks on the prepared baking sheets (12 breadsticks on each). Bake for 12 to 15 minutes, or until golden and soft. Serve warm.

Makes 24 bread sticks

All-purpose flour, for dusting

1 can (13.8 ounces) whole-grain pizza dough, such as Pillsbury Artisan

2 tablespoons (¼ stick) unsalted butter, melted

1 cup shredded Cheddar cheese

1½ teaspoons caraway seeds

1 teaspoon salt

½ teaspoon freshly ground black pepper

Soft Whole-Wheat Sandwich Bread

1¼ teaspoons active dry yeast

½ cup lukewarm
   (100°F to 110°F) water

¾ cup warm milk

3 tablespoons unsalted butter,
   melted

2 tablespoons sugar

1½ teaspoons salt

1 large egg yolk

1½ cups whole-wheat flour

2 cups all-purpose flour

Safflower or canola oil

There is nothing quite liked home-baked bread. Now, I know it takes time and care to make a yeast-risen bread from scratch, but I'm telling you, it is well worth the effort. So every once in a while, I put the brakes on life and I make an honest-to-goodness whole-wheat bread. When I bite into a sandwich made with two pillow-soft slices of this whole-wheat loaf, I say a little thank-you to myself for setting aside the time.

1. Grease a 9 by 5-inch loaf pan with cooking spray.

2. Sprinkle the yeast over the lukewarm water in a small bowl.

3. In a medium bowl, whisk together the milk, butter, sugar, salt, and egg yolk. In a large bowl, whisk together the whole-wheat flour and all-purpose flour. Add the yeast mixture to the milk mixture along with 1 cup of the flour mixture and stir to combine. Add another 2 cups of the flour mixture and stir until you've formed a rough dough. Add the remaining flour mixture in ¼-cup amounts if the dough seems too wet.

4. In the bowl of an electric mixer fitted with the hook attachment, knead the dough for 6 to 8 minutes (or knead the dough by hand on a lightly floured surface). Scrape the dough into another large bowl—it will be very sticky. Add a little oil to the bowl. Roll the ball of dough into the bowl and cover all sides with the oil. Cover with a damp kitchen towel and let the dough rise in a warm place until doubled, about 1 hour.

5. Scrape the dough into the prepared loaf pan, making sure the dough spreads to the ends and sides of the pan. Let the dough rise until doubled, about 30 minutes more.

6. Meanwhile, preheat the oven to 375°F.

7. Bake the bread for 35 to 45 minutes, until golden brown. The bread should sound hollow if tapped on the bottom. Remove the loaf from the pan and let it cool completely on a wire rack before slicing.

Makes one 9-inch loaf / Serves 16

Sweet Potato-Raisin Muffins

On Halloween, you'll find me baking these delicious muffins for my grandsons. The muffins' festive orange color and flavor are the perfect pre–trick-or-treat nibble for little ones. For myself, I like to enjoy these muffins at breakfast with a great big steaming cup of coffee.

1. Preheat the oven to 350°F. Grease a 12-cup muffin tin with cooking spray.

2. In a large bowl, whisk together the flour, baking powder, baking soda, salt, and pumpkin pie spice. In another large bowl, combine the brown sugar, sweet potato, oil, eggs, and orange zest. Using a rubber spatula, gently fold the sweet potato mixture into the flour mixture. Stir in the raisins.

3. Scrape the batter into the prepared muffin tin, filling the cups about three-quarters full. Bake for 25 to 30 minutes, until puffed and golden brown and a toothpick inserted into the center of a muffin comes out clean. Let the muffins cool in the pan for 5 minutes, then remove them and place on a wire rack to cool. Enjoy these muffins warm or at room temperature.

Makes 12 muffins

3 cups all-purpose flour

2 teaspoons baking powder

1 teaspoon baking soda

1 teaspoon salt

1 tablespoon pumpkin pie spice

¾ cup packed light brown sugar

2 cups cooked, mashed sweet potato (about 2 small)

⅔ cup canola or safflower oil

4 large eggs

2 teaspoons finely grated orange zest

½ cup raisins

HIDDEN VEGGIES
I try to get vegetables into meals and snacks whenever I can, both for myself and my grandsons. These muffins are a perfect example. The sweet potato bakes in the muffins and tastes so good that little ones don't even know they are eating a serving of vegetables.

Buttermilk Corn Muffins

1 cup buttermilk

2 large eggs

4 tablespoons (½ stick)
  unsalted butter, melted

¼ cup honey

1 teaspoon pure vanilla extract

½ teaspoon finely grated
  orange zest

1 cup fine cornmeal

1 cup all-purpose flour

1½ teaspoons baking powder

1 teaspoon baking soda

*I can literally eat these muffins for breakfast, lunch, and dinner.
In the morning, I like them with some all-fruit jam slathered on top.
At lunch, I enjoy them with a piping-hot bowl of soup. And at dinner,
I use them to sop up any sauces on my plate. They are moist and
chewy with a nice little sweetness. It's true I have never actually met
a muffin I didn't like. But this one, well, this one I positively love.*

1. Preheat the oven to 375°F. Grease a 12-cup muffin tin
   with cooking spray.

2. In a medium bowl, whisk together the buttermilk, eggs,
   butter, honey, vanilla, and orange zest. In a separate medium
   bowl, whisk together the cornmeal, flour, baking powder,
   and baking soda. Add the flour mixture to the buttermilk
   mixture and stir until just combined.

3. Scrape the batter into the prepared muffin tin, filling the
   cups three-quarters full. Bake for 12 to 15 minutes, until
   golden along the edges and a toothpick inserted into the
   center of a muffin comes out clean. Let the muffins cool in
   the pan for 5 minutes on a wire rack, then turn the muffins
   out when they are cool enough to handle.

Makes 12 muffins

Cheddar Chive Muffins

While I love a sweet muffin, my heart belongs to a cheesy savory muffin. You may be thinking to yourself, "Now Paula, a cheese muffin, is that really in your new-and-improved diet?" Well, yes it is, honey, because I use half the amount of cheese I used to use. Now that's what I call progress.

1. Preheat the oven to 425°F. Grease a 12-cup muffin tin with cooking spray.

2. In a large bowl, whisk together the all-purpose flour, whole-wheat flour, baking powder, baking soda, salt, black pepper, and cayenne. In a medium bowl, combine the butter, buttermilk, and egg. Fold the buttermilk mixture into the flour mixture until combined. Fold in the chives and 1 cup of the Cheddar.

3. Scrape the batter into the prepared muffin tin, filling the cups three-quarters full. Sprinkle the tops with the remaining ½ cup Cheddar.

4. Bake for 25 minutes, turning the pan halfway through baking. Let the muffins cool in the pan for 5 minutes, then remove them and place on a wire rack to cool.

Makes 12 muffins

1½ cups all-purpose flour

½ cup whole-wheat flour

1 tablespoon baking powder

¼ teaspoon baking soda

¾ teaspoon salt

½ teaspoon freshly ground black pepper

¼ teaspoon cayenne pepper

4 tablespoons (½ stick) unsalted butter, melted and cooled

1 cup buttermilk

1 large egg

3 tablespoons chopped fresh chives

1½ cups shredded extra-sharp Cheddar cheese

Oat Muffins with Blueberries

2 cups all-purpose flour

1½ teaspoons baking powder

1 teaspoon baking soda

1 cup buttermilk

2 extra-large eggs

½ cup packed light brown sugar

¼ cup canola or safflower oil

1 teaspoon pure vanilla extract

½ cup old-fashioned rolled oats

1 cup blueberries,
   fresh or frozen, thawed

These sweet oat muffins are absolutely bursting with berries. My son Bobby tried them and couldn't stop raving. He pointed out to me that I'd used two of the super foods he tries to eat as often as possible. Turns out oats and blueberries are just about the best things for you. Oats have been found to lower your chance of heart disease, and because they are packed with fiber, they help regulate blood glucose levels. If that wasn't enough for me, he informed his mama that blueberries were high in antioxidants, which also help to keep you healthy. My goodness, and here I was just thinking I'd created a tasty muffin. Turns out I'd devised a super muffin!

1. Preheat the oven to 375°F. Lightly grease a 12-cup muffin tin with cooking spray.

2. In a large bowl, whisk together the flour, baking powder, and baking soda. In a separate bowl, whisk together the buttermilk, eggs, brown sugar, oil, and vanilla. Add the buttermilk mixture and the oats to the flour mixture and stir until just combined. Gently fold in the blueberries.

3. Scrape the batter into the prepared muffin tin, filling the cups three-quarters full. Bake for 15 minutes, until a toothpick inserted into the center of a muffin comes out clean (watch out for blueberries). Let the muffins cool in the pan for 5 minutes, then remove them and place on a wire rack to cool.

Makes 12 muffins

Coconut Banana Bread

1 cup all-purpose flour

1 cup whole-wheat flour

¾ teaspoon baking soda

½ teaspoon salt

4 tablespoons (½ stick) unsalted butter, at room temperature

⅔ cup packed light brown sugar

2 large eggs

1½ cups mashed ripe banana (from about 3 bananas)

¼ cup plain yogurt

3 tablespoons apple juice or apple cider

½ teaspoon pure vanilla extract

½ cup plus 1 tablespoon unsweetened flaked coconut

Thanks to the yogurt and banana in this bread, I can get away with just four tablespoons of butter and still wind up with a rich, moist loaf. With the help of natural apple juice or cider, I can get away with just two thirds of a cup of brown sugar. These small changes add up to big health benefits. And I'm the living proof.

1. Preheat the oven to 350°F. Grease a 9 by 5-inch loaf pan with cooking spray.

2. In a large bowl, whisk together the all-purpose flour, whole-wheat flour, baking soda, and salt.

3. In the bowl of an electric mixer fitted with the paddle attachment, or using a hand-held mixer, beat the butter and brown sugar together until creamy and smooth. Add the eggs, one at a time, beating well after each addition and scraping down the sides of the bowl periodically. Beat in the banana, yogurt, apple juice, and vanilla. Gradually add the flour mixture, beating at low speed and scraping the sides of the bowl, just until combined. Using a rubber spatula, stir in ½ cup of the coconut.

4. Spoon the batter into the prepared loaf pan and sprinkle with the remaining 1 tablespoon coconut. Bake for 65 to 75 minutes, until a toothpick inserted into the center of the loaf comes out clean. Let the bread cool in the pan for 10 minutes on a wire rack, then remove it from the pan and cool completely on a wire rack before slicing and serving.

Makes one 9-inch loaf / Serves 12

Chocolate Chip-Zucchini Nut Bread

This good-for-you zucchini loaf was a happy surprise to me when I lifted it out of the oven and tried a slice for the first time. It's sweet, nutty, and chocolaty, y'all, even though I found ways to reduce the sugar and cut the fat. I was so proud of this bread I went straight back to the kitchen and made up a few more loaves to deliver to Jamie, Bobby, and Bubba. Success like this just has to be shared.

1. Preheat the oven to 350°F. Grease a 9 by 5-inch loaf pan with cooking spray.

2. In a large bowl, mix together the zucchini, brown sugar, oil, yogurt, eggs, and vanilla.

3. In a medium bowl, whisk together the flour, salt, baking powder, baking soda, cinnamon, and nutmeg. Fold the flour mixture into the zucchini mixture. Then fold in the walnuts and chocolate chips.

4. Pour the batter into the prepared loaf pan and bake for 40 minutes, rotating the pan halfway through the baking time. The bread is done when a toothpick inserted into the middle of the loaf comes out clean.

5. Let the bread cool in the pan for 10 minutes on a wire rack. Remove the bread from the pan and cool completely before cutting and serving.

Makes one 9-inch loaf / Serves 12

1½ cups grated zucchini

⅔ cup packed light brown sugar

⅓ cup olive oil

⅓ cup Greek yogurt

2 large eggs

1 teaspoon pure vanilla extract

1½ cups all-purpose flour

¾ teaspoon salt

½ teaspoon baking powder

½ teaspoon baking soda

1½ teaspoons ground cinnamon

¼ teaspoon freshly grated nutmeg

½ cup chopped walnuts

½ cup bittersweet chocolate chips

OIL ADVANTAGE
Olive oil is a much better choice over butter when you can use it. While I'll be sticking with butter in my cakes for the most part, this zucchini bread is a great place to use the oil. Thanks to the olive oil, the bread has a nice light texture. And olive oil has monounsaturated fats, rather than saturated fats, which are much better for my body.

Cheesy Rosemary Beer Bread

2 cups self-rising flour

1 cup whole-wheat flour

2 teaspoons salt

2 tablespoons sugar

1½ cups shredded Cheddar cheese

2 tablespoons chopped fresh rosemary

2 tablespoons warmed honey

1 can (12 ounces) lager-style beer

2 tablespoons (¼ stick) unsalted butter, melted

This hearty loaf will fill your house with the heady aromas of Cheddar and rosemary. It's a warming antidote to a cold winter day. I think the nutty whole wheat goes so nicely with the beer and cheese.

1. Preheat the oven to 375°F. Grease a 9 by 5-inch loaf pan with cooking spray and cover the base with parchment paper.

2. In a large bowl, whisk together the self-rising flour, whole-wheat flour, salt, and sugar. Stir in the Cheddar and rosemary and coat well in the flour mixture. Stir in the honey and beer until just combined. The dough will be sticky.

3. Press the dough into the prepared loaf pan and brush the top of the loaf with the butter. Bake for 45 to 50 minutes, until a toothpick inserted into the center of the loaf comes out clean. Let cool for 10 minutes before turning out and slicing.

Makes one 9-inch loaf / Serves 12

SINK OR SWIM
Make sure you get the shredded Cheddar good and coated with the flour before you mix in the honey and beer. This will ensure that the cheese doesn't sink to the bottom of the batter while the bread is baking, giving you a nice even distribution of cheese throughout the loaf.

11

Pies and Cakes

*N*o cookbook of mine would be complete without a pies and cakes chapter, y'all. While it's true I'm indulging in fewer of these treats of late, I haven't cut them out entirely. Heavens, no! They are still very much a part of my life, only now I enjoy them in moderation. You might say that I've found I can still have my cake and eat it too!

I look upon the pies and cakes from my old books and recipes as my special-occasion foods. I satisfy myself with half a slice of these treats on the weekends or at gatherings with family and friends. But I've also developed a whole arsenal of new desserts that I can feel confident consuming on a more regular basis. These new recipes feature much less fat and sugar, but still taste decadently delicious.

The thing is, pies and cakes are a part of my history and the history of Southern cooking. Why, yes, you could go and pick yourself up a pie or cake from the store any day you choose, but, really, there is nothing quite like a pie made at home by someone who loves you. My grandmother and my mother made these treats for me and taught me how to make them for my children. And today, my boys and I are busy passing that tradition on to the next generation. When my sweet grandkids perch on a stool by my kitchen counter and help me whip up a ***Vanilla Buttermilk Pie*** (page 321) or a ***Coconut Cake*** (page 334), I'm taken right back to the days when I was the one perched on that stool with my Grandmama Paul.

◄ *Matthew hard at work.*

I am so excited to unveil for you ***Paula's New Flaky Piecrust*** (page 325). It's so devilishly good that I think you're going to be amazed at how much healthier I've managed to make it. It's flaky, light, and buttery, but instead of including ¼ cup vegetable shortening, it features 2 to 4 tablespoons of Greek yogurt. When you're filling that piecrust with good-for-you, real ingredients like sweet potato in the **Light and Luscious Sweet Potato Pie** (page 324), you can feel pretty good about your dessert choices.

I've even developed ways to lighten up my sinful cakes. You'll still find me using butter, but a whole lot less of it. With this approach, I was able to lighten up even the richest cakes in my repertoire, like ***Gooey Butter Cake*** (page 328) and ***Italian Cheesecake*** (page 336).

One thing this chapter is packed with is fruit. Filling your pies and cakes with nature's own candy is the best way to make desserts just a little bit better for you. Not much of a hardship there, if you ask me. There is always a fruit in season that I love in my baked goods. For the fall months, I've created a twist on the classic apple pie with my ***Apple Cherry Pie*** (page 316). And in the summertime, I bake Georgia's luscious summer peaches into a ***Peaches and Cream Cheesecake*** (page 337) that you don't want to miss.

And there is chocolate and peanut butter to be had still. ***Chocolate Velvet Pie*** (page 317) is a creamy treat you can whip up in no time flat. No baking necessary— just pop it in the fridge for an hour or so to set and you have a pie the whole family will be falling all over. Of course, if you have a ***Creamy Peanut Butter Pie*** (page 320) around, the children just might take that one for themselves. My grandkids sure can't get enough of it.

I think it's so nice when something brings the whole family together. What better place for that to happen than at the kitchen table? When you're all together at the table enjoying delicious, homemade food, the good times are bound to follow. And that's what it's all about, folks.

Sunny Citrus Meringue Pie

With half the butter, a lot less sugar, and fewer eggs than my old meringue pie, the citrus flavor in this dessert takes center stage. This sweet, tart dessert is all about the sunny orange, lemon, and lime essences.

1. In a large pot, whisk together the cornstarch and 1 cup of the sugar. Slowly whisk in the boiling water. Bring to a boil and whisk until the sugar and cornstarch dissolve.

2. In a medium bowl, whisk together the egg yolks. Slowly whisk in the cornstarch mixture, a spoonful at a time, until completely combined. Scrape the mixture back into the pot and cook over medium-high heat, stirring constantly, until the mixture is bubbling thickly. Remove from the heat and whisk in the lemon zest, orange zest, lime zest, lemon juice, orange juice, lime juice, and butter. Pour the mixture into the piecrust and cool until just warm to the touch.

3. Preheat the oven to 350°F.

4. In the bowl of an electric mixer fitted with the whisk attachment, or using a hand-held mixer, whisk together the egg whites, cream of tartar, salt, and vanilla at medium speed until foamy. Beat in the remaining ¼ cup sugar, 1 tablespoon at a time. Beat the mixture on high speed until stiff peaks form. Spread the meringue over the surface of the cooled filling, using the back of a spatula or spoon to form pretty peaks.

5. Bake for about 15 minutes, until golden brown on top. Transfer the pie to a wire rack to cool completely, 2 to 3 hours.

Serves 8 to 10

⅓ cup cornstarch

1¼ cups sugar

1½ cups boiling water

2 large eggs, separated

1 teaspoon finely grated lemon zest

1 teaspoon finely grated orange zest

1 teaspoon finely grated lime zest

¼ cup fresh lemon juice

¼ cup fresh orange juice

1 tablespoon fresh lime juice

2 tablespoons (¼ stick) unsalted butter, cut into small bits

1 9-inch prepared graham cracker piecrust

¼ teaspoon cream of tartar

Pinch of salt

½ teaspoon pure vanilla extract

Apple Cherry Pie

6 apples (about 3 pounds), peeled, cored, and chopped

¼ cup packed light brown sugar

2 teaspoons ground cinnamon

½ teaspoon ground nutmeg

1 teaspoon ground ginger

2 teaspoons pure vanilla extract

1 tablespoon unsalted butter

½ cup dried cherries, finely chopped

¼ cup water

2 tablespoons all-purpose flour, plus more for dusting

2 batches Paula's New Flaky Piecrust (see page 325) or 2 9-inch unbaked prepared piecrusts

1 large egg

This here is basically my classic apple pie recipe, minus half the fat and more than half the sugar. I like to use a blend of Granny Smith and Golden Delicious apples to achieve just the right amount of tartness balanced by just the right amount of sweetness. And the dried cherries add plenty of good-for-you richness all by themselves.

1. Preheat the oven to 375°F.

2. In a medium saucepan, combine the apples, brown sugar, cinnamon, nutmeg, ginger, vanilla, butter, cherries, and water. Cover and simmer, stirring occasionally, over medium heat for 10 minutes, or until the apples begin to soften. Remove from the heat to cool. Once the mixture has cooled, add the flour to the saucepan and stir until combined.

3. On a lightly floured surface, roll each batch of dough into a 10-inch circle (skip this step if you are using prepared piecrusts). Carefully transfer one circle of pie dough to a 9-inch pie plate. Whisk the egg with 1 teaspoon water in a small bowl. Brush the egg wash lightly over the edges of the dough.

4. Pour the apple filling into the pie plate. Top with the second circle of dough. Using your fingers or a fork, crimp together the edges of the dough to seal the pie. Cut a slit in the top of the pie to allow steam to escape. Lightly brush the top with egg wash.

5. Bake for 45 to 50 minutes, until a piece of apple is easily pierced with a knife. Allow the pie to cool a bit and serve warm, topped with scoops of vanilla ice cream.

Makes one 9-inch pie / Serves 8 to 10

SPLURGE A LITTLE
I give myself a cheat day now and again. On those days, I indulge in some higher calorie dishes that aren't a daily part of my diet anymore. Cheat days give me something to look forward to after a job well done.

Chocolate Velvet Pie

I didn't call this pie chocolate velvet for just any old reason, y'all. It is rich, smooth, and very creamy. It tastes decadent and sumptuous, even though it's made with low-fat cream cheese and sugar-free whipped topping. Keep this one in mind next time you're craving a midweek treat. If you're making it for company or to bring to a gathering, you can make it look super special by decorating the top with some extra whipped topping. Make a quick piping bag by snipping off one corner of a resealable plastic sandwich bag. Fill the bag with whipped topping and squeeze out swirly designs all over the top of the pie. Have fun with it!

1 package (11½ ounces) semisweet chocolate chips

1 package (8 ounces) low-fat cream cheese (Neufchâtel), at room temperature

1 teaspoon pure vanilla extract

1 container (8 ounces) sugar-free or regular frozen whipped topping, thawed, plus more for decorating

1 9-inch prepared graham cracker piecrust

1. In a medium microwave-safe bowl, microwave the chocolate chips on medium-high power for 1 minute and stir. Microwave at 30-second intervals, stirring in between, until smooth and fully melted. Cool to room temperature.

2. In the bowl of an electric mixer fitted with the paddle attachment, or using a hand-held mixer, beat the cream cheese and vanilla until smooth. Scrape down the sides of the bowl and gradually mix in the cooled chocolate until combined.

3. Using a rubber spatula, gently fold in the whipped topping in two batches. Spoon the filling into the piecrust and smooth the top with a rubber spatula. Refrigerate until firm, about 1 hour. Serve cold or at room temperature. If you like, decorate the pie with more whipped topping.

Serves 8 to 10

Old-Fashioned Strawberry Pie

All-purpose flour, for dusting

Paula's New Flaky Piecrust
(see page 325) or 1 9-inch
unbaked prepared piecrust

1 package (0.3 ounce) sugar-free
strawberry gelatin

2 tablespoons cornstarch

1 cup water

2 pounds fresh strawberries

An old-fashioned fruit pie like this should be eaten outdoors when the sun is shining bright. Next time you are firing up the barbecue or packing a picnic basket, be sure to have one of these pies made up in your fridge. Fresh strawberries, cool gelatin, and a flaky piecrust combine to make this a summertime classic.

1. Dust a work surface with a small handful of flour. Roll the dough into a 12-inch round about ¼ inch thick. Use it to line a 9-inch pie plate, folding over the excess edges of the dough and crimping them if you like. Chill in the refrigerator for 30 minutes or up to overnight (cover lightly with plastic wrap if chilling for more than 2 hours). Skip this step if you are using a prepared piecrust.

2. When you are ready to bake the pie, preheat the oven to 375°F.

3. Use a fork to prick the bottom of the pie a couple times. Line the dough up the sides with parchment paper or aluminum foil and fill with dried beans or pie weights. Bake for 20 minutes, then reduce the oven temperature to 350°F. Remove the beans or pie weights and the paper or foil, return to the oven, and bake for 5 minutes. Remove the piecrust and let it cool.

4. In a small saucepan, whisk together the gelatin and cornstarch. Whisk in the water and bring to a simmer. Whisk continuously for about 5 minutes, scraping the bottom of the pan. Once the mixture has thickened, pour it into a medium bowl and continue to whisk for 1 to 2 minutes. Let the mixture cool for 15 minutes, whisking occasionally. The gelatin should be runny.

5. Rinse, dry, and hull the strawberries. Place them in a decorative pattern on the bottom of the cooled piecrust. Pour the gelatin over the berries and place the pie in the refrigerator until firm, about 1 hour. Once the pie is set, slice and serve.

Serves 8 to 10

BOUNTY OF BERRIES
When it's berry season, I vary this pie by making it with just about any berry there is. Sometimes it's blueberries, sometimes it's blackberries, and sometimes it's raspberries. But it's always delicious.

Creamy Peanut Butter Pie

1 package (8 ounces) low-fat cream cheese (Neufchâtel), at room temperature

2 tablespoons confectioners' sugar

½ teaspoon pure vanilla extract

1 cup creamy regular or natural peanut butter, softened

1 container (8 ounces) sugar-free or regular frozen whipped topping, thawed

1 9-inch prepared graham cracker piecrust

If there is one thing I've learned through my recent health experiences it is this: Always read the labels, y'all. You'd be amazed at what you find out. Take peanut butter, for instance. Did you know that regular peanut butter actually contains fewer carbs than low-fat peanut butter? I'm talking almost half the amount of carbs! And natural peanut butter contains even fewer than regular. Cutting carbs is key to keeping my diet in balance, so no need to go with the light stuff when I'm feeling like a little peanut butter pie. Isn't life just full of surprises?

1. In the bowl of an electric mixer fitted with the paddle attachment, or using a hand-held mixer, beat the cream cheese, confectioners' sugar, and vanilla until smooth. Add the peanut butter and beat, scraping down the sides of the bowl, until thoroughly combined. Using a rubber spatula, gently fold in the whipped topping in two batches.

2. Spoon the filling into the piecrust and smooth the top with a rubber spatula. Refrigerate until firm, at least 2 hours. Serve cold or at room temperature.

Serves 8 to 12

Vanilla Buttermilk Pie

I love the way the sweet vanilla flavor of this pie marries so nicely with the tangy buttermilk. And I also love that I have cut the sugar dramatically. Have no fear though, because with a little help from apple juice concentrate, this pie remains a sweet treat. I grew up eating this pie and I intend to grow old eating this pie. With these few simple changes, that dream has just become a reality.

1. Dust a work surface with a small handful of flour. Roll the dough into a 12-inch round about ¼ inch thick. Use it to line a 9-inch pie plate, folding over the excess edges of the dough and crimping them if you like. Chill in the refrigerator for 30 minutes or up to overnight (cover lightly with plastic wrap if chilling for more than 2 hours). Skip this step if you are using a prepared piecrust.

2. Position an oven rack in the middle of the oven. Preheat the oven to 350°F.

3. In a medium bowl, whisk together the sugar, flour, and cornstarch. Add the eggs and apple juice concentrate and whisk thoroughly to combine. Whisk in the buttermilk and vanilla.

4. Place the piecrust on a rimmed baking sheet and place the baking sheet on the middle oven rack. Pull the rack out a bit and pour the buttermilk mixture into the crust (this will prevent spills you might otherwise have getting the pie into the oven). Bake until the crust browns, then cover the pie loosely with aluminum foil. Continue to bake until the filling is fully set at the edges and just a bit wiggly in the center, about 40 minutes total. Let the pie cool completely (and I do mean completely) on a wire rack before slicing. Serve with strawberries alongside.

Serves 8 to 10

1 tablespoon all-purpose flour, plus more for dusting

Paula's New Flaky Piecrust (see page 325) or 1 9-inch unbaked prepared piecrust

½ cup sugar

1 tablespoon cornstarch

4 large eggs

¼ cup frozen apple juice concentrate, thawed

1½ cups buttermilk

1 teaspoon pure vanilla extract

Sliced fresh strawberries, for serving

FRUITFUL ENDINGS
I take any opportunity
I can to work fruits into
my day. Dessert is a
great place to add them
to the plate. Whether
baked right into the
dessert or served
alongside, fruit's a
great complement to
sweet endings.

All-New
Peach Cobbler

This new cobbler of mine has only half the sugar of my original recipe and a quarter of the butter. But it's got 100 percent of the great peachy taste. The cobbler topping is out of this world, I tell you. My favorite part of this dessert is the sweet golden edges of the topping. I always cut myself off an end piece and let the rest of the family fall all over the middle.

1. Preheat the oven to 350°F. Grease a 13 by 9-inch baking dish with the butter.

2. In a large bowl, whisk together the flour, sugar, baking powder, cinnamon, and salt. Whisk in the milk and vanilla until smooth. Pour the batter into the prepared baking dish and arrange the peach slices on top. Drizzle over the reserved juice. Bake for about 40 minutes, until lightly golden and firm to the touch.

Serves 8 to 10

2 tablespoons (¼ stick) unsalted butter

1½ cups all-purpose flour

½ cup sugar

2¼ teaspoons baking powder

¼ teaspoon ground cinnamon

Pinch of salt

1½ cups milk

½ teaspoon pure vanilla extract

2 cans (15 ounces each) sliced peaches in juice, drained, with ¼ cup juice reserved

Light and Luscious Sweet Potato Pie

2 sweet potatoes
(about 1¾ pounds)

All-purpose flour, for dusting

Paula's New Flaky Piecrust
(see page 325) or 1 9-inch
unbaked prepared piecrust

3 large eggs

⅔ cup milk

½ cup packed light brown sugar

2 tablespoons (¼ stick)
unsalted butter, melted

1 teaspoon pure vanilla extract

1 teaspoon ground cinnamon

¼ teaspoon ground nutmeg

¼ teaspoon salt

In so many households at Thanksgiving time, pumpkin pie reigns high. Not so in the Deen household. We are all about the sweet potato pie in my neck of the woods. If you've never had the pleasure of tasting one before, give this pie here a try. I've skipped the cream and extra butter in this version, making for a lighter pie with a more concentrated sweet potato flavor.

1. Preheat the oven to 400°F. Line a rimmed baking sheet with aluminum foil.

2. Cut a slit in the top of each sweet potato. Bake until very tender, about 1 hour. Cool completely. Peel away the potato jackets. Mash or puree the potatoes until smooth (you should have about 1½ cups of mash).

3. Position an oven rack in the lower third of the oven and reduce the oven temperature to 350°F. Place a rimmed baking sheet on the rack to preheat.

4. Dust a work surface with a small handful of flour. Roll the dough into a 12-inch round about ¼ inch thick. Use it to line a 9-inch pie plate, folding over the excess edges of the dough and crimping them if you like. Chill in the refrigerator for 30 minutes or up to overnight (cover lightly with plastic wrap if chilling for more than 2 hours). Skip this step if you are using a prepared piecrust.

5. In a large bowl, whisk together the mashed sweet potato and the eggs. Whisk in the milk, brown sugar, butter, vanilla, cinnamon, nutmeg, and salt. Pour the mixture into the chilled piecrust. Place the pie on the hot baking sheet and bake for 40 to 50 minutes, until the edges of the filling are puffed and lightly set. Cool completely, at least 4 hours, before serving.

Serves 8

Paula's New Flaky Piecrust

I have redesigned my famous piecrust, y'all. This is a piecrust I can enjoy on a more regular basis. And that is lucky because I like to have a pie on hand for when I get visitors stopping by. I make this dough in my food processor, but if you like to make it by hand, that works too. The dough will keep in the fridge for three days or so and in the freezer for three months, ensuring that you always have the makings of a Southern hospitality pie on hand.

1 cup all-purpose flour

¼ teaspoon salt

1 teaspoon sugar

4 tablespoons (½ stick) cold unsalted butter, cut into small bits

2 to 4 tablespoons regular or low-fat Greek yogurt

1. In a food processor, pulse together the flour, salt, and sugar just until combined. Add the butter and pulse until the mixture resembles coarse meal. Add the yogurt, 1 tablespoon at a time, and pulse just until the dough comes together, taking care not to overwork the dough. You should be able to bring the dough together in a ball.

2. Place the dough on a sheet of plastic wrap and press it into a flat disk. Wrap well and refrigerate for at least 30 minutes before rolling out.

Makes enough for one 9-inch piecrust

BLIND BAKING TIP

1. Dust a work surface with a small handful of flour. Roll the dough into a 12-inch round about ¼ inch thick. Use it to line a 9-inch pie plate and chill in the refrigerator for 30 minutes or up to overnight (cover lightly with plastic wrap if chilling for more than 2 hours).

2. When you are ready to bake the pie, preheat the oven to 375°F. Use a fork to prick the bottom of the pie a couple of times. Line the dough up the sides with parchment paper or aluminum foil and fill with dried beans or pie weights. Bake for 20 minutes. Remove the beans or pie weights and the paper or foil, return to the oven, and bake for 5 minutes.

Red Velvet Cake with Cream Cheese Frosting

CAKE

1 box (16 ounces) sugar-free
yellow cake mix

2 teaspoons or more red food dye

¼ cup Dutch-process
cocoa powder, sifted

FROSTING

2 packages (8 ounces each)
low-fat cream cheese
(Neufchâtel), at room
temperature

1 teaspoon pure vanilla extract

2 cups confectioners' sugar, sifted

This is hands down the easiest, most delicious red velvet cake I know. I challenge any of your guests to figure out you took a cake mix shortcut in preparing the cake. It's moist and flavorful and just as pretty as a picture. By using Neufchâtel in the frosting, I was able to cut out tons of fat without sacrificing a beautiful fluffy texture.

1. Preheat the oven to 350°F. Grease two 9- or 8-inch round cake pans with cooking spray.

2. To make the cake: In a large bowl, prepare the cake mix according to the package directions. Add the red dye and cocoa powder and stir until combined. Add more food coloring, depending on how red you want the cake to be. Make sure no cocoa or yellow cake mix lumps remain in the batter. Scrape the batter into the prepared cake pans and bake according to the package directions. Let the cakes cool in their pans on a wire rack.

3. To make the frosting: While the cakes are cooling, in the bowl of an electric mixer fitted with the paddle attachment, or using a hand-held mixer, whip the cream cheese until fluffy and smooth and no lumps remain, 2 to 3 minutes. Add the vanilla and confectioners' sugar and mix until combined.

4. Remove the cooled cakes from their pans and use a serrated knife to level off the tops, until even. Place 1 cake layer, cut side down, on a cake stand or platter. Spread one third to one half of the frosting over the surface of the cake. Top with the second layer, cut-side down, and frost the top and sides with the remaining frosting. Serve at room temperature.

Serves 9 to 12

Gooey Butter Cake

CAKE

1 box (16 ounces) sugar-free
   yellow cake mix

½ cup buttermilk

1 large egg

1 tablespoon unsalted butter,
   melted, plus 2 teaspoons,
   melted, for brushing the cake

FILLING

6 ounces low-fat cream cheese
   (Neufchâtel), at room
   temperature

2 large eggs

⅓ cup confectioners' sugar

⅔ cup buttermilk

1 teaspoon pure vanilla extract

*My son Bobby has taken a crack at a lighter version of my
Gooey Butter Cake and I reckon he's done a heck of a job.
But because this is one of my signature desserts, I felt I had to
throw my hat in the ring too. Well, bless my soul if I didn't come
upon yet another version of Gooey Butter Cake that I'd be proud
to serve to my guests.*

1. Preheat the oven to 350°F. Lightly grease a 13 by 9-inch
   baking dish with cooking spray.

2. To make the cake: Place the cake mix in a large bowl.
   In a small bowl, whisk together the buttermilk, egg, and
   1 tablespoon of the butter you melted. Add the buttermilk
   mixture to the cake mix, stirring just until blended. Scrape
   the batter into the prepared baking dish and use a spatula
   to spread the batter evenly over the bottom of the pan.
   You may need to use your hands to help pat out the batter
   because the batter will be pretty thick.

3. To make the filling: In the bowl of an electric mixer fitted
   with the paddle attachment, or using a hand-held mixer,
   beat the cream cheese at medium speed until smooth. Add
   the eggs, confectioners' sugar, buttermilk, and vanilla and
   beat well, continuously scraping down the sides of the bowl.
   Gently pour the cream cheese filling over the batter in the
   baking dish.

4. Bake for 35 to 40 minutes, until the center is almost firm,
   but still gooey. Remove from the oven, brush the top of the
   cake with the remaining 2 teaspoons melted butter, and
   let it cool for 15 minutes before serving.

Serves 12

Carrot Apple Snacking Cake

This is a lovely little snacking cake that is perfect for the late-afternoon doldrums when it's not quite time for dinner but lunch has faded into the distance. I get away with only ¾ cup sugar in this confection because the carrots, apple, and applesauce provide natural sweetness. And do make sure you use a juice that is all natural, with no added sugars. Those sneaky hidden sugars are just as unhealthy for you.

1. Preheat the oven to 350°F. Grease a 13 by 9-inch baking dish with cooking spray.

2. In a large bowl, whisk together the all-purpose flour, whole-wheat flour, baking powder, baking soda, salt, cinnamon, and nutmeg. In a medium bowl, whisk together the eggs, sugar, oil, and applesauce. Fold the applesauce mixture into the flour mixture just until combined. Stir in the carrots, apple, walnuts, and vanilla.

3. Scrape the batter into the prepared baking dish. Bake for 30 to 40 minutes, until a toothpick inserted into the center of the cake comes out clean. Let the cake cool completely in the dish on a wire rack before cutting into pieces.

Serves 12

1 cup all-purpose flour

½ cup whole-wheat flour

1½ teaspoons baking powder

1 teaspoon baking soda

½ teaspoon salt

1½ teaspoons ground cinnamon

½ teaspoon ground nutmeg

4 large eggs

¾ cup sugar

½ cup canola or safflower oil

½ cup natural applesauce

2 cups finely grated carrots
(3 to 4 large carrots)

1 cup peeled, cored, and grated apple (about 1 large apple)

1 cup walnuts, toasted

1 teaspoon pure vanilla extract

Flourless Chocolate Fudge Cake

*I thought I'd died and gone to chocolate heaven the first time
I tasted this cake. It's that richly, decadently chocolaty. With no
flour to dilute the full chocolate impact, I needed only a half cup
of sugar to add just the right amount of sweetness. This one is
for all you chocoholics out there. With love, from Paula.*

6 large eggs, separated

12 ounces bittersweet chocolate,
  chopped

9 tablespoons unsalted butter,
  cut into small bits

½ cup sugar

1. Preheat the oven to 325°F. Grease a 9-inch springform pan
   with cooking spray. Line the bottom with parchment paper
   and spray the top of the paper.

2. In the bowl of an electric mixer fitted with the whisk
   attachment or with a hand-held mixer, beat the egg whites
   until stiff peaks form.

3. In a medium microwave-safe bowl, melt the chocolate and
   butter in the microwave at 30-second intervals, stirring in
   between, until smooth. Whisk in the sugar until combined.
   Allow the chocolate mixture to cool.

4. Whisk the egg yolks into the chocolate mixture, one at a
   time. Using a rubber spatula, gently fold the whipped egg
   whites into the chocolate mixture in batches. Pour the batter
   into the prepared pan and bake for 40 minutes, or until the
   cake begins to pull away from the sides of the pan.

5. Let the cake cool for 1 hour before gently releasing it from
   the springform pan.

Serves 8 to 10

GLUTEN FREE
**Lots of people are cutting flour out of their diets
these days and going completely gluten free.
A flourless cake gives them an opportunity to
enjoy their dessert without the unwanted flour.**

Blueberry Streusel Coffee Cake

I like to make this streusel cake when I'm having some ladies over for coffee. It makes the house smell so warm and inviting. I always know that when I put this cake out, we'll get to talking long into the afternoon.

STREUSEL

2 tablespoons (¼ stick) unsalted butter, melted

Pinch of salt

2 tablespoons all-purpose flour

2 tablespoons old-fashioned rolled oats

2 tablespoons granulated sugar

2 tablespoons packed light brown sugar

½ teaspoon ground cinnamon

⅛ teaspoon freshly grated nutmeg

CAKE

1½ cups all-purpose flour

1 teaspoon baking powder

¼ teaspoon baking soda

½ teaspoon salt

8 tablespoons (1 stick) unsalted butter

½ cup granulated sugar

2 large eggs

1 teaspoon pure vanilla extract

⅔ cup regular or light sour cream

½ cup fresh or thawed frozen blueberries

1 teaspoon finely grated lemon zest (optional)

1. Preheat the oven to 350°F. Grease an 8-inch square cake pan or baking dish with butter, canola oil, or cooking spray.

2. To make the streusel: In a medium bowl, mix together the butter, salt, flour, oats, granulated sugar, brown sugar, cinnamon, and nutmeg until the streusel mixture begins to clump together.

3. To make the cake: In a medium bowl, whisk together the flour, baking powder, baking soda, and salt.

4. In the bowl of an electric mixer fitted with the paddle attachment, or using a hand-held mixer, beat the butter and granulated sugar at medium speed until creamy and smooth, 1 to 2 minutes. In a medium bowl, whisk together the eggs, vanilla, and sour cream. Beat one third of the flour mixture into the butter mixture. Beat in half the sour cream mixture. Repeat with the remaining flour and sour cream mixtures, ending with the last remaining flour mixture. Mix, just until incorporated, scraping down the sides of the bowl. Fold in the blueberries and lemon zest (if using).

5. Pour the batter into the prepared cake pan and top evenly with the streusel. Bake for about 45 minutes, or until a toothpick inserted into the center of the cake comes out clean. Let the cake cool in the pan, then slice and serve.

Serves 8 to 10

Potluck Apple Nut Cake

Applesauce and vanilla yogurt do wonders for this charming cake. The sweetness and moisture that they bring to the table allowed me to cut the sugar and oil way, way down. This is the perfect make-ahead cake that tastes even better the next day. Now, don't you just love things that get better with age?

1. Preheat the oven to 350°F. Lightly grease a 9-inch square cake pan with cooking spray.

2. In a small bowl, combine the apple, walnuts, butter, brown sugar, and ½ teaspoon of the cinnamon. Toss until the apple is thoroughly coated, then set aside while you prepare the cake batter.

3. In the bowl of an electric mixer fitted with the paddle attachment, or using a hand-held mixer, beat together the granulated sugar and eggs. Add the applesauce, yogurt, and oil and beat until combined.

4. In a medium bowl, whisk together the all-purpose flour, pastry flour, baking powder, baking soda, nutmeg, clove, and the remaining 1 teaspoon cinnamon.

5. With the mixer on low, beat the flour mixture into the applesauce mixture just until combined. Pour the batter into the prepared pan and scatter the apple and nut mixture over the top. Bake for about 40 minutes, or until a toothpick inserted into the center of the cake comes out clean. Let the cake cool completely on a wire rack.

Serves 9 to 12

1 apple, peeled, cored, and chopped

½ cup chopped walnuts

2 tablespoons (¼ stick) unsalted butter, melted

1 tablespoon light brown sugar

1½ teaspoons ground cinnamon

½ cup granulated sugar

2 large eggs

1 cup natural applesauce

¾ cup low-fat or regular vanilla yogurt

¼ cup canola or safflower oil

1 cup all-purpose flour

1 cup whole-wheat pastry flour

2 teaspoons baking powder

½ teaspoon baking soda

¼ teaspoon ground nutmeg

Pinch of ground clove

A IS FOR APPLE
Applesauce is actually well known in baking circles as a substitute for extra fat in a cake. It can take the place of up to half the oil or butter in a cake and allow you to drop an egg or two. Plus, it offers a sweet mellow flavor in the mix. So, even if you aren't making an apple-based cake, applesauce can be a real handy tool to cut down the fat in your baked goods.

Coconut Cake

CAKE

2⅓ cups cake flour, sifted, plus more for dusting

2½ teaspoons baking powder, sifted

½ teaspoon salt

8 tablespoons (1 stick) unsalted butter, at room temperature

1 cup sugar

2 large eggs, at room temperature

1 large egg white, at room temperature

2 teaspoons pure vanilla extract

1½ cups light unsweetened coconut milk

FROSTING

⅔ cup sugar

3 tablespoons water

2 large egg whites, at room temperature

¼ teaspoon cream of tartar

⅛ teaspoon salt

1 teaspoon pure vanilla extract

⅔ cup unsweetened shredded coconut

I've been making this cake for Jamie's birthday ever since he was a little boy. When I set about changing my diet, it was high on my list to tinker with so I'd be able to share it with him for many more birthdays to come. Between the cake and the frosting, I have managed to cut half the amount of sugar in this dessert, without sacrificing the beautiful flavor.

1. Preheat the oven to 350°F. Lightly grease two 8-inch round cake pans with butter, canola oil, or cooking spray. Dust with flour, tapping out any excess.

2. To make the cake: In a large bowl, whisk together the flour, baking powder, and salt.

3. In the bowl of an electric mixer fitted with the paddle attachment, or using a hand-held mixer, beat together the butter and sugar until very light and fluffy, about 4 minutes. Be sure to scrape down the sides of the bowl occasionally to incorporate all the sugar into the butter. Add the whole eggs, one at a time, beating well after each egg is added to thoroughly combine. Add the egg white, then the vanilla. Stop and scrape down the sides of the bowl and beat for 1 minute. With the mixer on low speed, alternate beating in the flour mixture and the coconut milk. Mix just until incorporated, scraping down the sides of the bowl occasionally.

4. Divide the batter between the prepared pans, smoothing the tops. Bake for about 30 minutes, or until a toothpick inserted into the center of each cake comes out clean. Let the cakes cool in the pans on wire racks for 10 minutes. Then invert the cakes out of the pans onto the racks and let them cool completely before frosting.

5. To make the frosting: Bring a medium saucepan filled one third of the way with water to barely a simmer. In a large heatproof bowl (one that will rest on top of the pan without touching the water), whisk together the sugar, water, egg whites, cream of tartar, and salt. Place the bowl over the simmering water and beat at high speed with a hand-held mixer for 7 minutes. The frosting should appear thick, glossy, and fluffy. Remove from the heat and stir in the vanilla.

6. Use a serrated knife to level the top of both cake layers. Place 1 cake layer cut side down, on a serving plate or cake stand. Spread about one third of the frosting on top of the cake. Sprinkle with 3 tablespoons of the shredded coconut. Place the second layer, cut side down, on top of the first. Spread the remaining frosting on top and around the sides of the cake. Sprinkle with the remaining shredded coconut over the top and sides of the cake.

Serves 10

CLEAN HOUSE
Household chores are a great way to sneak some exercise into your busy day while still getting the things on your list done. I burn calories while tending to my garden, then treat myself to a little something sweet when I'm done.

Italian Cheesecake

4 cups (32 ounces) part-skim
ricotta cheese

⅔ cup sugar

¼ cup all-purpose flour

½ cup half-and-half

1 tablespoon amaretto liqueur

1 teaspoon pure vanilla extract

1 teaspoon pure almond extract

1 teaspoon finely grated
orange zest

4 large eggs

This is a different style cheesecake from the kind I usually whip up. Instead of using cream cheese, I make it the way the Italians have been making it for years on end, using ricotta cheese. The ricotta makes it feather light and airy. I like to serve this cake with some pretty little orange slices on the side. As they say across the ocean, buon appetito!

1. Preheat the oven to 350°F if you are using a silver 9-inch springform pan. If you are using a dark nonstick 9-inch springform pan, preheat the oven to 325°F. Grease the pan with cooking spray.

2. In the bowl of an electric mixer fitted with the paddle attachment, or using a hand-held mixer, beat the ricotta, sugar, flour, and half-and-half at medium speed until combined. Add the amaretto, vanilla, almond extract, and orange zest. Mix until combined. Add the eggs, one at a time, beating after each addition to incorporate the eggs. Be sure to scrape down the sides of the bowl so that the whole mixture is combined. Pour the mixture into the springform pan.

3. Bake for 1 hour and 20 minutes, or until the edges are set but the center still jiggles. Let the cheesecake cool to room temperature, then use a knife to loosen it from the sides of the pan. Enjoy this cake at room temperature or cold.

Serves 10 to 12

Peaches and Cream Cheesecake

This ultracreamy cheesecake is so scrumptious, I can't help but cut myself a healthy slice whenever I'm indulging in this treat. Because of all the luscious peaches beaten into the batter, you get delicious, delicate peach flavor in every bite, without the calories of regular cheesecake.

1. Preheat the oven to 325°F.

2. In a medium bowl, toss the graham cracker crumbs with the melted butter until thoroughly combined. Press the mixture evenly into the bottom and just slightly up the sides of a 9-inch springform pan.

3. In the bowl of an electric mixer fitted with the paddle attachment, or using a hand-held mixer, beat the cream cheese, sugar, and vanilla on low speed until smooth. Add the eggs, one at a time, beating after each addition until incorporated and scraping down the sides of the bowl. Add the peach slices, increase the speed to medium, and blend until the peaches are broken down into small chunks.

4. Pour the filling into the prepared piecrust and bake for about 1 hour, or until the edges of the cheesecake are set but the center still jiggles. Let the cheesecake cool completely at room temperature before covering with plastic wrap and refrigerating for 8 hours or overnight.

Serves 10 to 12

1½ cups graham cracker crumbs

4 tablespoons (½ stick) unsalted butter, melted

3 packages (8 ounces each) low-fat cream cheese (Neufchâtel)

¾ cup sugar

1 teaspoon pure vanilla extract

4 large eggs

1 can (15 ounces) sliced peaches in juice, thoroughly drained

KINDEST CUT
Get yourself a hot, dry knife (heated up under hot running water, then wiped dry with a towel) to cut wedges from your cheesecake. The wedges will come out nice and clean.

12

Other Tempting Desserts and Beverages

My mama used to say to me at the dinner table, "Slow down, Paula, your food's not gonna up and run away!" But for years on end, I ate my food way too fast. I have finally come to realize that food is best eaten slowly, allowing you to savor each and every bite. And that is especially true when you are eating these tempting desserts that look so darn good on the plate you can't wait to gobble them up. You see it actually takes a full twenty minutes for your stomach to tell your brain that you've had enough. And in that twenty minutes, you could be eating way past the point of fullness. So what I do now is, I take my time with my food. That has helped me more fully appreciate the food I'm eating.

And what a lot there is to appreciate in this chapter! Each bite of these decadent delights should be savored. This chapter's got a little bit of everything that's sweet and yummy, from *Gingered Apple Crisp* (page 341) to *Homemade Vanilla Ice Cream* (page 347) to *Chocolate-Banana-Walnut Bread Pudding* (page 353). You see, now that y'all are eating healthy, you need little rewards here and there to tell yourself, "Job well done."

While you'll still find plenty of chocolate, peanut butter, and creamy goodness in my sweet treats, just as in my pies and cakes, you're also going to see tons and tons of fruit. Take my *Homey Baked Apples* (page 342), for instance. The apples' natural sugars are helped along by only three tablespoons of apple juice. And that's no-sugar-added apple juice, mind you! The **All-New Peach Melba** (page 354) not only features peaches but a whole pint of raspberries in the delectable raspberry sauce I smother it in. And the **Everyday Frozen Peach and Banana Treat** (page 356) is a little indulgence that Michael and I can feel good about having on an almost daily basis, usually just after we've taken our evening walk around the neighborhood.

I always like to have cookies in the kitchen. I don't care whether you're young or old, not many people will turn down a cookie when offered one. For my grandkids, it's got to be **Peanut Butter and Jelly Cookies** (page 349). These little sandwich cookies are a protein-packed nibble that helps to perk them up after the school day. And I've developed a healthier cookie for myself to indulge in. My **Granola Cookies** (page 350) have all the goodness of a granola bar rolled up into cookie form.

Apart from my food, I also had to think twice about the beverages I was consuming. It's proven that sugary drinks can pose serious health risks. You may think you are just wetting your mouth when in actuality you are taking in tons of sugar and calories with that sugary sip. Quitting cola was no big chore for me but, as a Southerner, a tall glass of sweet tea is nearly sacred. I developed **New Southern Iced Tea** (page 359) so that I could have my beloved iced tea, with just a little bit of honey instead of a whole lot of sugar.

I love me a sweet nibble now and again. I'm grateful I've been able to develop ways to keep that happiness in my new lifestyle. But most of all, I'm grateful I've learned to take it slowly, savor the treat, and thank my lucky stars that I'm still here for the next bite.

Gingered Apple Crisp

These warm baked apples are highlighted by sweet candied ginger and topped off with a crunchy, buttery, crisp topping. If it's pears you've got in the fruit bowl, you can use those in place of the apples. Or, if you like, go on ahead and try a mix of both fruits.

1. Preheat the oven to 350°F.

2. To make the apples: In a large bowl, combine the apples, lemon zest, lemon juice, and ginger.

3. To make the topping: Place the flour in a medium bowl. Cut in the butter using two forks or your hands until the mixture resembles coarse meal. Stir in the brown sugar, oats, lemon zest, cinnamon, and nutmeg and combine well.

4. Spread the apples into the bottom of an 8- or 9-inch square baking dish. Add the topping in an even layer, clumping bits of topping together with your fingers. Bake for 45 to 55 minutes, until the topping is crisp and golden brown and the apples are tender. Serve warm.

Serves 8

APPLES

5 cups thinly sliced apples

½ tablespoon finely grated lemon zest

2 tablespoons fresh lemon juice

¼ cup chopped crystallized ginger

TOPPING

½ cup all-purpose flour

5 tablespoons unsalted butter, cut into small bits

⅓ cup packed light brown sugar

¾ cup quick-cooking rolled oats

1 tablespoon finely grated lemon zest

1½ teaspoons ground cinnamon

¼ teaspoon freshly grated nutmeg

BEST ZEST
This recipe includes a fair amount of lemon zest, giving it a nice, bright, light taste. To zest your lemons, use a fine grater such as a Microplane. Rub the lemon along the grater just to remove the bright yellow exterior. Be sure not to rub too hard in one spot. You don't want to get down to the bitter white pith below the yellow. This works for any citrus zest.

Homey Baked Apples

3 large apples

1 tablespoon unsalted butter, cut into small bits

3 tablespoons no-sugar-added apple juice

½ teaspoon ground cinnamon

⅛ teaspoon ground allspice

When September and October come around and apples are at their peak, this is one of the many ways I like to enjoy them. It doesn't get much more warm and comforting than apples baked with cinnamon and allspice and just a hint of buttery goodness. Serve them with a scoop of reduced-sugar vanilla ice cream (or a tiny scoop of the regular kind), and you have yourself the perfect accompaniment to a chilly fall day.

1. Preheat the oven to 375°F.

2. Core the apples and cut them in half lengthwise. In a medium baking dish, place the apple halves, skin side down.

3. Dot the apples with the butter and drizzle with 2 tablespoons of the apple juice. Sprinkle with the cinnamon and allspice.

4. Cover the dish with aluminum foil and bake for 15 minutes. Uncover, drizzle with the remaining 1 tablespoon apple juice, and bake for 20 minutes more, or until the apples are easily pierced with a knife.

Serves 6

Homemade Ginger Applesauce

In the fall, when apples seem to be just about everywhere you look, I set to work on preparing jars of my homemade applesauce. I tell you, there is nothing like it. Every year I come up with new flavors to add to my sauces. My ginger sauce has got to be one of the more popular varieties. I like to use a mix of different-colored apples so that my sauce comes out a pretty pink color. And I always make enough for several jars so I can give them out to family and friends. Slap a pretty bow on one and you've got yourself a sweet little homemade gift.

1 tablespoon unsalted butter

½ tablespoon fresh ginger, peeled and finely chopped

2 green apples, skin on, cored, and thinly sliced

2 red apples, skin on, cored, and thinly sliced

1 tablespoon honey

½ teaspoon ground cinnamon

Pinch of salt

Juice of ½ lemon

¾ cup water

1. In a medium pot, heat the butter over medium-high heat until melted. Add the ginger and cook for 2 minutes. Add the apple slices, honey, cinnamon, salt, and lemon juice. Stir to combine. Add the water and bring the mixture to a boil. Simmer the applesauce for 20 minutes, until the apples have broken down and are tender.

2. Set a food mill or coarse sieve securely above a bowl and push the applesauce through in batches. Thin out the sauce with extra water, if you think it needs it.

Serves 4 to 6

RUN OF THE MILL

I make this sweet, fragrant sauce using a food mill. But don't you worry if you haven't got this tool in your kitchen appliance drawer. You can also make this sauce using a colander or sieve to push the pulp through. If you do use a colander, though, you may want to peel your apples first. That way you won't give yourself a great big muscle ache from pushing those apples through.

Christmas Trifle

1 box (16 ounces) sugar-free
yellow cake mix

2 cups sugar-free raspberry
preserves

2 tablespoons water

2 pints fresh raspberries

2 cups heavy cream

2 tablespoons confectioners'
sugar

Fresh mint, for garnish

It may be called a Christmas trifle, but I enjoy this delicious decadence at special-occasion meals at any time of the year. After all, what is there not to like about cake, cream, and fruit? These days I make my trifle with sugar-free products, but this can most certainly be made with full-sugar products as well. And while this version features beautiful raspberries, I just as often use blueberries, strawberries, or blackberries. There are two cups of cream in this trifle, so I treat it as a special indulgence. But a little does go a long way. Those couple cups of cream stretch out to serve twelve.

1. Preheat the oven according to the cake mix package directions. Grease a 13 by 9-inch baking dish with cooking spray.

2. Prepare the cake according to the package directions and pour the batter into the prepared baking dish. Bake according to the package directions.

3. While the cake is baking, add the preserves and water to a small saucepan. Bring to a simmer. Add 1 pint of the raspberries and carefully stir to combine. Cook for 2 to 3 minutes and remove from the heat.

4. In the bowl of an electric mixer fitted with the whisk attachment, or using a hand-held mixer, whisk together the cream and sugar until soft peaks form, about 3 minutes. Be careful not to overmix.

TRUE TRIFLE
This dessert is so very pretty and always makes a grand entrance when served at the table. Be sure to serve it in a clear bowl or dish so that your guests can see the beautiful layers. I highly recommend a trifle dish, which is a clear, straight-sided bowl with a wineglasslike stem at the bottom.

5. Once the cake is cool, cut it into 1-inch-thick slices. Line the bottom of a 3-quart clear bowl or trifle dish with one third of the cake slices. Top with one third of the preserves. Smooth one third of the whipped cream on top with a rubber spatula, reaching the edges of the bowl. Repeat with another layer of cake, preserves, and whipped cream. Layer the last of the cake, preserves, and whipped cream, ending with the whipped cream. Decorate with the remaining 1 pint raspberries and garnish with mint. Serve at room temperature or chilled.

Serves 12

Not Yo' Mama's Banana Pudding

1 sleeve graham crackers (about 7 crackers)

6 to 8 bananas, peeled and sliced

2½ cups milk

2 packages (1 ounce each) instant sugar-free vanilla pudding

1 package (8 ounces) low-fat cream cheese (Neufchâtel), at room temperature

1 container (8 ounces) sugar-free frozen whipped topping, thawed

If you're watching your sugar intake like I am these days, you'll be relieved to see this recipe. I've rejiggered my famous banana pudding with a whole lot less sugar. I tell you, it's absolutely delicious. And I can feel good about having it just about any old day of the week.

1. Line the bottom of a 13 by 9-inch baking dish with the graham crackers and layer the bananas on top.

2. In a large bowl, combine 2 cups of the milk with the pudding mix. Blend well using a hand-held mixer. In a medium bowl, beat the cream cheese until smooth. Add the remaining ½ cup milk to the cream cheese and mix until smooth. Using a rubber spatula, fold the whipped topping into the cream cheese mixture. Fold the cream cheese mixture into the pudding in two batches until well combined.

3. Pour the pudding mixture over the crackers and bananas. Place a piece of plastic wrap directly on top of the surface of the pudding. Refrigerate for 2 hours, or until the graham crackers have softened and the pudding is set.

Serves 12

Homemade Vanilla Ice Cream

Homemade vanilla ice cream is one of the simple, sweet indulgences in life. And this recipe is just as delicious and satisfying, if a bit less indulgent. While it is still real vanilla ice cream, there is not a drop of cream or a single egg yolk in the mix. For flavoring, I like to use a vanilla bean pod in the custard. The vanilla seeds give the ice cream a pretty speckled look that I love. If you haven't got a vanilla pod on hand, though, extract will do just fine.

2 cups half-and-half

1 cup milk

$\frac{2}{3}$ cup sugar

$\frac{1}{8}$ teaspoon salt

1 vanilla bean pod, split, or 2 teaspoons pure vanilla extract

1. In a heavy saucepan over medium heat, combine the half-and-half, milk, sugar, and salt. Using a small sharp knife, scrape the insides of the vanilla bean into the pan and drop in the pod. Bring the mixture just to a simmer and cook, stirring, until the sugar dissolves, about 5 minutes. Remove from the heat (if using vanilla extract, stir into the pan at this point) and cover with a lid to let the mixture steep for 30 minutes.

2. If you are using it, remove and discard the vanilla pod. Cover the mixture with plastic wrap and chill in the fridge until cold, at least 2 hours or overnight. Freeze the mixture in an ice-cream maker according to the manufacturer's instructions. Serve soft and custardy right away or place the ice cream in an airtight freezer container with a tight-fitting lid and freeze until firm, at least 4 hours.

Makes about 1 quart

KEEP IT REAL
See what I've done here in this recipe? I have slashed the fat, all the while using real, honest-to-goodness ingredients. Whenever I can do so, I like to use natural ingredients to lighten up my foods.

Oatmeal Raisin Cookies

⅓ cup pecans

1¾ cups old-fashioned rolled oats

½ cup all-purpose flour

½ teaspoon baking powder

¼ teaspoon baking soda

½ teaspoon salt

1 teaspoon ground cinnamon

¼ teaspoon freshly grated nutmeg

Pinch of ground cloves

4 tablespoons (½ stick) unsalted butter, at room temperature

½ cup packed light brown sugar

1 large egg

1 teaspoon pure vanilla extract

2 tablespoons natural applesauce

¾ cup raisins

PLAY WITH ME
I like to stay active by playing with my grandkids. If you've ever played with two young boys, you'll know it's great exercise! But besides that, it's fun, keeps me feeling young, and brings me closer to two of the most special people in my life.

This is the classic oatmeal raisin cookie I bet y'all grew up on. Here, though, I dial back the sugar and sweeten it with a kiss of applesauce. My grandsons can't get enough of these yummy cookies after a busy day playing with Grandma.

1. Preheat the oven to 375°F. Line two rimmed baking sheets with parchment paper.

2. In a food processor, pulse the pecans until finely chopped, then pour into a small bowl and set aside.

3. Place ¼ cup of the oats in the processor and finely grind into oat flour. Place the oat flour in a medium bowl. Add the remaining 1½ cups oats, the flour, baking powder, baking soda, salt, cinnamon, nutmeg, and cloves. Whisk together until combined.

4. Place the butter and sugar in the processor and pulse until well combined and fluffy. Using a rubber spatula, scrape down the sides of the bowl, then add the egg and vanilla while continuing to pulse. Once the mixture is well combined, add the applesauce and pulse until mixed. Scrape down the sides of the bowl and pulse one more time.

5. Add the oat mixture to the processor and pulse until a dough is formed. Use a spatula to scrape the dough back into a medium bowl and fold in the finely chopped pecans and the raisins.

6. Drop the batter by the rounded tablespoonful (a mini ice-cream scoop is great for this) onto the prepared baking sheets. Bake, one sheet at a time, for 10 to 12 minutes, until the cookies are set around the edges and light golden brown, turning the sheets halfway through. Let the cookies cool slightly on the pans, then place them on wire racks to cool completely.

Makes about 24 cookies

Peanut Butter and Jelly Cookies

Your eyes are not deceiving you. This cookie doesn't contain a lick of butter. It's a light, cakey cookie that has a wonderful peanut butter flavor. I sandwich two cookies together with all-fruit preserves in the middle to make a little peanut butter and jelly cookie that is oh so cute. I like to use raspberry preserves, but feel free to use whatever flavor you or your little ones like best.

¾ cup packed light brown sugar

½ cup regular or natural peanut butter, creamy or crunchy

½ cup canola or safflower oil

2 large eggs

1 teaspoon pure vanilla extract

1⅓ cups all-purpose flour

¼ teaspoon salt

¾ teaspoon baking soda

⅓ cup all-fruit preserves

1. In the bowl of an electric mixer fitted with the paddle attachment, or using a hand-held mixer, beat the brown sugar, peanut butter, oil, eggs, and vanilla at low speed until creamy and smooth.

2. In a medium bowl, whisk together the flour, salt, and baking soda. Add the flour mixture to the peanut butter mixture and stir just until combined. Refrigerate for 1 hour.

3. Place an oven rack in the upper third of the oven. Preheat the oven to 375°F.

4. Drop the batter by the tablespoonful (a mini ice-cream scoop is great for this) onto two ungreased cookie sheets. Bake, one sheet at a time, for 8 to 10 minutes, until the bottom edges start to turn golden (keep a close watch as these cookies do burn quickly). Let the cookies cool on the sheets before moving to wire racks.

5. Spread the preserves on the flat sides of half the cookies, then top them with the remaining cookies, flat side down.

Makes 15 sandwich cookies

SKIP THE PRESERVES
If it's just peanut butter cookies you're in the mood for, skip the preserves and enjoy these cookies individually, without turning them into sandwiches.

Granola Cookies

4 tablespoons (½ stick) unsalted butter

½ cup packed light brown sugar

¼ cup olive oil

1 large egg

1 teaspoon pure vanilla extract

1 cup whole-wheat pastry flour

½ teaspoon baking soda

½ teaspoon ground cinnamon

¼ teaspoon salt

1 cup old-fashioned rolled oats

⅔ cup finely chopped walnuts

⅔ cup dried cranberries

½ cup sunflower seeds

I never really thought I'd see myself becoming a granola cookie kind of gal. But, lo and behold, I absolutely love these chewy, nutty cookies. I'm not going to go so far as to call these cookies health food. But, if you eat them in moderation, they're a pretty good choice when you're craving something sweet. I've said it before and I'll say it again. It's about moderation, folks, not deprivation.

1. Preheat the oven to 350°F. Line 2 rimmed baking sheets with parchment paper.

2. In the bowl of an electric mixer fitted with the paddle attachment, or using a hand-held mixer, beat together the butter and brown sugar until light and fluffy. Slowly beat in the oil until fluffy and smooth. Beat in the egg and vanilla until combined.

3. In a large bowl, whisk together the pastry flour, baking soda, cinnamon, and salt. Beat the flour mixture into the butter mixture just until combined. Using a wooden spoon, stir in the oats, walnuts, cranberries, and sunflower seeds.

4. Drop rounded tablespoons of dough onto the prepared baking sheets, 1½ inches apart. Bake for 10 to 12 minutes, until golden. Let the cookies cool several minutes on the baking sheets, then transfer them to a wire rack to cool completely. Repeat with the remaining dough.

Makes about 24 cookies

Rice Pudding

I could hardly believe it myself, but as it turns out, brown rice is downright delicious when baked into a rice pudding. When you think about it, it makes sense actually. Brown rice has a wonderful nutty flavor that is the perfect complement to dried cherries, cinnamon, and nutmeg. Because I've always been crazy about nuts in my desserts, this came as a happy surprise to me.

2½ cups milk

3 large eggs, lightly beaten

1 cup cooked brown or white rice

½ cup sugar

½ cup dried cherries, coarsely chopped

1 teaspoon pure vanilla extract

¼ teaspoon salt

½ teaspoon ground cinnamon

¼ teaspoon ground nutmeg

½ teaspoon freshly grated orange zest

1. Preheat the oven to 325°F. Grease an 8-inch square baking dish with cooking spray.

2. In a large bowl, whisk together the milk and eggs until combined. Stir in the rice, sugar, cherries, vanilla, salt, cinnamon, nutmeg, and orange zest. Spoon the mixture into the prepared baking dish.

3. Place the baking dish in a 13 by 9-inch pan and carefully pour water into the pan to a depth of 1 inch. Bake for about 1½ hours, or until the rice pudding is lightly browned and set. Cool slightly and place in the fridge for at least 30 minutes. Cut into squares to serve.

Serves 8

LEFTOVER LOVER
This rice pudding is a great place to use leftover rice from dinner the night before.

Chocolate-Banana-Walnut Bread Pudding

Because I'm not eating as much bread as I used to, I find that I always have extra pieces of bread lying around and going stale. What better way to put them to good use than to whip up an oldie but a goodie like this? Bread pudding never seems to disappoint and a bread pudding featuring bananas, chocolate, and walnuts is a surefire crowd-pleaser. I often use leftover crostini for this here dish, but feel free to use French bread too. This pudding recipe is a much lighter version of what I used to make, but it is just as scrumptious. When you get a load of how fast it disappears, you'll see what I mean.

1. Preheat the oven to 350°F. Lightly grease an 8-inch square baking dish with cooking spray.

2. Place the bread in a large bowl.

3. In a medium bowl, whisk together the milk, sour cream, ⅓ cup of the sugar, the eggs, and nutmeg. Add the milk mixture to the bread, stirring gently to combine. Let stand for 15 minutes.

4. Spoon the mixture into the prepared baking dish. Evenly sprinkle the chocolate chips over the top and slide the banana slices in between the bread slices. Top with the walnuts and sprinkle over the remaining 1 tablespoon sugar. Bake for 55 minutes to 1 hour, until the center is set.

Serves 6 to 8

1 small loaf stale bread, sliced ½ inch thick

1¼ cups milk

¼ cup regular or light sour cream

⅓ cup packed light brown sugar, plus 1 tablespoon

3 large eggs

½ teaspoon freshly grated nutmeg

⅓ cup semisweet chocolate chips

2 bananas, peeled and sliced

½ cup walnuts, chopped

All-New Peach Melba

PEACHES

4 fresh peaches, sliced
   (about 2 cups), or 1 bag
   (10 ounces) frozen peach
   slices, thawed

1 tablespoon superfine sugar,
   as needed

¼ teaspoon pure vanilla extract

RASPBERRY SAUCE

1 pint raspberries

2 tablespoons confectioners'
   sugar

1 teaspoon fresh lemon juice

Regular or reduced-sugar vanilla
   ice cream, for serving

I find this melba works best with fresh peaches, if you can get your hands on them. But if you can't, no matter, it's still delicious. If you happen to have super-sweet peaches (such as Georgia peaches—the absolute best!), then you may not even need to add any sugar to the fruit. Go ahead and give them a taste first to see if you think you will.

1. To make the peaches: In a medium bowl, add the peaches and sprinkle with 1 tablespoon superfine sugar, as needed. Add the vanilla and stir to combine. Let the peaches soak and soften for 15 to 20 minutes.

2. To make the raspberry sauce: In a blender or food processor, puree the raspberries, confectioners' sugar, and lemon juice, until smooth. Add water to thin it out, if you think it needs it. Strain the seeds, if you like.

3. Place a scoop of vanilla ice cream in a bowl. Add the peach slices and juices and drizzle with raspberry sauce.

Serves 4

SOFTEN UP

What you're doing when you soak the peaches here is macerating them. To macerate fruit means to soak it in a liquid to soften it up and load it up with flavor. Most times, that flavoring is booze, so if you're feeling adventurous, go on ahead and add a shot of sweet wine to these peaches as they sit.

Very Berry Gelatin Cups

*These delightful gelatin cups are almost too pretty for words.
I like to make them in all sorts of different glasses. Sometimes
I use dainty sherry glasses, sometimes it's cute squat tumblers,
and other times I use decorative punch glasses. Whatever I decide
to make them up in, though, they are refreshing, delicious, and
fun to eat: a dessert that's guaranteed to make you smile.*

1 package (0.3 ounces) sugar-free strawberry gelatin

1 cup boiling water

1 container (6 ounces) nonfat strawberry Greek yogurt

½ cup frozen raspberries

½ cup fresh blueberries

⅓ cup sugar-free whipped topping, thawed

1. In a medium bowl, dissolve the gelatin in the boiling water. Refrigerate until thickened, 30 to 45 minutes. Whisk the yogurt into the gelatin and divide among four 8-ounce dessert glasses. Refrigerate until firm, 2 to 3 hours.

2. Meanwhile, place the raspberries in a microwave-safe bowl and defrost in the microwave for 1 minute, until completely thawed. Set a fine-mesh strainer over a small bowl and strain the juice from the raspberries into the bowl. Refrigerate the juice until time to serve (discard the solids).

3. When the gelatin is set, top each glass with 2 tablespoons of the blueberries, followed by a dollop of whipped topping and a drizzle of the raspberry juice.

Serves 4

NO CITRUS NECESSARY
If I were using cream instead of Greek yogurt in this gelatin treat, I would need to add a good dose of lemon juice to brighten it up. That's not necessary here because the Greek yogurt gives the dessert a tangy finish all by itself.

Everyday Frozen
Peach and Banana Treat

4 very ripe bananas,
   peeled and sliced

2 ripe peaches, peeled, pitted,
   and chopped (about ¾ cup)

½ teaspoon pure almond extract

1 to 2 teaspoons honey (optional)

If you've got some browning bananas on your counter, this is the dessert to throw them into. Ripe bananas and peaches provide all the sweetness you need in this everyday treat. And I mean it when I say everyday! Michael and I have a cup of this on most nights. It's the perfect ending to a fine home-cooked meal.

1. Spread the banana slices on a large plate and freeze for 1 to 2 hours until semifrozen but not solid.

2. In a food processor, puree the bananas until smooth. If they stick, stop and scrape down the sides of the bowl and process again. Once smooth, pulse in the peaches, almond extract, and honey (if using). Serve immediately. Freeze leftovers in an airtight freezer container with a tight-fitting lid. Just before serving, thaw slightly and process again.

Makes about 1 quart

Pineapple Coconut Ice Pops

1 can (13½ ounces) light unsweetened coconut milk

1 can (6 ounces) pineapple juice

½ teaspoon coconut extract

1 package (1 ounce) sugar-free instant vanilla pudding

When the Georgia summer really gets going, a homemade ice pop is the most refreshing way to beat the heat. These pineapple and coconut pops are a sweet and creamy treat that will satisfy both kids and adults.

1. Shake the can of coconut milk well before opening. In a large bowl, whisk the coconut milk with the pineapple juice and coconut extract. Add the package of pudding and whisk until the mixture has thickened.

2. Pour the mixture evenly into 3-ounce ice pop molds and insert wooden pop sticks. Freeze until firm.

Makes 6 ice pops

COOK TOGETHER This is the perfect dessert to make with the little ones in your life. They'll have so much fun with it. Get them in on the act, especially when you are making something healthy. Good habits start young, y'all!

New Southern Iced Tea

Is there anything more refreshing on a hot summer's day than a nice tall glass of iced tea? Well, I surely do not think so. I've been enjoying sweet tea since I was knee high to my mama's leg. It is still my drink of choice, even though I've cut the sweetness way, way down. I've added lemon slices for a nice bright zing and a little honey for sweetness.

5 black tea bags, preferably Luzianne

1 quart water

3 tablespoons honey, plus more to taste

Lemon slices, for serving

Place the tea bags in the bottom of a large pitcher. Bring the water to a boil, pour the water over the tea bags, and let them steep for 5 minutes. Remove the tea bags and squeeze out any excess liquid before discarding them. Stir in the honey until it is completely dissolved. Fill tall glasses with ice and pour in the tea. Serve with lemon slices.

Makes 1 quart tea / Serves 4 to 6

HONEY, HONEY

While the carbs in honey are basically equal to what you'll find in white sugar, there is a health benefit to honey over sugar. Because honey contains more fructose than white sugar, a small amount tastes sweeter. And that sweet hit helps you use less in your food.

Pomegranate-Ginger Ale Punch

1 cup pomegranate juice

1 cup pineapple juice

4 orange slices

Diet ginger ale, for serving

Pomegranate juice is chock-full of healthful antioxidants, so I enjoy it in as many ways as possible. This festive punch is one of my favorite libations. When I'm having a crowd over, I double or triple the recipe and serve it in a lovely crystal punch bowl.

In a small pitcher, combine the pomegranate juice, pineapple juice, and orange slices and stir well. Add enough ice to come halfway up the side of the pitcher, then top with the ginger ale. Stir again and serve.

Serves 4

Acknowledgments

It seems that each new day I find another reason to be thankful for the people around me. When trials and tribulations come my way, my loved ones are there to inspire me and to cheer me on. The four Fs, in no particular order, are Family, Friends, Fans, and Faith, and they are near and dear to my heart.

My utmost gratitude goes out to the team who captured the deliciousness of each dish. Thanks go to photographer Ben Fink, food stylists Lori Powell and Maria Del Mar Sacasa, and prop stylist Meghan Erwin Hack. And thanks also go to Fishs Eddy, Prop Workshop, and Prop Haus for the beautiful props used in this book.

I owe an ocean of thanks to my fabulous Deen Team, the pillar of my days, who help me navigate my schedule and my life: Brandon Branch, Theresa Feuger, Hollis Johnson, Sarah Meighen, and Cassie Powers. Thanks to Phyllis Hoffman and her tip-top staff who publish my beautiful magazine, *Cooking with Paula Deen*. Thanks to Gordon Elliott, executive producer extraordinaire and a man who has been a very dear friend for over fourteen years. Thanks to my hairstylist Jamie Cribbs, my makeup artist Courtney Fix, and my wardrobe stylist Dimpy Sethi, all of whom always make me look and feel pretty. Thanks to Jaret Keller, a man I have grown to love so much and who always has my back.

◄ **1** *Michelle Reed and a Ginny hug for my grandson Henry Reed.*
2 *Jack Deen, Anthony and Ashley Groover, Bubba Hiers, and Sandy Nevils, holding John Reed.* **3** *My Deen boys Jamie, Jack, and Bobby.* **4** *Henry Reed and Matthew Deen loving my chicken.* **5** *Some of my girls getting ready to chow down: Ashley; Sandy, with John; Michelle; and Claudia (left to right).*

Heaps of thanks to my faithful and hardworking staff at The Lady & Sons. They are a fabulous team who will do everything to ensure that each guest has a wonderful Southern meal. I'm so proud of our new restaurant, Paula Deen's Family Kitchen, in Pigeon Forge, Tennessee, and I owe a debt of gratitude to all who worked so hard to open this beautiful restaurant. None of it would have been possible without Bob McManus. Bob; Sid, Jim, Doug, and Kevin Blalock; and Darby Campbell have created a wonderful vacation destination at Pigeon Forge, and I'll be there every chance I get.

I have been fortunate to have partners who capture my style, remain true to my recipes, and provide the highest quality products. Thanks to Universal Furniture, which, for over six years, has been creating the beautiful and best-selling Paula Deen furniture line. I can never thank Meyer Corporation enough for creating all of my cookware, which has enabled me to create the most delicious food for my family and friends.

How do I thank someone who has helped me to take control of my business? Steven Nanula, CEO of Paula Deen Ventures, with his amazing business sense, sheer determination, and unwavering belief in me, has brought stability to my life. He is the short stack to my maple syrup. Steve has assembled a world-class team: Nick Gallegos, David Loglisci, and Nicholas Longano, my knights in shining armor; Cheryl Lanoye, whose pencil very rarely leaves the paper; and my P.J., who has captured my personality on every page of this book. I could not have done this without each of you.

And, of course, I thank my incredible family: my dear husband, Michael Groover, the man who brings so much laughter into my life; my two handsome sons, Jamie and Bobby; my lovely daughters-in-law, Brooke and Claudia; the Groover kids, Anthony and Michelle, and their spouses, Ashley Groover and Daniel Reed; and all my grandsons, Jack, Matthew, Henry, John, and Sullivan. Thanks to my baby brother, Bubba, and my niece, Corrie. Also hugs and thanks to Michael's brothers, Father Hank and Nick; the entire Groover family; and my darlin' Aunt Peggy Ort. Y'all are so special to me—thank you for being there.

And, as always, a big Paula Deen hug goes out to all my fans. You will never know how much your support has meant to me over the years. You have stuck with me through thick and thin, and you inspire me every day.

This is the most open and honest accounting of my journey to a new me, and I hope it inspires you to take that journey for yourself. In telling my story, maybe, just maybe, I can help a few of you out there to uncover all the very best that there is inside of you.

Index

vegetable(s), xxi, xxiii, xxvii, 223–57, 303
Beans, Baked, **244**, 245
and Beef Barley Soup, 88
blanching, 55
Broccoli, Crispy Broiled, 257
Brussels Sprouts and Bacon, 243
Cauliflower Casserole,
Mediterranean, 239
and Chickpea Soup, with Orzo, 92
Corn, Grilled, with Parmesan and
Mayonnaise, **155**, 242
Eggplant, Crispy Baked, with
Parmesan, 234
Green Bean Casserole,
New-Fashioned, 247
Green Beans Almondine, 251
Greens, Braised Southern, Best, **125**, 225
Green Tomatoes, Oven-Fried, 232, **233**
Lima Beans and Vidalia Onions,
Sautéed, 256
Okra, Hot-Roasted, 238
Okra and Tomatoes, Stewed, 235
Peas and Ham, Creamy, 240, **241**
Potatoes, Twice-Baked, with
Variations, 231
Potatoes Gratiné, Southern, **254**, 255
Roasted, Fusilli with Ricotta and, 117
Succotash, The Lady's New, **236**, 237
Sweet Potato Balls, Nutty, 229
Sweet Potatoes, Mashed, with
Bourbon, 230
Tomato Pie, 226
Turnips and Greens, Sautéed, 246
Veggie Cobbler, 252, **253**
Winter Vegetable Soup, 78
Yams, No. 7, New, 227
Zucchini Boats with Tomato, Rice, and
Olives, 248, **249**
See also root vegetables; salad(s);
specific vegetables

Vidalia onion(s):
and Beet Salad with Creamy
Horseradish Dressing, **52**, 53
and Cauliflower Soup, Creamy, 74
and Lima Beans, Sautéed, 256

waffles, 279
Chicken and, Lighter, 178
Four-Grain, with Dried Cherry–
Pineapple Sauce, 278–79
walnuts:
Apple Nut Cake, Potluck, 333
Chocolate-Banana-Walnut Bread
Pudding, **352**, 353
Chocolate Chip–Zucchini Nut
Bread, 309
Cinnamon Apple Granola with
Cranberries and, 286
Granola Cookies, 350
Roasted Root Vegetable Salad with
Honey, Goat Cheese, and, 59
watermelon:
Cajun Gazpacho, 70
Watermelon Cucumber Salad with
Fresh Basil, 46, **47**
wheat, bulgur, 179
whole-wheat flour, 289
Whole-Wheat Biscuits, Everyday, 296
Whole-Wheat Sandwich Bread,
Soft, 302
See also bread(s)
whole-wheat pasta, 95–96, 111
See also noodles; pasta; pasta salads
wild rice, 28
Mushroom Soup with, 84
Salad, Picnic, with Cranberries and
Pecans, 45
winter squash:
Salad, with Apple, Pecans, and
Parmesan Dressing, 56, **57**

The **Bag Lady** Foundation

In 1989, after her marriage of 27 years ended in divorce, Paula was left with only $200, and money was tight while she was raising her sons Jamie and Bobby. She tried hanging wallpaper, working as a bank teller, and selling real estate and insurance. She then started a catering service, making sandwiches and meals, which her sons Jamie and Bobby delivered, and named it "The Bag Lady." Deen's home business soon outgrew her kitchen, and from there…the "Deen dream" took off. In 2012 Paula Deen established The Bag Lady Foundation.

The mission of The Bag Lady Foundation is to improve the well-being, health and independence of women, children and families, with a focus in two areas.

Nourishment

Providing food, food education and support of community efforts to feed the hungry.

Nurturing

Providing support to organizations that help women in need get back on their feet and become self-sufficient.

Of the foundation's mission, Paula says, "There is nothing worse than a child or a family going to bed hungry. And, of course, coming from where I came from, supporting the needs of single moms is something that is near and dear to my heart. I want women to feel the same kind of empowerment that has helped guide me to where I am today."

The Bag Lady Foundation receives funding through charitable contributions, as well as a portion of proceeds from Paula Deen Foods sales.

Visit thebagladyfoundation.org

PAULA DEEN®

A Family OF COMPANIES

Paula Deen's FAMILY KITCHEN

the Lady & Sons

PAULA DEEN® STORE

Paula Deen® NETWORK

PDV
PAULA DEEN VENTURES

PAULA DEEN® FOODS

Paula Deen's GENERAL STORE

PAULA DEEN Home

Paula Deen® CHANNEL

cooking with Paula DEEN

Paula Deen's RECIPE QUEST

Visit PAULADEEN.COM